A PLUME BOOK

TOP SECRET RECIPES STEP-BY-STEP

TODD WILBUR is the bestselling QVC cookbook author. He's appeared on *The Oprah Winfrey Show*, *Today*, and *Good Morning America*, among others. He lives in Las Vegas.

TOP SECRET RECIPES®

STEP-BY-STEP

1 2 3

SECRET FORMULAS WITH PHOTOS FOR DUPLICATING YOUR FAVORITE FAMOUS FOODS AT HOME

BY TODD WILBUR

WITH PHOTOGRAPHS BY THE AUTHOR

A PLUME BOOK

PLUME
An imprint of Penguin Random House LLC
375 Hudson Street
New York, New York 10014
penguin.com

P REGISTERED TRADEMARK—MARCA REGISTRADA
ISBN: 978-0-14-219696-0

LIBRARY OF CONGRESS CATALOGING-IN-PUBLICATION DATA
has been applied for.

Printed in China
10 9 8 7 6 5 4 3

Designed by Todd Wilbur

To my beloved kale.
Sorry for not mentioning you in this book.
Some relationships are better left private.

CONTENTS

THANKS

Clare Ferraro, Becky Cole, Liz Keenan, Sandra Dear, and everyone else at Penguin Random House who worked so hard on my books, and who have supported me over the more than two decades that I've been publishing there.

MeLinda Baca, for her indispensable help on this book and for all of her hard work over the many years at Top Secret Recipes HQ.

Perry Rogers, Colin Smeeton, Rishi Daulat, and Shannon Doucett at PR + Partners.

Rabih Gholam, Cris Abrego, Scott Teti, and everyone on our crew at 51 Minds; and Jayson Dinsmore and Melanie Moreau at CMT. You all helped make our CMT TV show, *Top Secret Recipe*, better than I ever could have imagined.

David Venable, Paula Bower, Christina Pennypacker, Lisa Commodari, and all of my friends at QVC.

Anthony Corrado for the book title *Joy of Cloning* (to be used at a future date).

To Howard Stern, for giving my ears something to do while my taste buds worked overtime. Thanks for so many years of making my lonely, tedious hours fiddling with food seem not so lonely and tedious.

Joe and Mary Essa, for the great Wolfgang Puck knives you see in just about every shot with a knife in it.

My driver, Brian Chaszar, for helping me obtain the goods (waffles) at a Waffle House in Indianapolis along with some crucial new hacking intel.

Jeremy Reed at Praxair in Vegas, for hooking me up with more than enough liquid nitrogen for the Dippin' Dots clone in this book.

And to my family—my beautiful wife, Pamela, and amazing daughter, Morea—for all your patience and understanding as I spent many long days and nights over the past few years locked up in my underground lab writing and shooting this book. I really missed you girls . . . let's eat out tonight!

The first title I gave this book when I started writing it more than three years ago was *Joy of Cloning*. Not because I was scheming to pick up new readers who stumbled upon my cookbook while searching for Irma S. Rombauer's *Joy of Cooking*—although I admit that wouldn't have been such a terrible thing—but really because, as Rombauer imparted in her culinary classic, the process of entertaining and creating delicious food for friends and family is a true joy. And I think that sentiment pertains as much, if not more, to this niche of cooking. There are practical reasons why we clone famous foods, which I will explore later in more detail, such as saving money and duplicating the taste of our favorite dishes with ingredients that we prefer. But the enjoyment we experience when everyone is amazed by the successful re-creation of a delicious dish they thought they could only get in a restaurant or in a package sets this type of cooking apart from any other.

Over time, as this book evolved from a cookbook with dozens of photographs into one with hundreds of photographs detailing each important step of every recipe, the current title, *Step-by-Step*, made more sense.

A NEW LOOK WITH PHOTOS

I considered using photographs when I began writing my first *Top Secret Recipes* cookbook in 1987. I studied photography in college—even took second place in an *L.A. Times* photography contest with ten thousand entries while I was in school—but at that time I only knew how to process

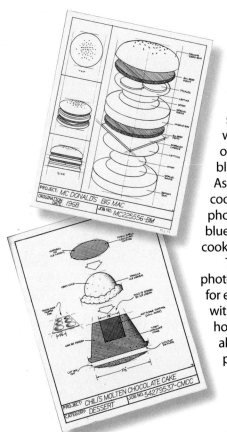

black-and-white photos in the darkroom, and digital cameras were not yet the norm. I wanted to use some art that I could make myself so I decided to illustrate the books with hand-drawn blueprint-style schematics that nicely suited the "top secret" theme of the books. Over a period of twenty-five years, working on a tiny worn-out drafting table using a combination of stenciling and freehand drawing, I inked a total of 450 blueprints to illustrate the first ten *Top Secret Recipes* cookbooks. As the years moved on I heard from an increasing number of cookbook buyers and *TSR* fans who expressed a strong desire for photographs in the cookbooks. I decided it was time to leave the blueprints behind and begin a new look for the *Top Secret Recipes* cookbooks with step-by-step color photos for each of the recipes.

This is the first copycat recipes cookbook that guides you with photographs through every important step of the replicating process for each of the brand-name clone dishes. By using the photos along with the instructions, you will now have a clearer understanding of how each part of each recipe is made, virtually guaranteeing that all of these famous dishes come out as intended, so that you will produce delicious and accurate copies of the popular brand-name foods that everyone loves to eat.

I kept the photos simple and shot many from a first-person perspective, helping you to see exactly how the cooking process should progress in front of you. Since I work alone, it's a little tricky to pose, focus, and shoot this way, but I dig the angle so it's worth the extra effort. When the last ingredient was added, I had shot more than 35,000 photos to get the 1,100+ pics that made it into the book.

WHAT'S IN *STEP-BY-STEP*

All 125 recipes in this cookbook are new, never-before-published recipes. Most of them (a total of 75) are formulas that I have not cloned in any of my cookbooks. I call them "First-Time Hacks." I chose these recipes from a long list of fan requests that I have compiled over many years and from researching what is popular in today's food business. Some of these items have been big sellers for many years like McDonald's McRib Sandwich (page 160), The Cheesecake Factory Stuffed Mushrooms (page 54), Carrabba's Italian Grill Steamed Mussels (page 47), Gatorade Orange Sports Drink (page 110), Ben & Jerry's Chocolate Chip Cookie Dough Ice Cream (page 24), and Legal Sea Foods Legal's Signature Crab Cakes (page 141). Some of the First-Time Hacks you'll find here are top-selling newer items like Chili's Chipotle Chicken Flatbread (page 76), McDonald's Premium Sweet Chili Chicken McWrap (page 155), and Wendy's Pretzel Bacon Cheeseburger (page 272).

The other fifty recipes in the book are what I call "Improved Hacks." These are some of my most popular classic clone recipes that I have gone back and re-hacked to make much better than my original previously published versions. I tapped into some new techniques and tricks that I've picked up over the last two and a half decades of cloning foods to make these classic recipes even better culinary carbon copies of their famous brand-name counterparts. For these improved hacks I chose my most popular recipes for which I had discovered new information that helps makes the recipes better, or recipes that needed an update because the original product formulas they clone had been altered. If you like my early version of KFC Cole Slaw, then you'll really like the new hack on page 133 where dairy is no longer in the ingredients list. If you're a fan of the Tony Roma's Ribs recipe I published almost twenty years ago, then you're going to be crazy about the new version in this book, which incorporates a restaurant trick I learned to make smoky ribs at home without a smoker (page 264). The Olive Garden Salad Dressing (page 174) is better now, as is Wendy's Chili (page 270), Applebee's Fiesta Lime Chicken (page 14), and El Pollo Loco Fire-Grilled Chicken (page 104), just to name a few.

EXECUTIVE PRODUCER
Cris Abrego

To make it clear which of the two categories a recipe falls under I have tagged each one with either "First-Time Hack" or "Improved Hack."

Eight of the recipes included here (some are Improved Hacks and some are First-Time Hacks) were developed from information I gathered on the eight episodes of my CMT TV show *Top Secret Recipe*. In the show I travel around the country in my food lab on wheels to the headquarters of some of the country's biggest food companies and attempt to re-create their famous products. I am given three days to gather enough information—using whatever sneaky means I can muster—to re-create a dish that can fool three judges in a blind

taste test. Sometimes I am successful, sometimes not so much. Three days is not a lot of time to hack dishes that were developed and perfected by these companies over years of research and development, so the task is a challenging one—especially when the judges are often picked by the company whose product I'm hacking.

Every recipe from the show is here: Cinnabon Classic Cinnamon

Roll (page 90), Chili's Grilled Baby Back Ribs (page 79), Dippin' Dots Banana Split Ice Cream (page 98), Domino's Large Cheese Pizza (page 101), KFC Original Recipe Fried Chicken (page 136), Mrs. Fields Chocolate Chip Cookies (page 168), Outback Steakhouse Bloomin' Onion (page 185), and P.F. Chang's Chicken Lettuce Wraps (page 201).

BETTER RECIPES, BETTER RESULTS

With this book I have made a few changes to the way I write recipes. These tweaks should help give you more consistent and reliable results that closely match the finished products I intend for you to create.

Because weight is often a more accurate way to measure certain ingredients like flour and powdered sugar, I specify weight measurements for ingredients that are best measured that way. I recommend that you get yourself a kitchen scale and measure ingredients by weight whenever possible. This measuring method will give you more consistent results, especially when baking. If you don't have a kitchen scale, don't worry. I also list the volume measurements for those ingredients.

Because the amount of salt in salted butter can vary from brand to brand, I am now creating all recipes with unsalted butter. This small change will help give you results that are closer to mine.

In previous *Top Secret Recipes* books I often use ingredient shortcuts to make the recipes easy, but this sometimes results in a finished product that could have tasted better if I had used a scratch method. For example, my previous version of Chili's Molten Chocolate Cake (page 82) called for a boxed cake mix for the cake and bottled fudge for the molten center. In this book I have redesigned the recipe by making the chocolate cake and fudge filling from scratch. It takes a little more time to write recipes this way, but by creating scratch versions of these formulas I can make adjustments in individual ingredients so that the finished product is a better clone of the original recipe. There are several other re-hacks in this book that I have converted to scratch recipes to give you improved results: the Hostess Twinkie (page 120), which formerly called for a box of pound cake mix, and the Red Lobster Cheddar Bay Biscuits (page 211), which called for Bisquick baking mix, are a couple other examples. I have also made an effort to create most of the First-Time Hacks in this book with scratch ingredients for more accurate and great-tasting clone recipes.

I have included an info box at the top of each recipe to give you an idea of the time required for each recipe and the difficulty level. I estimated the time required for the active and inactive preparation of each recipe. The "Active Prep" time is the hands-on time required to make the recipe, while the "Inactive Prep" time is the passive time required to make the recipe, such as when ingredients are marinating or something is baking.

In addition, I have estimated the difficulty of each recipe by tagging the recipe with either "Easy," "Medium," or "Hard." If you are a novice cook I suggest you use only the recipes that are either "Easy" or "Medium" difficulty. These recipes make up the bulk of the recipes in this book. There are, however, a handful of recipes here that I consider to be "Hard." A little more cooking experience is suggested for these recipes and the time required to make these recipes is considerably longer. You up for the challenge? Don't be scared. They're not impossible recipes—just a little harder than the other ones.

WHY CLONE FAMOUS FOODS?

It was in 1987 that I received a chain letter in the mail claiming to be the real secret recipe for a Mrs. Fields Chocolate Chip Cookie. It was not, of course. But this chain letter with a mediocre recipe for chocolate chip cookies printed on it was widely popular across the country and caused quite a stir. People who made the recipe and had never tried a Mrs. Fields Cookie assumed that Mrs. Fields Cookies were as ordinary as the cookies produced with the recipe. The chain letter also claimed that the recipe was obtained by a woman who had purchased it at one of the cookie stores for $2.50 but was then charged $250.00 on her credit card for the purchase. This prompted the Mrs. Fields Cookie company to place signs in all their stores disclaiming the recipe as well as the story about the woman's purchase and overcharging. Debbi Fields later wrote about the incident in her book, *One Smart Cookie*, referring to the situation as "The Recipe Problem."

When I saw the signs pop up in the cookie stores, it struck me that this ridiculous little chain letter must have become very popular—and it didn't even make a good cookie! It became obvious to me that America had a fascination with copycat recipes for famous brand-name foods, and a book filled with a bunch of recipes like these might be a winner. For the next five years I spent all my free time learning how to reverse-engineer popular foods, and I started by making a much better version of the Mrs. Fields Chocolate Chip Cookie than the one in the chain letter. Eventually I had created a collection of recipes that duplicated the taste and appearance of iconic American brand-name foods, and I set out to find a publisher for the book.

That first book, called *Top Secret Recipes*, came out in 1993 and sold better than expected. I appeared on several popular TV and radio talk shows in the following weeks responding to various questions about my food-hacking process, my favorite cloned recipes, and which secret formulas were the most difficult to reverse-engineer.

One of the questions that I got most often back then—and still today—is, "Why would anyone want to duplicate a famous food item that they can just go out and buy?" In a short radio or TV interview it's hard to hit on all of the reasons why America loves to clone food and why this specialty niche of cooking is more popular today than ever before, but this is the perfect place to give you my full list:

Cost: It is almost always cheaper to clone these food items at home than it is to purchase the original items at restaurants or in stores. Through cost analysis I have found that re-creating these dishes in your own kitchen costs an average of around half of what the original product will cost you. Cloning famous food at home is a great way to save some coin.

Customization: With these recipes you have the freedom to customize brand-name dishes to suit your taste preferences and nutritional needs. You may wish to substitute reduced-fat ingredients for those with full fat, such as mayonnaise or sour cream. You may prefer to use organic ingredients, or use wheat buns when sesame seed buns are called for. You may choose to substitute ground turkey for ground beef because you don't eat red meat. You now have the freedom to make these dishes the way you like them and treat yourself to a special version of the item that is not available where the original is sold.

Discontinuation: Someone once said to me, "Why would I ever want to make a Twinkie at home when I can just go out and buy a Twinkie? It's not like they're ever gonna stop selling Twinkies!" But in November 2012, that's exactly what happened. Due to a labor dispute, Hostess closed the doors to its baking facilities and we became a Twinkie-less country until the company reopened with new owners in July of the following year. There are gobs of other famous foods that have been discontinued over the years, many of them indefinitely. Having these secret recipes is the only way to enjoy the taste of our favorites long after they are gone.

Scarcity: In the holiday months of 2008 a memo was sent to all Starbucks stores announcing a shortage of the Pumpkin Cream Cheese Muffins. Demand was so high that year that supplies were dwindling and the chain would run out before the holidays had even arrived! In November 2009 historic amounts of rain closed the plant in Atlanta that makes Eggo Waffles and another Kellogg's plant in Rossville, Tennessee, was closed indefinitely for repairs. These two closures reduced Eggo production by 50 percent and the country was faced with a nationwide shortage of Eggos that left grocery store freezer shelves empty for weeks. With clone recipes at the ready for popular items such as these (both of which I previously cloned in another book and on our website at TopSecretRecipes.com), scarcity of your favorite food products is no longer an issue.

Location: When you were in Indianapolis you had the best shrimp cocktail of your life at St. Elmo Steak House and now you're back home in Poughkeepsie with a deep craving for it. Good thing you have a clone recipe for St. Elmo Steak House World Famous Shrimp Cocktail on page 240 to satisfy your otherwise insatiable urge, so that you can treat yourself to a food that's only available in a specific part of the country. It's also nice to have a handy clone recipe for the famous Hashbrown Casserole from Cracker Barrel (page 94) when the closest Cracker Barrel Restaurant to your house is a six-hour drive away. And it's pouring rain.

Mixed-up Menu: You want to make a meal with an appetizer of Loaded Potato Skins from T.G.I. Friday's (page 258), Chili's Grilled Baby Back Ribs (page 79) as the entrée with some Marie Callender's Famous Golden Cornbread (page 147) on the side, and Applebee's Maple Butter Blondie (page 17) for dessert. This would be an impossible meal to get at any one restaurant and you're not about to drive around town picking everything up. Using the recipes in this book, you have the unique ability to assemble amazing feasts that feature a combination of your favorite signature dishes from a variety of different restaurants.

Fun and Adulation: Cloning famous foods at home is fun. When you decide to make something to eat at home to serve to your friends and family, why not make something you love from your favorite restaurant chain? It's an entertaining culinary challenge and an engaging experience to find out if you are successful. And when you are, it's always nice to hear the words of amazement. This is the *joy of cloning* that I write about at the beginning of this introduction. There's no other niche of cooking that offers the same culinary experience. You are in for a treat.

THE JOY OF CLONING

On my end, creating these clones of famous food is about the challenge of it, solving the puzzle, discovering the secrets—knowing that I was successful at re-creating the familiar flavors we love. Hearing great comments from fans and seeing all the positive reviews for my recipe creations over the years is my reward. My joy begins before the clones are complete, during the creation of the recipes, even as frustrating and tedious as the task can be at times. My pleasure comes from the process, especially when it yields a great result. My joy is in the hacking—the snooping, the exploring, and the experimenting, and knowing that the pure pleasure I get from my work will translate into beautiful and delicious dishes in your home unlike those you have made from any other cookbook.

I am certain that you will have many great times in your kitchen with this book. And I hope that later on down the road you will come back for another joy-filled helping.

To all my friends—happy cloning!

APPLEBEE'S MOZZARELLA STICKS

🏆 First-Time Hack

⏱ Active Prep: 20 min.
Inactive Prep: 3 hrs.

E🌡 Difficulty: Easy

👥 Yield: 12 sticks

I realized that I had never assembled a hack of the great mozzarella sticks from America's largest casual restaurant chain when I was working up a lower-fat version of this recipe for *The Dr. Oz Show* (you can get that recipe at TopSecretRecipes.com). Mission finally accomplished. Now you can make your own delicious and easy culinary carbon copy of Applebee's popular finger-food appetizer that the *Huffington Post* claims is one of the best in the biz.

½ cup **plain bread crumbs (such as Progresso brand)**
1 tablespoon **grated** Parmesan cheese
¾ teaspoon **Italian seasoning herb blend**
¼ teaspoon plus ⅛ teaspoon **salt**
¼ teaspoon **garlic powder**
2 large **eggs, beaten**
1 cup **whole milk**
½ cup **all-purpose flour**
12 1-ounce **mozzarella cheese sticks**
6 to 12 cups **vegetable oil**

ON THE SIDE (FOR DIPPING)
½ **cup marinara sauce**

1 Combine the bread crumbs with the Parmesan cheese, Italian seasoning, salt, and garlic powder in a medium bowl. Combine the beaten eggs with the milk in another medium bowl. Pour the flour onto a plate.

2 Working one at a time, dip a cheese stick into the egg/milk mixture, then coat it with flour. Let it sit in the flour for a bit so that the flour sticks. Dip the floured cheese stick back into the egg/milk mixture, then coat it with the seasoned bread crumbs. Arrange the

breaded cheese sticks on a wax paper–lined baking sheet and place them in your freezer for 3 hours.

3 Preheat the oil in a deep fryer or large saucepan with a thermometer attached to 350 degrees F.

4 Fry the frozen cheese sticks 3 or 4 at a time in the hot oil for 1½ to 2 minutes or until they are light brown and you see cheese beginning to ooze out. Drain on a rack or paper towel–lined plate. Serve the mozzarella sticks with warmed marinara sauce on the side for dipping.

APPLEBEE'S ORIENTAL CHICKEN SALAD

 Improved Hack

 Prep Time: 30 min.

 Difficulty: Medium

 Yield: 2 large salads (Can split to serve 4)

This classic signature salad was a popular staple on Applebee's menu way before I first cloned it back in 1997. With Applebee's still going strong some eighteen years later, it's about time I share a new version of the recipe with some tweaks that make an already good clone recipe even better. The improved sweet-and-sour Asian dressing formula here yields a finished product that tastes much more like Applebee's current offering, and the breaded chicken is even more like the real deal.

This new recipe produces two giant entrée-size salads that can easily be split up to feed a hungry tribe of four. And if you want to make this fairly simple recipe even easier, you can use frozen pre-breaded chicken fingers and bake or fry them to top your salads. These days Applebee's also offers this salad with the option of grilled chicken on top, so I have included a marinade and quick instructions for that variation in the Tidbits at the end.

DRESSING

½ cup **mayonnaise**
3 tablespoons **honey**
5 teaspoons **rice wine vinegar**
1 tablespoon **lime juice**
1 tablespoon **Grey Poupon Dijon mustard**
1 teaspoon **granulated sugar**
½ teaspoon **sesame oil**

CHICKEN

2 skinless **chicken breast fillets**
1 cup **all-purpose flour**
2 teaspoons **salt**
1 teaspoon **granulated sugar**
¾ teaspoon **ground black pepper**
½ teaspoon **garlic powder**
½ teaspoon **onion powder**
1 large **egg, beaten**
1 cup **milk**
4 to 6 cups **vegetable oil**

SALAD

6 cups coarsely chopped **romaine lettuce**
2 cups sliced **napa cabbage**
1 cup thinly sliced **red cabbage**
½ cup julienned or shredded **carrot**
¼ cup chopped **green onion (green part only)**
¼ cup **sliced almonds**
¾ cup **crispy chow mein noodles**

1. Whisk together the dressing ingredients in a small bowl. Cover and chill the dressing until it's needed.

2. Cover the chicken breasts with plastic wrap and pound them with a kitchen mallet to about ¼ inch thick. Slice the breasts in half lengthwise to make four long fillets.

3. Mix together the flour, salt, sugar, pepper, garlic powder, and onion powder in a shallow bowl or a pie pan. Whisk together the egg and milk in another shallow bowl or pie pan.

4. Working with one fillet at a time, first coat the chicken with the dry breading, then dip it into the egg/milk mixture. Coat the fillet with breading again, then dip it back into the liquid and once again in the breading until well-coated. Arrange the breaded fillets on a plate until the oil is hot.

5. Fill a sauté pan with oil to about an inch deep. Heat the oil to 325 degrees F.

6. When the oil is up to temperature, fry the breaded chicken for 5 to 7 minutes or until golden brown. Drain on a rack or paper towel–lined plate.

7. Build the salad by tossing together the romaine lettuce, cabbages, and carrot.

8. Divide the salad onto two plates and sprinkle each with green onion. Sprinkle the sliced almonds over each salad, followed by the chow mein noodles.

9. Slice the chicken into bite-size chunks and arrange it on the top of each salad. Serve your salads with the dressing on the side.

TIDBITS If you would like to use grilled chicken rather than breaded fried chicken on

11

your salad, combine 3 cups water, 1 tablespoon salt, ½ teaspoon garlic powder, and ¼ teaspoon hickory-flavored liquid smoke. Pound 2 skinless chicken breast fillets flat and marinate in the brine solution for 3 hours. When done marinating, blot each chicken breast dry, rub with oil, and grill (on a barbecue or indoor grill pan) until done. Lightly pepper each fillet while grilling. Slice the chicken into bite-size chunks and arrange it over the top of each salad prepared as in the above recipe.

You can also use pre-grilled frozen chicken breasts prepared as instructed on the package.

APPLEBEE'S MEXICAN RICE

First-Time Hack

Active Prep: 5 min.
Inactive Prep: 30 min.

E Difficulty: Easy

Yield: 4 servings

Here's an easy side dish that can be served with just about any entrée but is especially great with the clone recipe for Applebee's Fiesta Lime Chicken on page 14. Be sure you are using converted rice for this recipe, not instant rice. And if you can't find poblano or red Fresno peppers, any mild red and green peppers will do the job.

1 tablespoon olive oil	**1 tablespoon** minced **poblano pepper**
1 cup uncooked converted rice	**1 tablespoon** minced **red Fresno pepper**
1 cup water	**1½ teaspoons** chili powder
1 cup chicken broth	**¾ teaspoon** salt
¼ cup frozen yellow corn	**1 teaspoon** lime juice

1 Heat up the olive oil in a medium saucepan over medium heat. When the oil is hot, add the rice and stir constantly until the rice begins to turn light brown, about 3 minutes.

2 Add the remaining ingredients except for the lime juice and bring the mixture to a boil, then reduce the heat to low and cover the pan. Cook for 30 minutes or until the rice has absorbed all of the liquid. Turn off the heat and stir in the lime juice.

APPLEBEE'S FIESTA LIME CHICKEN

👍 Improved Hack

🕐 Active Prep: 30 min.
Inactive Prep: 1 hr.

M🌡 Difficulty: Medium

👥 Yield: 4 servings

When I first cloned this dish in 2007 it was called Tequila Lime Chicken. Was the tequila removed from the recipe and the name to satisfy concerned teetotaling Applebee's customers? I really don't know. What I do know, however, is that this dish is still one of the chain's best sellers.

Upon examining the dish at the restaurant recently I discovered that the chicken is brushed with a zesty lime sauce before the Mexi-ranch sauce is applied. I'm not sure if the restaurant's version of the dish has always included this step, but I do know that my first version of the recipe did not, so it was my responsibility and resolute duty, as a dedicated food hacker, to instantly get cracking on an improved hack of this fine dish. The zesty lime sauce clone is here now, as are improvements for the Mexi-ranch sauce and chicken marinade. At the restaurant, the dish is served with a side of delicious Mexican rice. If you'd like to do the same, you'll find a new clone of that simple recipe on page 13.

ZESTY LIME SAUCE
2 tablespoons vegetable oil
1 tablespoon white vinegar
2 teaspoons lime juice
½ teaspoon Grey Poupon Dijon mustard
½ teaspoon minced garlic
½ teaspoon granulated sugar
¼ teaspoon ground black pepper
⅛ teaspoon salt
⅛ teaspoon dried oregano
⅛ teaspoon dried thyme
Pinch of crushed red pepper flakes

MEXI-RANCH SAUCE
⅔ cup mayonnaise
⅓ cup sour cream
3 tablespoons whole milk
2 tablespoons diced Roma tomato
2 tablespoons diced onion
1 tablespoon white vinegar
1 tablespoon finely minced cilantro
1 teaspoon paprika
¼ teaspoon ground cayenne pepper
¼ teaspoon garlic powder
⅛ teaspoon salt
⅛ teaspoon ground black pepper
⅛ teaspoon dried dill weed
⅛ teaspoon ground cumin

PICO DE GALLO

1 cup diced Roma tomatoes (about 2 tomatoes)
¼ cup diced red onion
2 tablespoons finely minced cilantro
1 teaspoon lime juice
⅛ teaspoon salt
⅛ teaspoon ground cayenne pepper

CHICKEN MARINADE

3 cups water
½ cup vegetable oil
1 tablespoon salt
1½ teaspoons granulated sugar
½ teaspoon garlic powder
½ teaspoon paprika
½ teaspoon ground black pepper
¼ teaspoon hickory liquid smoke

4 skinless chicken breast fillets
1⅓ cups shredded cheddar/Jack cheese blend

GARNISH
Fried tortilla strips
4 lime wedges

❶ Combine all of the ingredients for the zesty lime sauce in a medium bowl. Whisk well, then set aside.

❷ Combine all of the ingredients for the Mexi-ranch sauce in a medium bowl. Cover and set this aside as well.

❸ Combine all of the ingredients for the pico de gallo, then cover and set it aside along with the two sauces.

❹ Prepare the chicken marinade by combining all of the ingredients in a large bowl. Pound the chicken breasts flat under a piece of plastic wrap with a kitchen mallet. Add the chicken to the marinade, then cover and chill it for 1 hour.

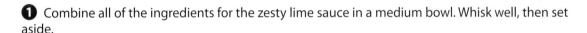

5 Preheat your barbecue grill to high about 30 minutes before the chicken is done marinating (you can also use a grill pan that is preheated over medium heat). When the chicken has marinated for 1 hour, remove it from the marinade and place it directly on a well-lubricated grill. Cook the chicken for 3 to 5 minutes per side or until done.

6 Assemble each dish by placing a chicken breast on a plate. Brush a little zesty lime sauce over the chicken, then spoon on some of the Mexi-ranch sauce. Sprinkle about 1/3 cup of cheese over the top of the chicken, then microwave it for 30 to 60 seconds on high heat to melt the cheese.

7 To serve, arrange the chicken breast on top of a bed of fried tortilla strips. Serve with the pico de gallo and a wedge of lime on the side.

APPLEBEE'S MAPLE BUTTER BLONDIE

👍 Improved Hack

🕐 Active Prep: 35 min.
Inactive Prep: 22 min.

M🌡 Difficulty: Medium

👥 Yield: 8 servings

This dessert, which used to be called the "White Chocolate & Walnut Blondie," has been through a few minor ingredient changes along with the name. The fantastic maple cream cheese sauce has been improved and delicious glazed pecans are now sprinkled over the top where there used to be super boring unglazed walnut pieces. I've improved every part of this recipe to more closely match the current version of the top-selling dessert at the huge casual chain. The original is served in a piping hot cast-iron skillet, which you can duplicate by preheating small pans on your stovetop. If you don't have small skillets, you can serve the dessert on a plate after warming up the blondie in your microwave. Done and done.

BLONDIE
1 cup (packed) light brown sugar
⅓ cup unsalted butter, softened
3 large eggs
2 teaspoons vanilla extract
9 ounces (1¾ cups) all-purpose flour
1½ teaspoons baking powder
¾ teaspoon salt
⅓ cup water
1 cup chopped walnuts
6 ounces white chocolate, chopped into chunks

GLAZED PECANS
2 tablespoons unsalted butter
¼ cup (packed) light brown sugar
2 tablespoons water
1 cup chopped pecans

MAPLE CREAM CHEESE SAUCE
8 ounces (1 cup) cream cheese, softened
4 ounces (1 cup) powdered sugar
2 tablespoons maple syrup
2 tablespoons unsalted butter, softened
¼ teaspoon salt

8 scoops of vanilla ice cream

❶ Preheat the oven to 350 degrees F.

❷ Combine the brown sugar with the butter, eggs, and vanilla in a large bowl. Beat well with an electric mixer on high speed until creamy.

❸ Combine the flour, baking powder, and salt in a medium bowl. Pour the dry mixture into the wet mixture along with the water and mix well with your mixer on low speed until combined. Add the walnuts and white chocolate and mix by hand. Spread the mixture

into a 9 x 13-inch baking pan that has been lined with a sling of aluminum foil or parchment paper (to help remove the blondie once baked). Bake for 22 to 26 minutes or until the top has browned. Remove from the oven and cool. When cool, slice the blondie lengthwise across the middle, then slice down three times, creating 8 even portions.

❹ Make the glazed pecans by melting the butter in a medium saucepan over medium heat. Add the brown sugar and water and heat until bubbling. Add the pecans and continue stirring for 2 to 3 minutes or until the water has cooked away. Remove the pan from the heat and continue stirring until the sugar crystallizes on the nuts. Pour the nuts out onto a plate to cool.

❺ Make the maple cream cheese sauce by combining all of the ingredients in a microwave-safe medium bowl with an electric mixer on medium speed until smooth. Heat up the sauce by zapping it in the microwave oven for 30 to 60 seconds on high until warm.

❻ Serve the dessert by heating up a small cast-iron skillet over medium heat for 3 to 4 minutes or until hot. Place one slice of the blondie into the pan, then spoon a scoop of ice cream on top. Pour the warm maple cream cheese sauce over the ice cream and sprinkle the dessert with about 2 tablespoons of the sugared pecans. You can also serve the dessert on a plate by heating up the blondie in the microwave for 20 to 30 seconds until warm, then topping the blondie with a scoop of ice cream, warm maple sauce, and nuts.

ARBY'S CURLY FRIES

 First-Time Hack

Active Prep: 25 min.
Inactive Prep:
2 hrs. 30 min.

M Difficulty: Medium

Yield: 2 servings

According to recent polls, these fries are considered either the #1 or #2 best fast-food fries in America—they flip-flop with McDonald's for the top spot (which I call "Lord of the Fries"). Much of what I know about how Arby's makes these fries comes from an episode of Food Network's *Unwrapped* that reveals what the potatoes go through during the automated prep process at a ConAgra Foods processing plant in Southern Washington. The potatoes are sliced at high speed, then they rush down a conveyor where they are blanched in hot water for 20 minutes to deactivate an enzyme in the potatoes that turns them brown and to help create the perfect texture when the potatoes are fried. The potatoes are then battered, par-fried for 30 seconds, frozen, and shipped to each Arby's restaurant where the cooking process is completed with a final frying step.

My process at home is simple and incorporates all these steps, but you will need to get yourself a curly fry slicer if you want fries that look just like those at Arby's. The one I used here from Progressive makes perfect slices and costs around 30 bucks. If you don't want to pony up for a slicer, you can also use this recipe with fries that are sliced on a mandoline or by hand. They won't be curly, but they'll still have the same amazing flavor and crispiness.

1 medium **russet potato**
6 to 12 cups **vegetable oil**

BATTER
3½ ounces (⅔ cup) **all-purpose flour**
2½ tablespoons **paprika**

1¼ teaspoons **salt**
¾ teaspoon **garlic powder**
¾ teaspoon **onion powder**
¾ teaspoon **ground cayenne pepper**
½ teaspoon **ground black pepper**
1 cup **water**

1 Cut off both ends of the potato, then slice the potato in a spiral curly fry slicer.

2 Remove the odd-shape little bits of potato and the slices that are too thin with the skin on them. Drop the rest into a large bowl and cover with water as hot as you can get it from your tap. Let the potato slices sit in the water for 20 minutes, then strain.

3 While the potato soaks in the water, preheat the oil in a deep fryer or a large saucepan with a thermometer attached to 375 degrees F.

19

4 Make the batter by whisking together the dry ingredients in a large bowl, then whisk in the water until smooth.

5 Drop the sliced potatoes into the batter and gently coat all of the pieces. Arrange the coated fries on a rack or screen so that the excess batter can drip off.

6 When the oil is hot, par-fry the fries for 30 seconds in batches, then freeze them for at least 2 hours. You can keep the fries for several days in a sealed container in the freezer at this point and finish the frying later, or go ahead and fry them now.

7 When you are ready to finish the fries, preheat the oil to 350 degrees F. Fry the fries for 2½ to 3 minutes or until crispy. Remove to a rack or paper towel–lined plate and lightly salt the fries. Serve them right away.

AUNTIE ANNE'S PRETZELS

Improved Hack

Active Prep: 30 min.
Inactive Prep: 2 hrs. 10 min.

M Difficulty: Medium

Yield: 6 pretzels

Even though dough is usually made up of just a handful of ingredients, knocking off the exact texture and taste of a well-known doughy product such as this is one of trickiest tasks in food hacking. Each small variation in the formula has a profound effect on the workability of the dough and the eventual texture of the bite. What kind of flour and yeast should be used? How long to knead the dough? Should the dough rise at room temperature, or in the refrigerator, and for how long? These are just a few of the many questions that must be answered to achieve a perfect clone, and in the weeks that I spent making this recipe over and over, I have come to some far-tastier conclusions than in my first hack of this recipe.

    Among the many changes are the addition of some bread flour to add more chewiness to the pretzel, and brown sugar to contribute a slight molasses flavor that was missing from my previous version. The baking soda bath formula here gives the pretzel a better color, the cooking temp has been adjusted, and the cinnamon sugar has now been perfected. Put it all together, with several other tweaks, and you will now produce some of the best homemade pretzels you'll ever eat. If you want to make your pretzels as authentic as they can be, snag some real pretzel salt online or in a specialty store. It makes a much better finished product than the kosher salt I mention as an alternative. The recipe here makes original salted pretzels and the popular cinnamon sugar pretzels just like those from Auntie Anne's.

DOUGH
6 tablespoons dark brown sugar
1¼ cups warm water (105 to 110 degrees F)
¼ teaspoon rapid-rise yeast
12 ounces (2¼ cups plus 2 tablespoons) all-purpose flour
5 ounces (1 cup) bread flour
1 teaspoon salt

BATH
½ cup baking soda
3 cups water

Pretzel salt (or kosher salt)
½ cup (1 stick) unsalted butter, melted

CINNAMON SUGAR
1 cup granulated sugar
2 teaspoons ground cinnamon

❶ Dissolve the brown sugar in the warm water. Add the yeast and mix until dissolved.

❷ In a separate large bowl combine the flours and salt. Pour in the yeast/sugar mixture and mix with a stand mixer on low until the dough forms a ball, or combine with a mixing spoon, then use your

hands to bring the dough together into a ball. Knead with a stand mixer or by hand for 5 minutes, then cover the dough in a bowl with a towel for 2 hours.

3 After 2 hours, preheat the oven to 450 degrees F, and make the bath by stirring the baking soda into the water in a medium bowl.

4 Spray a little nonstick cooking spray onto a smooth rolling surface. Place the dough there and then divide it into 6 portions that weigh 4½ ounces each.

5 Working with one portion of dough at a time, roll the dough into a rope that is approximately 36 inches long. Bring both ends up to form a "U," then twist the ends all the way around once and press the ends (the "feet") down onto the bottom of the pretzel.

6 Hold the pretzel where the feet are attached and dip it into the water bath, then blot the bottom briefly on a towel to remove the excess liquid. Place the pretzel onto a parchment paper–lined baking sheet and sprinkle with pretzel salt, unless you are making cinnamon-sugar pretzels. Repeat with the remaining pretzels.

7 Bake the pretzels for 5 minutes, then rotate the pan and bake for 5 to 7 more minutes or until nicely browned.

8 When the pretzels come out of the oven, transfer them to a plate or a screen and brush them with the melted butter. Sprinkle a little more salt onto the salted pretzels.

9 If you are making the cinnamon-sugar pretzels, combine the sugar and cinnamon in a medium bowl and spoon the cinnamon-sugar over the buttered (but not salted) pretzels until well-coated on both sides.

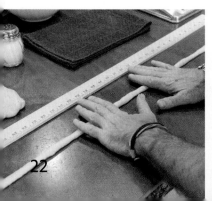

BEN & JERRY'S CHOCOLATE CHIP COOKIE DOUGH ICE CREAM

First-Time Hack

Active Prep: 30 min.
Inactive Prep:
2 hrs. 30 min.

Difficulty: Medium

Yield: 5 cups

Chocolate Chip Cookie Dough ranks in the top five biggest sellers from the famous Vermont duo's wide assortment of eclectic chunky ice cream flavors. No surprise there really. It's a simple combination of vanilla ice cream, chocolate bits, and little chunks of delicious cookie dough that appeals to just about everyone with a mouth. But before I could even think about how to make the cookie dough and semisweet chocolate bits for this clone, I had to figure out how to make a creamy vanilla ice cream base that tastes just like Ben & Jerry's.

Part of the secret is in finding a way to keep the ice cream creamy and to delay melting so that it doesn't form unpleasant ice crystals when it refreezes. The way to do that is to add in some of the same thickening agents found in the original. These natural gums help to stabilize the ice cream, delaying any ice crystal formation. But where do we get the food gums we need? We'll just add a little fat-free half-and-half and Egg Beaters to the mix! These products contain the important ingredients needed to make super creamy ice cream with no crunchy ice crystals, just like the pros do. We'll also use the Egg Beaters in the cookie dough since the dough is not cooked and Egg Beaters are made from pasteurized egg that is safe to eat raw. Just before you scoop the ice cream out of your ice cream maker (yes, you will need an ice cream machine for this recipe), you mix in the little cookie dough chunks and the chocolate bits and get it into the freezer as quickly as possible to set up.

ICE CREAM
2 cups heavy cream
1¼ cups fat-free milk
½ cup fat-free half-and-half
½ cup granulated sugar
¼ teaspoon salt
2 large egg yolks
3 tablespoons Egg Beaters (original)
1½ teaspoons vanilla extract

COOKIE DOUGH
3 tablespoons unsalted butter, softened
2 tablespoons granulated sugar

2 tablespoons dark brown sugar
1 tablespoon Egg Beaters (original)
¼ teaspoon vanilla extract
⅛ teaspoon salt
2 ounces (6 tablespoons) all-purpose flour
2 tablespoons semisweet mini chocolate chips, chopped

CHOCOLATE CHUNKS
¼ cup semisweet mini chocolate chips

YOU WILL ALSO NEED
Ice cream maker

❶ Combine the cream, milk, half-and-half, ¼ cup sugar, and salt in a 2- or 3-quart saucepan over medium heat. Stir often as the mixture heats until it begins to steam, 5 to 7 minutes.

❷ While the cream mixture heats, combine the egg yolks, Egg Beaters, and remaining ¼ cup sugar in a medium bowl with an electric mixer on high speed for 1 minute or until the mixture turns light yellow.

❸ When the cream mixture is hot, pour a little into the bowl with the egg yolks while mixing to temper it (so you don't cook the yolks). Continue mixing while adding a little more of the hot cream mixture, and then add a little more while still mixing. Now that the mixture has been tempered you can safely add the remaining hot mixture into the egg yolks. Mix well and then pour the entire contents of the bowl back into the saucepan and put it back over medium heat.

❹ Heat the ice cream base while stirring often until it begins to bubble and steam, 4 to 6 minutes. Turn off the heat and add the vanilla

extract. Pour the ice cream base into a bowl or storage container, cover it, and place it in your freezer for 2 hours.

❺ While the ice cream base chills, make the chocolate chip cookie dough by combining the butter, sugars, Egg Beaters, vanilla, and salt in a medium bowl with an electric mixer. Mix for about 1 minute. Add the flour and mix just until combined. Before adding the 2 tablespoons of mini chocolate chips, be sure you have chopped them up into smaller bits (about the size of rice) with a knife. Mix in the chopped mini chips.

❻ Form the dough into marble-size balls with your hands, then press the balls slightly flatter into disks. Place all of the dough chunks into a container and into the freezer.

❼ Heat up the ¼ cup of semisweet mini chips in a small glass or ceramic bowl in your microwave for 30 seconds. Stir gently until the chocolate is smooth. Spoon the chocolate out onto a wax paper–covered baking sheet. Place another piece of wax paper over the top of the chocolate, then press another smaller baking sheet down onto the chocolate to flatten it out

to about ¹/₁₆ inch. Place the pans with the chocolate between them into your freezer to set up.

❽ When the ice cream base has cooled for a couple hours, it's time to make the ice cream. Place a medium glass or ceramic bowl in your freezer, then pour the ice cream base into your ice cream maker and turn it on. When the ice cream is done, stop the machine and remove

the paddle. Break the flattened semisweet chocolate into chunks and drop it along with the cookie dough chunks into the ice cream and quickly mix it up.

❾ Spoon the ice cream into the frozen bowl you had placed in the freezer. Press a piece of plastic wrap down onto the surface of the ice cream (to keep the air out and ice crystals from forming), cover the bowl, and freeze.

BOSTON MARKET MEATLOAF

Boston Market has one of the best home-style meatloaf recipes around and it's one of the most popular recipes I've cloned. When I first hacked it I cloned the chain's hickory ketchup by mixing barbecue sauce and sugar with tomato sauce. It was a good solution, but I recently discovered that the sauce could be even better with just a few additional ingredients that makes it more like ketchup made from scratch. I also determined that the recipe should yield more sauce so that you have extra for pouring over the top of the meatloaf when it's served.

A few other important tweaks here include adding ground pork and an egg into the mix with the ground sirloin for a richer meatloaf, plus using bread crumbs (as Boston Market does) rather than just flour in the mix for a much better, toastier flavor. Throw it all into a small loaf pan (8 x 4-inch) and in under an hour you'll be ready to serve up this new improved Boston Market Meatloaf hack.

HICKORY KETCHUP
1 15-ounce can (1½ cups) tomato sauce
3 tablespoons Kraft original barbecue sauce
½ teaspoon white vinegar
⅛ teaspoon salt
⅛ teaspoon garlic powder
⅛ teaspoon onion powder

MEATLOAF
1¼ pounds ground sirloin
½ pound ground pork
½ cup plain bread crumbs
1 large egg
1 tablespoon minced dry onion
½ teaspoon salt
¼ teaspoon garlic powder
¼ teaspoon ground black pepper

❶ Preheat the oven to 400 degrees F.

❷ Make the hickory ketchup by combining all of the ingredients in a small saucepan over medium heat. When the mixture begins to bubble, reduce the heat and simmer for 5 minutes. Cool.

❸ Combine ¾ cup of the hickory ketchup with the ground meats and other ingredients in a large bowl. Use your hands to mix until all of the ingredients are well combined.

4 Press the meatloaf into an 8 x 4-inch meatloaf pan. Use your fingers to make the top of the meatloaf smooth and slightly domed, then cover the pan with foil. Bake for 30 minutes, remove the foil, then pour ¼ cup of the remaining hickory ketchup over the top of the meatloaf. Bake again, uncovered, for 20 to 25 more minutes or until the meatloaf has browned around the edges.

5 Cool for 10 minutes, pour out any fat, then remove the meatloaf from the pan and cut it into 8 slices. Serve 2 slices per plate with extra hickory ketchup poured over the top.

BUBBA GUMP SHRIMP CO. SEAFOOD HUSH PUPS

 First-Time Hack

 Active Prep: 30 min.
Inactive Prep: 30 min.

 Difficulty: Medium

Yield: 2 dozen

This restaurant spin-off from the Tom Hanks movie *Forrest Gump*, which opened its first location in Monterey, California, in 1996, has now grown to over 40 restaurants around the world. As you may guess, many of the dishes feature shrimp that has been boiled, broiled, poached, breaded, fried, or stuffed, along with many other seafood—and a nice selection of non-seafood—menu items. The top appetizer pick at the restaurant chain is its spin on hush puppies that are filled with shrimp and a white fish called hoki. Hoki is not an easy fish to find in stores, but you can substitute with true cod, which is very similar in taste and texture. In fact, McDonald's uses hoki and cod interchangeably in its Fillet-O-Fish sandwich. You'll need only a small 4-ounce fillet along with 4 large shrimp—each getting quickly poached in a fish sauce broth for great savory flavor—to make a couple dozen hush puppies. The delicious remoulade sauce is also conveniently hacked here for your dipping pleasure.

REMOULADE SAUCE
½ **cup** mayonnaise
2 **tablespoons** milk
2 **teaspoons** finely minced cilantro
2 **teaspoons** finely minced garlic
1 **teaspoon** finely minced red bell pepper
1 **teaspoon** lemon juice
1 **teaspoon** paprika
⅛ **teaspoon** ground black pepper
Pinch of salt

HUSH PUPPIES
4 **cups** water
⅓ **cup** fish sauce
1 **4-ounce** cod fillet
4 **ounces (4 large)** uncooked shrimp, **peeled and deveined**

5 **ounces (1 cup)** all-purpose flour
2 **tablespoons** yellow cornmeal
1½ **teaspoons** baking powder
¾ **teaspoon** salt
¼ **teaspoon** garlic powder
¼ **teaspoon** onion powder
¼ **teaspoon** white pepper
Pinch of ground cayenne pepper
½ **cup** frozen yellow corn (**not sweet**)
¼ **cup** thinly bias-sliced green onion
2 **large** eggs
¾ **cup** milk
¼ **cup (½ stick)** unsalted butter, **softened**
1 **cup** panko bread crumbs

2 **cups** vegetable oil

1. Make the remoulade sauce by combining all of the ingredients in a medium bowl. Cover and chill until needed.

2. Combine the water and fish sauce in a medium saucepan over high heat and bring to a boil. Reduce the heat so that the liquid is just simmering, then add the fish fillet. Poach the fish for 5 minutes or until done, then remove it from the liquid to a plate. Turn off the heat. Add the shrimp to the pan and let it sit in there for 2 minutes, then take the shrimp out of the liquid and cool it on a plate with the fish. When cool, chop the fish fillet and shrimp into pieces about the size of shelled peanuts.

3. Combine the flour, cornmeal, baking powder, salt, garlic powder, onion powder, white pepper, and cayenne in a large bowl. Add the fish, shrimp, corn, and green onion and mix well. Beat 1 egg, combine it with ¼ cup of milk, then add it to the flour mixture along with the butter to form a stiff batter. Chill the batter for 30 minutes uncovered in your refrigerator.

4. While the batter is chilling, heat up the oil in a medium saucepan to 325 degrees F. Pour the bread crumbs into a medium bowl. Beat the remaining egg and mix it with the remaining ½ cup of milk in another medium bowl.

5. When the batter has rested, form it into balls that are about the size of walnuts. Dip each ball into the egg/milk mixture, then roll it in the bread crumbs and set the balls aside on a plate or sheet pan until they are all breaded.

6. Fry the hush puppies in the hot oil, several at a time, for 3 to 4 minutes or until golden brown. Serve with remoulade sauce on the side for dipping.

BUBBA GUMP SHRIMP CO. SHRIMP NEW ORLEANS

 First-Time Hack

 Active Prep: 30 min.
Inactive Prep: 10 min.

 Difficulty: Easy

 Yield: 2 entrées

The menu describes this dish as "an authentic recipe from our staff in the French Quarter! Lots of tender shrimp broiled with butter, garlic, and spices, and served with jasmine rice." The broiled shrimp recipe here is pretty basic stuff, but it's the amazing Worcestershire-based cream sauce that will get you hooked on this popular entrée. After all the shrimp is gone you'll be looking around for other things to dip in the sauce that's left over. That's why you get a slice of toasted garlic bread along with every dish. Oh, thank you.

RICE
1½ cups water
½ teaspoon salt
1 cup uncooked jasmine rice

NEW ORLEANS SAUCE
6 tablespoons unsalted butter
2 tablespoons finely minced onion
2 teaspoons finely minced garlic
⅓ cup chicken broth
5 tablespoons Worcestershire sauce
1 teaspoon lemon juice
1 teaspoon dried thyme
½ teaspoon dried basil
½ teaspoon ground black pepper **(coarse ground or freshly cracked)**
¼ teaspoon ground cayenne pepper
¼ teaspoon salt
1 cup heavy cream

SHRIMP
2 teaspoons paprika
1 teaspoon salt
¾ teaspoon ground black pepper
¾ teaspoon garlic powder
½ teaspoon onion powder
Pinch of ground cayenne pepper
24 large raw tails-on shrimp (31/40 per pound)
2 tablespoons unsalted butter, melted

GARNISH
¼ cup diced Roma tomato
¼ cup chopped green onion **(green part only)**

ON THE SIDE (OPTIONAL)
2 slices toasted garlic butter bread **(see Tidbits)**

1 Prepare the rice by bringing the water and salt to a boil in a medium saucepan over high heat. Add the rice, reduce the heat to low, and cover the pan. Cook for 15 to 20 minutes, then turn off the heat.

2 Make the sauce by melting the butter in a small saucepan over medium heat. Add the onion and garlic and cook for 1 minute, then add the chicken broth, Worcestershire sauce, lemon juice, thyme, basil, black pepper, cayenne, and salt and cook for 3 more minutes. Reduce the heat to medium/low and stir in the cream. When the sauce comes back up to a simmer, cook for 10 more minutes or until it starts to thicken. Turn off the heat and cover the sauce to keep it warm until later.

3 Preheat the broiler to high.

4 Combine the seasoning for the shrimp in a small bowl. Pierce each of the shrimp onto two skewers to keep them from curling up when cooked. You'll need 4 long skewers (to hold 12 shrimp on each pair) or 8 smaller skewers (6 shrimp on each pair). Brush the shrimp with the melted butter and sprinkle the shrimp with the seasoning. Arrange the shrimp on a baking sheet and broil for 3 to 4 minutes on the top rack or until the shrimp begins to char and blacken. Flip the shrimp over halfway through the broiling.

5 Prepare each dish by pressing the cooked rice into a 4-inch sauce bowl. Invert the bowl onto the center of a serving plate, then remove the bowl. Spoon a hefty portion of sauce around the rice and arrange 12 shrimp in the sauce around the rice with the tails pointing up. Sprinkle each dish with 2 tablespoons of diced tomato and 2 tablespoons of chopped green onion. Serve each dish with a slice of toasted garlic butter bread, if desired.

TIDBITS You can easily make garlic butter bread by adding a pinch of salt and a pinch of garlic powder to a tablespoon of melted butter. Brush the butter over each side of a thick slice of French bread or hoagie roll (sliced on the bias). Toast both sides in a hot skillet until browned.

33

BURGER KING STUFFED STEAKHOUSE BURGER

 First-Time Hack

Active Prep: 20 min.
Inactive Prep: 2 hrs.

 Difficulty: Easy

Yield: 4 burgers

In January 2011 Burger King introduced the fast-food world's first stuffed burger. Spicy bits of real jalapeño and little chunks of cheddar cheese are embedded in the quarter-pound beef patty, which is flame-broiled and stacked on a specialty bun with lettuce, tomato, and an excellent spicy poblano sauce. Making the burger is no big secret: just chop up jalapeños and cheddar cheese and work them into the ground beef, then freeze the patties so that they hold their shape when grilled. The freezing step also prevents the cheese from melting too much.

The poblano sauce is the best part of this recipe, although I had to design the formula to make much more than you will use on these four burgers because there needs to be enough volume for your food processor or blender to work its magic. If you have an extremely small food processor, you can certainly cut the sauce recipe in half and there will be plenty for all your burgers. If you go with the whole recipe, you'll have extra sauce left over to spread on other home-styled sandwiches or to use as a spicy dip for finger foods such as grilled artichokes or onion rings.

CREAMY POBLANO SAUCE

1 cup mayonnaise
2 tablespoons minced fresh poblano (pasilla) chile pepper
2 tablespoons ketchup
¾ teaspoon ground chipotle chile pepper
½ teaspoon lime juice
¼ teaspoon salt
¼ teaspoon ground cumin

BURGERS

2 medium jalapeños, seeded and finely diced (about ¼ cup)
3 ounces medium cheddar cheese, finely diced (about ⅓ cup)
1 pound ground beef

Salt
Ground black pepper
4 kaiser rolls or corn-dusted buns
8 tomato slices
4 iceberg lettuce leaves, coarsely chopped

1 Make the creamy poblano sauce by adding all of the ingredients to a small food processor or a blender. Process on high until the poblano pepper is barely visible. Spoon the sauce into a covered container and refrigerate it until needed.

2 Use your hands to mix the finely diced jalapeños and cheddar cheese with the ground beef. Divide the beef into 4 equal portions, roll each into a ball, and press onto a wax paper–lined baking sheet into the shape of patties that are slightly larger than the diameter of your buns. Lay

another sheet of wax paper on top of the patties and freeze the patties for at least 2 hours.

3 When the beef patties are frozen, preheat your barbecue grill or indoor grill to high heat. Cook the beef patties for 3 to 4 minutes per side or until done. Lightly salt and pepper the patties when you drop them onto the grill.

4 While your patties cook, preheat an indoor griddle or skillet to medium/high heat and brown the faces of the top and bottom buns.

5 Spread a generous portion of the poblano sauce on the face of the top buns.

6 When the beef is cooked, place each patty on the bottom buns.

7 Add two tomato slices on top of each beef patty, followed by a handful of chopped lettuce.

8 Flip the top bun over onto the burger and serve.

CAFE RIO CREAMY TOMATILLO DRESSING

🏅 First-Time Hack

🕐 Active prep: 5 min.
Inactive prep: 30 min.

E 🌡 Difficulty: Easy

👥 Yield: 2 cups

This fast-growing 73-unit chain offers up a variety of dishes inspired by the cuisine of Northern Mexico's Rio Grande, Southern Texas and New Mexico. Flour tortillas are skillfully hand-made all day long and stuffed with fire-grilled chicken or steak, or with pulled chicken breast or signature Cafe Rio Sweet Pork Barbacoa (page 37). If it's not a burrito that you crave, you can order a salad made with cilantro-lime rice, beans, and your choice of meat, and then have it topped off with a drizzling of this delicious Creamy Tomatillo Dressing, which you can now duplicate yourself in a matter of minutes for your own home salad masterpieces.

1 **cup** mayonnaise
2 **medium** tomatillos, **quartered**
¼ **cup chopped** cilantro
1 **tablespoon minced** garlic
1 **tablespoon minced** jalapeño (½ **jalapeño, seeded**)
1 **pkg. Hidden Valley Ranch Salad Dressing & Seasoning Mix (regular or buttermilk)**

❶ Combine all of the ingredients in a blender and blend on high speed until the jalapeño and garlic are well chopped up, about 30 seconds.

❷ Pour the dressing into a container with a lid and chill for about 30 minutes before use.

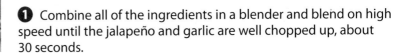

CAFE RIO
SWEET PORK
BARBACOA

 First-Time Hack

Active Prep: 15 min.
Inactive Prep:
5 hrs. 30 min.

E Difficulty: Easy

Yield: 8 servings

When building your burritos, tacos, or tostada salads there are several delicious fire-grilled and pulled meats to choose from at Cafe Rio, but the signature dish that everyone raves about is the Sweet Pork Barbacoa. The slow-braised pork is fork tender and comes in a sweet sauce that is flavored with a certain popular soft drink. Over the years I have debunked several culinary rumors of Coca-Cola being used in some secret recipes, but in this case I have confirmed that the rumors are indeed true. Coca-Cola *is* the secret ingredient that helps give this pork its sweet flavor.

For this clone you'll use the soda in the braising liquid and then again in the sweet sauce after the pork is shredded—you'll need a total of 72 ounces of Coke, or the same amount that's in a six-pack of cans. It's best if you can find Mexican Coke, which is made with real sugar rather than high-fructose corn syrup that's found in the U.S. version, but even the U.S. Coke makes a very tasty finished product. Use this pork in homemade burritos and tacos, and on salads with rice, beans, mixed greens, guacamole, cheese, and pico de gallo.

5 lb. pork shoulder

BRAISING LIQUID
48 ounces (4 12-ounce cans) Coca-Cola
2 cups chicken broth
½ cup (packed) dark brown sugar
1 tablespoon garlic powder
1 tablespoon onion powder
2 teaspoons salt

SAUCE
24 ounces (2 12-ounce cans) Coca-Cola
2 10-ounce cans mild enchilada sauce
1 cup (packed) dark brown sugar
1 teaspoon salt
½ teaspoon garlic powder
½ teaspoon onion powder

❶ Trim any excess fat from the pork shoulder roast.

❷ Combine all of the ingredients for the braising liquid in a large stockpot or Dutch oven over medium/high heat. Cook until the sugar dissolves, then carefully lower the pork into the liquid and cover. When the liquid comes to a full boil, reduce the heat and simmer for 4 hours. Turn the pork over every hour or so.

3 After 4 hours remove the pork from the liquid and discard the liquid. Cool the pork for 45 minutes to 1 hour or until you can handle it. Shred the pork into chunks, discarding any large portions of fat.

4 Clean out the pot, then pour all of the sauce ingredients into it over medium/high heat. Cook until the sugar dissolves, then add the pork back to the pot. Bring the sauce to a boil, then reduce the heat and simmer for 45 minutes, stirring occasionally to help shred the pork into smaller pieces, until the sauce reduces by about one-quarter of its original volume. The sauce will thicken as the pork cools. Use tongs to remove the pork from the sauce to serve.

CAFE RIO TRES LECHES CAKE

 First-Time Hack

Active Prep: 20 min.
Inactive Prep: 30 min.

 Difficulty: Medium

 Yield: 5 cakes

This hack of the decadent tres leches cake that's made fresh daily at Cafe Rio is an easy scratch sponge cake soaked with a generous mixture of evaporated milk, condensed milk, and cream and then chilled for several hours. There's also whole milk in the cake batter here, so we should call this "cuatro leches cake" if we want to be more accurate about it. The chain prepares the dessert in 4-inch foil tart pans, which can be tough to find in stores, so I use the more common and easier-to-find 5-inch potpie pans for this recipe. Homemade cream and sliced strawberries top off this Top Secret version of what is the best tres leches cake you'll find at any chain.

7½ ounces (1½ cups) all-purpose flour
1 teaspoon baking soda
1 teaspoon baking powder
¼ teaspoon salt
4 large eggs, separated
1 cup granulated sugar
¾ cup whole milk
1 teaspoon vanilla extract
1 12-ounce can evaporated milk
1 14-ounce can sweetened condensed milk
1¼ cups heavy cream

WHIPPED CREAM
1 cup heavy cream
2 tablespoons powdered sugar
¼ teaspoon vanilla extract

GARNISH
Sliced strawberries
5 mint sprigs

① Preheat the oven to 350 degrees F.

② Mix the flour with the baking soda, baking powder, and salt in a medium bowl and set it aside.

③ Beat the egg whites in a large bowl with an electric mixer on high speed until the whites form stiff peaks. Gradually add the sugar while beating. Beat in the yolks one at a time, mixing well after each addition.

④ Add the flour mixture a little bit at a time along with the milk, alternating the addition of each. Add the vanilla.

⑤ Rub each of five 5-inch foil potpie pans with some shortening or softened butter, or coat with nonstick cooking spray. Fill each pan halfway with batter and arrange the pans on a baking sheet. Bake for 25 to 30 minutes or until the tops have browned. Rotate the pan halfway through the baking time.

6 While the cakes bake, combine the evaporated milk, condensed milk, and cream in a medium bowl with an electric mixer on medium speed for 1 minute. When the cakes come out of the oven and while they are still warm, use a fork to poke several holes with quick jabs in the top of each cake. Pour the milk mixture into a 9 x 13-inch baking pan. Remove all of the cakes from their pans and invert them into the milk mixture for about a minute, then flip them all over to soak on the other side for another 30 seconds. Pour about ½ cup of the milk mixture back into each cake

pan and replace the cakes in the pans. Use up all of the milk mixture. Loosely cover the pans and chill the cakes until cold, about 3 hours or overnight.

7 When you are ready to serve the cakes, use an electric mixer to whip the cream in a medium bowl with the sugar and vanilla until stiff.

8 To serve the cakes, remove each one from the pans and place them on individual serving plates. Top each with sliced strawberries, whipped cream, and a sprig of mint.

THE CAPITAL GRILLE CREAMED CORN WITH SMOKED BACON

- First-Time Hack
- Prep Time: 15 min.
- Difficulty: Easy
- Yield: 4 servings

This 49-unit fine-dining eatery owned by Darden Restaurants—the company that operates the much more casual Olive Garden and Bahama Breeze chains—is an upscale steakhouse with mouthwatering entrée choices and an award-winning wine list. But the most-requested dishes on my "to clone" list from this chain come from the great selection of side dishes, including this addicting and easy-to-make creamed corn. What makes it so tasty is the smoky and salty flavor of the bacon and bacon fat—can't go wrong with a little bacon fat—complemented by a bit of sugar plus the added sweetness of the fresh corn, cooked just enough so that it still has a nice crunch to it. This recipe requires a little sugar, but if you are using a super sweet corn, you can cut the sugar listed here in half.

2 slices thick bacon, cooked and chopped
1 tablespoon bacon fat (from the cooked bacon)
4 ears of yellow corn
1 tablespoon unsalted butter
⅔ cup heavy cream
4 teaspoons granulated sugar
Pinch of salt
½ tablespoon all-purpose flour
¼ cup water

1 Cook the bacon until crispy in a large sauté pan over medium heat. Reserve 1 tablespoon of the bacon fat and chop the cooked bacon into small pieces.

2 Slice all of the corn from the cobs using a sharp knife.

3 Wipe out the sauté pan you used to cook the bacon and place it over medium/high heat. Add the bacon fat and the butter.

4 When the butter has melted, add the corn to the pan along with the bacon, cream, sugar, and salt. Stir the flour into the water in a small bowl and add the solution to the corn. Cook for 4 to 6 minutes or until the cream has thickened and the corn is cooked but still a little firm, stirring often. Pour the creamed corn into a dish and serve immediately.

THE CAPITAL GRILLE LOBSTER MAC 'N' CHEESE

 First-Time Hack

 Active Prep: 25 min.
Inactive Prep: 5 min.

E Difficulty: Easy

Yield: 4 servings

A video clip of an appearance that I discovered online from TV station WPRI in Rhode Island features Capital Grille chef Matthew Gallagher demonstrating the technique his restaurant uses to create its signature Lobster Mac 'N' Cheese side dish. Chef Gallagher explains that the chain uses four cheeses in the sauce: a soft cheese, a hard cheese, a flavorful cheese, and a sharp cheese, but he doesn't tell us exactly what those cheeses are.

After a trip to the restaurant to question the server, I discovered that the soft cheese is mascarpone, the flavorful cheese is Havarti, and the sharp cheese is white cheddar. My server said that the hard cheese is Parmesan, but after studying the menu and discovering Grana Padano being used to stuff the olives of the chain's 601 martini cocktail, I'm more inclined to use that in the recipe instead. If you can't find Grana Padano, go with the similar Parmigiano-Reggiano, or less expensive Parmesan.

The chain uses claw meat for the dish, which probably comes from the freshly cooked lobster it serves as entrées, but it's tough to find claw meat in stores without buying a whole fresh lobster. For this clone use the meat from two lightly poached medium lobster tails, which are much easier to procure. The restaurant uses campanelle pasta because it holds onto the sauce, but feel free to use bow tie pasta, tube-shaped pasta, even pasta shaped like dinosaurs if that's the mood you're in.

CRUMB TOPPING
1 tablespoon unsalted butter
½ cup panko bread crumbs
1 tablespoon grated Parmesan cheese

5 ounces lobster meat (2 small tails)
8 ounces uncooked campanelle pasta
   (12 ounces when cooked)

6 cups water
1 tablespoon plus **¼ teaspoon** salt
1¾ cups heavy cream
4 ounces (½ cup) mascarpone cheese
3 ounces (1 cup) shredded Havarti cheese
2 ounces (¾ cup) grated Grana Padano or
   Parmigiano-Reggiano cheese
1 ounce (¹/₃ cup) shredded white cheddar cheese

① Preheat the oven to 400 degrees F.

② Prepare the crumb topping by melting the butter in a small pan over medium heat, then add the bread crumbs. Cook for 3 to 4 minutes, stirring often, until the crumbs are browned. Pour the crumbs into a small bowl and stir in the Parmesan cheese. Set aside.

3 Poach the lobster tails in the shells for 2 minutes in boiling water. Remove the meat from the shells and chop it into large chunks. Set aside.

4 Prepare the pasta by dropping it into a 2½- to 3-quart saucepan filled with 6 cups of water plus 1 tablespoon of salt boiling over high heat. Cook the pasta for 8 minutes. It will still be very al dente (tough) at this point. Drain the pasta but don't rinse it.

5 Make the sauce by combining 1½ cups of cream with the remaining ¼ teaspoon salt in a medium saucepan over medium heat. When the cream begins to bubble, reduce the heat and add the mascarpone, Havarti, and Grana Padano (or Parmigiano-Reggiano).

Cook while stirring often for 3 minutes or until the sauce is smooth.

6 Pour the remaining ¼ cup of cream into a large skillet over medium heat. Add the lobster and cook for 2 to 3 minutes to heat up the lobster. Pour the cheese sauce into the pan along with the cooked pasta and add the cheddar cheese. Cook for 3 to 4 minutes until the cheese sauce begins to thicken a bit, then pour it all into an oven-safe serving dish. Use a small spoon to bring several chunks of lobster to the top (looks better this way!). Bake the mac and cheese in the oven for 4 to 5 minutes or until it begins to bubble around the edges.

7 Sprinkle the dish with the bread crumbs just before serving.

THE CAPITAL GRILLE CLASSIC CRÈME BRÛLÉE

 First-Time Hack

Active Prep: 15 min.
Inactive Prep: 45 min.

E Difficulty: Easy

Yield: 4 servings

For years now I've been on the lookout for a great chain restaurant crème brûlée to clone for one of my books, but hadn't located a really fantastic formula to hack until I tried this one. The Capital Grille's Classic Crème Brûlée is a perfect blend of sweet and creamy with amazing flavor that comes from real vanilla bean. If you want an easy dessert to impress that you can prepare a day or two in advance of the sit-down, this is your recipe. When it comes time to serve the brûlée, sprinkle each serving with a little white sugar and caramelize it with a small chef's torch (if you don't already have one, you can find them online or at kitchen stores for around 15 bucks). Add a garnish of fresh seasonal berries plus a sprig of mint, and serve up the goodness.

2 cups heavy cream
1 vanilla bean, split and scraped
6 egg yolks
⅓ cup granulated sugar
½ teaspoon vanilla extract

TOPPING
2 tablespoons granulated sugar

GARNISH
Fresh seasonal berries (blueberries, raspberries, blackberries, sliced strawberries)
Mint leaves

1 Preheat the oven to 300 degrees F.

2 Combine the cream with the vanilla bean and the pulp in a small saucepan over medium/high heat and cook, stirring, until the cream begins to bubble, then turn off the heat. Cover the pan and let it sit for 15 minutes. Remove the vanilla bean after the cream cools and strain the cream.

3 Beat the egg yolks, sugar, and vanilla in a medium bowl with a wire whisk or electric beater for about 1 minute, until thick and creamy and light yellow in color. Add the cream a little bit at a time while stirring gently so as not to make any bubbles. If there is any foam on top of your liquid wait until most of it goes away, then transfer the liquid to 4 crème brûlée dishes or ramekins.

4 Arrange the dishes or ramekins in a roasting pan and place it in the oven. Add hot water to the pan until it is about halfway up the side of the dishes or ramekins. Bake for 35 to 40 minutes or just

until the brûlée is set and no longer jiggles in the center. Carefully remove the dishes from the hot water, cool to room temperature, then cover and refrigerate for at least 4 hours or overnight.

5 To prepare for serving, remove the crème brûlée from the fridge and sprinkle each serving with about ½ tablespoon of sugar.

Shake the dish back and forth to evenly spread the sugar over the top of the brûlée. Use a chef's torch in a sweeping motion to caramelize the sugar on top until crispy and brown. Let the crème brûlée sit for a couple of minutes so that the sugar cools, then sprinkle the dessert with a handful of fresh berries and a mint leaf and serve.

CARRABBA'S ITALIAN GRILL COZZE IN BIANCO (STEAMED MUSSELS)

 First-Time Hack

 Active Prep: 15 min.
Inactive Prep: 20 min.

 Difficulty: Easy

 Yield: 2 servings

When mussels are prepared right they can be a great starter dish for a variety of meals. I think Carrabba's version—which is one of the chain's signature dishes—is the best you'll find at any casual chain in the country, and now you can make a perfect copy with minimal effort in your own kitchen. Carrabba's uses mussels that are grown off the coast of Prince Edward Island in Canada. They are small and sweet, so try to find these mussels for your clone, and be sure to clean the mussels well before steaming them. Make faces happy by serving some crusty bread on the side for dipping into the leftover lemon butter sauce.

26 to 32 small mussels

LEMON BUTTER SAUCE
½ cup (1 stick) unsalted butter
1 teaspoon minced garlic
2 teaspoons dry white wine (Chablis)
2 teaspoons lemon juice
⅛ teaspoon salt
⅛ teaspoon white pepper
¼ cup heavy cream

2 tablespoons extra virgin olive oil
2 tablespoons chopped onion
1 tablespoon chopped garlic
¼ cup dry white wine (Chablis)
2 tablespoons Pernod liqueur
½ lemon
¼ cup coarsely chopped fresh basil

ON THE SIDE (OPTIONAL)
Crusty bread for dipping

1 Clean the mussels before you prepare them. Remove any beards from the mussels and let them soak in cold water for 20 minutes so that they expel any sand.

2 While the mussels soak, make the lemon butter sauce by melting the butter in a small saucepan over low heat. Add the garlic and cook slowly for 5 minutes, but do not let the garlic brown. Add the wine, lemon juice, salt, and white pepper; raise the temperature just a little bit and cook for another 3 minutes or until simmering. Turn off the heat. When the sauce stops bubbling, whisk in the cream. Turn the heat to low and cook for about 3 minutes, whisking often, until the sauce is hot and thick. Cover and turn off the heat.

3 Heat the oil in a large sauté pan over medium heat and add the cleaned mussels. Cover the pan and cook for 1 minute.

4 Add the onion and garlic to the pan with the mussels and toss or stir well. Cover and cook for 1 minute.

5 Add the white wine and Pernod to the pan. Cover and cook for another 2 minutes or until all of the mussels have opened. Toss the mussels with the sauce a couple of times while cooking.

6 Use the lid of the pan to hold all of the mussels in while draining off the liquid in the pan. Squeeze the juice out of the lemon into the pan, then add all of the lemon butter sauce to the pan along with the basil. Toss well and pour into a serving dish. Serve with some bread on the side, if desired.

CARRABBA'S ITALIAN GRILL POLLO ROSA MARIA

First-Time Hack

Active Prep: 30 min.
Inactive Prep: 12 min.

Difficulty: Medium

Yield: 4 servings

The secret to the signature flavor of the most popular grilled dishes at Carrabba's, including the Pollo Rosa Maria, is a top secret grill baste that is applied to the food as it cooks. According to servers at the chain, the base formula contains butter, oil, vinegar, and seasoning, and it flames up big time when applied to the chicken, giving the dish a fantastic smoky flavor. Carrabba's famous lemon butter sauce and mushrooms top the chicken breasts stuffed with Fontina cheese and prosciutto for an impressive signature entrée that can now be perfectly duplicated by you.

GRILL BASTE
¼ **cup (½ stick)** unsalted butter
¼ **cup** extra virgin olive oil
1 **tablespoon** balsamic vinegar
1 **teaspoon** white wine vinegar
2 **teaspoons minced** garlic
1 **teaspoon minced fresh** parsley
½ **teaspoon** salt
½ **teaspoon** ground black pepper
¼ **teaspoon** dried oregano
¼ **teaspoon** dried basil
¼ **teaspoon** crushed red pepper flakes

LEMON BUTTER SAUCE
½ **cup (1 stick)** unsalted butter
1 **teaspoon minced** garlic
2 **teaspoons** dry white wine **(Chablis)**

2 **teaspoons** lemon juice
⅛ **teaspoon** salt
⅛ **teaspoon** white pepper
¼ **cup** heavy cream

MUSHROOMS
1 **tablespoon** unsalted butter
1 **tablespoon** extra virgin olive oil
8 **ounces (3 cups) sliced** mushrooms
¼ **teaspoon** salt
¼ **teaspoon** ground black pepper
1 **tablespoon chopped fresh** basil

4 **6-ounce skinless** chicken breast fillets
4 **¼-ounce slices** prosciutto
4 **½-ounce slices** Fontina cheese
Salt
Ground black pepper

1 Preheat your grill to high.

2 Make the grill baste by combining all of the ingredients in a small saucepan and bringing it to a simmer over medium heat. Turn off the heat when the mixture begins to bubble in the middle of the pan.

3 Make the lemon butter sauce by melting the butter in a small saucepan over low heat. Add the garlic and cook slowly for 5 minutes, but do not let the garlic brown. Add the wine, lemon juice, salt, and white pepper, then raise the temperature just a little bit and cook for another 3 minutes or until

simmering. Turn off the heat. When the sauce stops bubbling, whisk in the cream. Turn the heat to low and cook for about 3 minutes, whisking often, until the sauce is hot and thick. Cover the pan and turn off the heat.

4 Prepare the mushrooms by combining the butter with the oil in a sauté pan over medium heat. When the butter has melted, add the sliced mushrooms, salt, and pepper and cook for 2 to 3 minutes or until the mushrooms are browned. Add the mushrooms to the lemon butter sauce along with the basil.

5 Make a deep slice through the middle of each chicken breast, but not all of the way through, making a flap that you can open.

Place a slice of prosciutto and a slice of Fontina cheese inside each chicken breast and close the flap over the fillings. Rub each chicken breast with a little olive oil and sprinkle with salt and pepper. Grill the chicken for 10 to 12 minutes until done. Flip the chicken over several times as it cooks and use a brush to baste the chicken breasts thoroughly with the grill baste each time you flip the chicken.

6 Serve the chicken breasts with the lemon butter sauce and mushrooms spooned over the top.

TIDBITS You can also cook the chicken using a grill pan on your stovetop preheated over medium heat.

THE CHEESECAKE FACTORY FRIED MACARONI AND CHEESE

🏅 First-Time Hack

🕐 Active Prep: 30 min.
Inactive Prep: 5 hrs.

🌡 Difficulty: Medium

👥 Yield: 4 to 6 servings

Grossing an average of over $10 million per restaurant each year, The Cheesecake Factory continues to ring up more dollars per store than any other chain in the U.S.

The fantastic cheesecakes make up a big part of that sales figure, but the chain's ginormous menu, which appeals to a wide variety of tastes, is what brings customers back over and over again. One of the top-selling items these days is the Fried Macaroni and Cheese appetizer that I discovered could be re-created at home by forming macaroni and cheese into balls, which are then frozen, breaded, and fried to a crispy golden brown. I made a simple formula here for the creamy marinara dipping sauce by adding heavy cream to bottled marinara sauce. I ran some taste tests and concluded that Newman's Own brand was a close match to the sauce served at the restaurant. Feel free, though, to use any marinara sauce you like.

This recipe will make twelve fried macaroni and cheese balls, which is enough to serve as an appetizer for four to six.

MACARONI AND CHEESE BALLS
4 ounces uncooked cavatappi or twisted elbows pasta
2 tablespoons unsalted butter
2 tablespoons all-purpose flour
2 cups whole milk
3 ounces (about 1 cup) shredded medium cheddar cheese
3 ounces (about 1 cup) shredded Monterey Jack cheese
3 ounces (about 1 cup) shredded Fontina cheese
1 teaspoon salt
2 large eggs, beaten

1 cup all-purpose flour
2 cups panko bread crumbs
6 to 12 cups vegetable oil

CREAMY MARINARA DIPPING SAUCE
1 cup bottled marinara sauce
½ cup heavy cream

GARNISH
Finely shredded Parmesan cheese
Sprig or two of fresh flat-leaf parsley

1 Prepare the macaroni by cooking the pasta in 6 cups of boiling water in a medium saucepan over high heat until tender (8 to 10 minutes). Strain the water from the pasta using a colander or large strainer.

❷ Make the cheese sauce by melting the butter in a medium saucepan over medium/low heat. Whisk in the flour and cook for a couple of minutes. Whisk in 1 cup of the milk, then add the cheeses and salt. Continue cooking, stirring often, until the sauce is smooth with no lumps of cheese. Stir in the pasta. Pour the mixture into a rectangular baking dish, cover, and refrigerate for 2 hours.

❸ When the macaroni and cheese is cold, slice it into 12 pieces with a knife (4 rows down and 3 across). Use your hands to remove each section, form it into a ball, and arrange each of the balls on wax paper. Freeze for 1½ hours.

❹ When the macaroni and cheese balls are frozen, combine the beaten eggs and the remaining 1 cup of milk in a small bowl, pour the flour into another small bowl, and pour the bread crumbs into a third small bowl.

❺ Roll each macaroni and cheese ball first in the flour, then dip it into the egg/milk mixture, and then roll it in the bread crumbs until well coated. Dip each ball back into the egg/milk for a second time and then roll it around in the bread crumbs again for a nice, thick breading. Arrange all of the breaded mac and cheese balls on the wax paper and let them rest in your refrigerator for 1½ hours or overnight.

❻ When you are ready to fry the macaroni and cheese balls, preheat the oil in a deep fryer or large saucepan with a cooking thermometer attached to 325 degrees F. Fry the balls, a few at a time, for 4 to 5 minutes or until brown. Drain the balls on a rack until they are all fried.

❼ While the macaroni and cheese balls are frying, combine the marinara sauce with the cream in a small bowl and heat it up in your microwave oven for 1 minute (or in a small saucepan over medium heat until hot).

❽ Pour the creamy marinara sauce into a serving dish and arrange the fried macaroni and cheese balls in the sauce. Sprinkle a little shredded Parmesan cheese over each of the macaroni and cheese balls. Add a sprig or two of parsley to the dish and serve.

THE CHEESECAKE FACTORY STUFFED MUSHROOMS

First-Time Hack

Active Prep: 20 min.
Inactive Prep: 20 min.

Difficulty: Medium

Yield: 4 servings

Despite years of numerous requests to clone the stuffed mushrooms at The Cheesecake Factory, I never ordered the popular appetizer before embarking on this food hacking mission. But let me tell you, once I had my first bite of these mushrooms, with the perfect stuffing, creamy Madeira wine sauce, and crispy Parmesan topping, I understood all the big raves. Not only is this one of the best appetizers on the chain's menu, but these are far and away the best stuffed mushrooms I've ever had. And the clone would have to be just as good no matter how long it took! After many hours in the lab washing mushrooms, chopping mushrooms, and eating them, I finally worked up this hack that I'm convinced would fool even the biggest fans of the dish in a side-by-side taste test.

SAUCE
⅓ cup minced mushroom stems (from mushrooms below)
1 tablespoon vegetable oil
2 tablespoons minced shallots
¼ cup Madeira wine
½ cup beef broth
½ cup heavy cream
⅛ teaspoon paprika
Pinch of salt
Pinch of ground black pepper

MUSHROOMS
20 medium white button mushrooms
¼ cup (½ stick) unsalted butter
2 teaspoons minced garlic
2 pinches of salt
2 pinches of ground black pepper
¼ cup Italian-style seasoned bread crumbs (such as Progresso brand)
½ cup shredded Fontina cheese

TOPPING
1 tablespoon unsalted butter, melted
¼ cup panko bread crumbs
¼ cup finely shredded Parmesan cheese
2 tablespoons finely minced fresh parsley
⅛ teaspoon salt

1 Make the sauce by removing all of the stems from the mushrooms, then mince some of the stems so that you have ⅓ cup. Heat up the oil in a small saucepan over medium heat. Add the mushroom stems and shallots and cook for 2 to 3 minutes or until the shallots and mushrooms begin to brown. Add the wine and, when it begins to bubble, cook for 1 to 2 minutes or until it reduces by half. Add the beef broth and cook for another 2 to 3 minutes or until the sauce reduces by about half. Strain the sauce through a wire mesh strainer to remove the mushroom stems and shallots. Rinse the saucepan and return the sauce to the pan (discard the mushroom stems and shallots). Add the cream, paprika, salt, and pepper and simmer for 7 to 10 minutes or until the sauce darkens and thickens—it should reduce by a little more than half.

2 Set aside the 12 most awesome-looking mushrooms, then finely mince the remaining mushrooms to make approximately 1 cup of minced mushrooms.

3 Melt 2 tablespoons of butter in a small sauté pan over medium heat. Add the 1 cup of minced mushrooms, garlic, salt, and pepper and sauté for 2 minutes or until just beginning to brown. Turn off the heat and gently stir in the seasoned bread crumbs (don't overmix). Pour the mixture into a medium bowl, then stir in the cheese.

4 Use your hands to form the stuffing into loose balls and press them into the mushroom caps. Set the stuffed mushrooms aside and preheat your oven to high broil.

5 Make the topping by melting 1 tablespoon butter over medium heat. Add the bread crumbs and cook, stirring often, until the bread crumbs begin to brown. Pour the bread crumbs into a small bowl. When the bread crumbs are cool, add the remaining topping ingredients.

6 Melt the remaining 2 tablespoons of butter. Arrange the stuffed mushrooms on a baking sheet and brush the tops and sides generously with the melted butter. Broil for 2 to 4 minutes or until the tops are brown.

7 Plate the mushrooms by pouring the sauce into a serving dish. Arrange the mushrooms on the sauce, sprinkle a little of the topping over the top of each of them (you will not use all of the topping), and serve.

THE CHEESECAKE FACTORY MASHED RED POTATOES

First-Time Hack

Active Prep: 5 min.
Inactive Prep: 25 min.

E Difficulty: Easy

Yield: 4 servings

I am including this new hack of the side dish served with some entrées at The Cheesecake Factory because it is the perfect companion for the much improved Chicken Madeira recipe (that I've included on page 58) or as a side for just about any dish you're cooking tonight. Because the skin on red potatoes is so thin, you save time by not having to peel them. I like that. Just quarter the potatoes, boil until tender, mash 'em up, add the remaining ingredients, and cook until hot.

2 pounds red potatoes, quartered
¼ cup (½ stick) unsalted butter
1 teaspoon minced garlic

⅔ cup heavy cream
1 teaspoon salt
1 teaspoon ground black pepper

1 Drop all of the quartered potatoes in a 3-quart saucepan of boiling water over medium heat and cook for 25 to 30 minutes, until tender when stuck with a knife. Drain the potatoes.

2 Pour the potatoes into a large mixing bowl and mash them well with a potato masher.

3 Rinse out the saucepan. Add the butter to it and place it over medium/low heat. When the butter has melted, add the minced garlic and cook for 2 minutes.

4 Add the potatoes back to the saucepan with the butter and garlic. Stir in the cream, salt, and pepper and cook, stirring often, until the potatoes are hot, about 10 minutes.

THE CHEESECAKE FACTORY CHICKEN MADEIRA

👍 Improved Hack

⟳ Active Prep: 30 min.
Inactive Prep: 30 min.

M🌡 Difficulty: Medium

👥 Yield: 4 servings

The secret to perfectly replicating The Cheesecake Factory's most popular chicken dish—which is thin chicken breast fillets topped with asparagus, cheese, mushrooms, and a Madeira sauce—starts with creating the perfect clone of the sauce. My first go at this dish revealed a simplified version of the sauce that, while quite delicious, does not duplicate the flavor or color as closely as I think it should. That's why I went back into the lab and spent several days working on just the sauce. After many attempts I found that infusing the sauce with flavor from carrots, celery, onions, and garlic, then straining and reducing the sauce to around one-quarter of its original volume, gave me a perfectly rich flavor that much more accurately mirrors the original. I also noticed that when I chilled the sauce from the restaurant, it solidified to the consistency of a Jell-O shot. A clue! I added unflavored gelatin to my version of the sauce, which gave it the perfect velvetiness of a collagen-infused stock reduction. It was now perfect. The full-size entrée at the restaurant includes two thin chicken breast fillets, but since this restaurant typically serves giant, often unfinishable portions, I've reduced this dish to one breast fillet per serving to give you a total yield of four servings. Of course you can always double up to make two bigger servings that end up looking just like those at the restaurant. You'll want to be very hungry for those plates.

MADEIRA SAUCE
2 tablespoons vegetable oil
½ cup diced carrots
½ cup diced onions
½ cup diced celery
2 teaspoons minced garlic
2 cups Madeira wine
1 tablespoon tomato paste
2 cups beef broth
2 tablespoons dark brown sugar
2 teaspoons unflavored gelatin (1 envelope)
⅛ teaspoon salt

2 skinless chicken breast fillets
2 tablespoons vegetable oil
2 large eggs, beaten
1 cup all-purpose flour
Salt
Ground black pepper
8 asparagus spears
2 tablespoons unsalted butter
2 cups sliced mushrooms
2 cups shredded mozzarella cheese

1 Make the Madeira sauce by heating up the oil in a 2½-quart saucepan over medium heat. Add the carrots, onions, celery, and garlic and cook for 3 minutes or until the vegetables begin to brown. Add the wine and tomato paste and cook for 5 to 7 minutes (once it begins to simmer) or until the wine reduces by half. Add the beef broth and cook for 10 to 15 minutes (once it begins to simmer) or until the sauce again reduces by half. Strain the sauce through a wire mesh strainer and rinse the pan. Whisk the brown sugar, gelatin, and salt into the strained sauce (discard what's left in the strainer), then pour the sauce back into the pan. Cook the sauce for another 5 to 7 minutes or until it reduces by half and thickens. You should have about 1 cup of sauce.

2 Make the chicken by slicing through the middle of each chicken breast, making 4 thinner chicken breast fillets. Cover the chicken with plastic wrap. Pound the fillets to about ¼ inch thick with a kitchen mallet.

3 Heat up the oil in a sauté pan over medium heat. Pour the beaten eggs into a plate or pie pan. Add the flour to another plate or pie pan. Dredge each chicken breast in the egg, coating both sides, then press it into the flour, coating both sides. Drop the chicken breasts into the hot sauté pan, sprinkle with salt and pepper, and cook for 3 to 4 minutes per side or until browned. Cover all of the chicken fillets when they are done to keep them warm.

4 Preheat your broiler to high heat.

5 Steam the asparagus in a steamer basket in a saucepan over boiling water for 3 to 4 minutes or until bright green.

6 Prepare the mushrooms by melting the butter in a sauté pan over medium/high heat. Add the sliced mushrooms, sprinkle with a little salt and pepper, and cook for 3 to 4 minutes or until the mushrooms begin to brown.

7 Assemble the entrée by placing the chicken breasts on a baking sheet. Cross two spears of asparagus over the top of each chicken fillet, then cover each with a generous pile of shredded mozzarella cheese.

8 Broil the chicken for 2 to 3 minutes or just until the cheese begins to brown.

9 Prepare each plate by placing a chicken breast on the serving plate. Spoon some mushrooms onto the chicken, then spoon a few tablespoons of Madeira sauce over the top.

THE CHEESECAKE FACTORY LOUISIANA CHICKEN PASTA

 First-Time Hack

 Active Prep: 40 min.
Inactive Prep: 12 min.

M🌡 Difficulty: Medium

👥 Yield: 4 servings

The menu describes this dish as "Parmesan-crusted chicken served over pasta with mushrooms, bell peppers, and onions in a spicy New Orleans sauce." Of the many great pastas on The Cheesecake Factory's menu, this one consistently ranks as a top choice, so a *Top Secret Recipes* hack was inevitable. To clone this recipe you must first start with the delicious, yet simple-to-make, New Orleans sauce, which is basically an alfredo sauce with a little paprika for color and cayenne pepper for kick. The chicken is breaded with a combination of panko bread crumbs and Parmesan cheese, and pan-fried to a golden brown. In true Cheesecake Factory style, this recipe makes four very large servings, but you can also serve this dish on one big platter for a nice family-style feast.

SPICY NEW ORLEANS SAUCE
½ cup (1 stick) unsalted butter
2 teaspoons minced garlic
2 cups heavy cream
¾ cup grated Parmesan cheese
2 teaspoons paprika
2 teaspoons lemon juice
½ teaspoon ground black pepper
½ teaspoon ground cayenne pepper
¼ teaspoon salt
¼ teaspoon dried oregano

1 pound farfalle pasta
4 skinless chicken breast fillets
1 cup all-purpose flour
2 large eggs, beaten

1 cup milk
1½ cups panko bread crumbs
1 cup shredded Parmesan cheese
1 teaspoon salt
½ teaspoon ground black pepper
Vegetable oil
2 cups sliced white button mushrooms
½ cup diced red bell pepper
½ cup diced yellow bell pepper
¼ cup chopped green onion (white and light green parts only)
4 teaspoons minced garlic

GARNISH
Minced fresh parsley

① Make the sauce by melting the butter in a medium saucepan over medium/low heat. Add the garlic and cook it slowly in the butter for 5 minutes. Don't let it brown.

❷ Whisk in the remaining ingredients, increase the heat to medium, and cook until the mixture begins to bubble. Reduce the heat and simmer the mixture for 12 to 15 minutes or until the sauce thickens.

❸ Prepare the farfalle pasta by dropping it into 4 to 6 quarts of boiling water in a large pot. Cook for 11 to 12 minutes, or until the pasta is done. Drain.

❹ Make two thinner chicken fillets from each chicken breast by slicing each one in half through the middle. Cover the chicken with plastic wrap and pound the fillets to about ¼ inch thick with a kitchen mallet.

❺ Pour the flour into a medium bowl. Combine the beaten eggs and milk in another medium bowl. Combine the bread crumbs, ½ cup of the Parmesan cheese, salt, and pepper in a third medium bowl.

❻ Preheat about ¼ inch of vegetable oil in a large sauté pan over medium heat.

❼ Bread the chicken by coating each fillet first with the flour, then dip it into the egg/milk mixture. Let the excess egg/milk drip off, then press each fillet into the bread crumbs/Parmesan. Flip each fillet over a couple of times to make sure it's well breaded.

❽ Cook the fillets in the hot oil for 3 to 5 minutes per side, until they are golden brown. Drain the fillets on a paper towel–lined plate.

❾ Prepare two servings at a time by heating 1 tablespoon of oil over medium/high heat. Add 1 cup of mushrooms, ¼ cup of red bell pepper, and ¼ cup of yellow bell pepper. Add 2 tablespoons green onion and 2 teaspoons garlic. Cook for 2 minutes or until the peppers begin to brown. Add half of the pasta to the pan and toss it until it's hot, then turn off the heat. Stir in half of the New Orleans sauce. Divide the pasta onto two serving plates. Arrange two breaded chicken fillets, chopped in half, on top of the pasta on each plate. Sprinkle each serving with parsley. Repeat for the remaining servings.

THE CHEESECAKE FACTORY FRESH STRAWBERRY CHEESECAKE

First-Time Hack

Active Prep: 20 min.
Inactive Prep: 5 hrs.
30 min.

M Difficulty: Medium

Yield: 12 servings

I've hacked many a cheesecake from The Cheesecake Factory in several *Top Secret Recipes* cookbooks but have yet to clone the cheesecake that's been the chain's top-seller for the last thirty years . . . until now. Here is a brand-new hack for the chain's original cheesecake recipe with fresh strawberries in strawberry glaze on top. One difference with this recipe versus any that I've previously cracked is the larger size of the cheesecake. This recipe will fill a 10-inch springform cake pan all the way to the top, giving you twelve big servings. When you cut some parchment paper to line the pan, be sure to make the paper that goes around the inside of the pan a little taller than the pan itself. This way, when the cheesecake swells up as it cooks, it won't overflow the pan. As the cheesecake cools it will come back down to about flush with the cake pan. Because the cake is so thick, you will cook it for 70 minutes in a 350 degree F oven, then you will turn the oven off and let the cake sit in there for 20 minutes more to cook through. Use strawberry glaze that's usually found in the produce department at your local grocery store.

CRUST
9 ounces (2 cups) graham cracker crumbs
2 tablespoons granulated sugar
¼ teaspoon ground cinnamon
½ cup (1 stick) unsalted butter, **melted**

CHEESECAKE FILLING
40 ounces (5 8-ounce pkgs.) Philadelphia
   cream cheese, **softened**

1⅔ cups granulated sugar
5 large eggs
½ cup sour cream
2½ teaspoons vanilla extract

36 fresh strawberries
2 cups strawberry glaze

OPTIONAL
Extra creamy canned whipped cream

1 Line the bottom and sides of a 10-inch springform cake pan with parchment paper. Make the parchment paper lining the side of the pan slightly higher than the pan to hold in the filling as it rises. Butter the pan to make the paper stick. Wrap foil around the bottom of the pan to keep it dry when in the water bath.

2 Combine the graham cracker crumbs with the sugar and cinnamon in a medium bowl. Stir in the melted butter, then press the crumbs into the bottom of the lined pan and about two-thirds of the way up the side. Use the bottom of a glass or bottle to press the crumbs flat. Place the pan in your freezer until you are ready to fill it.

3 Preheat the oven to 350 degrees F. Fill a pan that is larger than the springform pan with ½ inch of water and place it in the center of the oven.

4 Make the cheesecake filling by combining the cream cheese with the sugar in a large bowl with an electric mixer on high

speed. When the mixture is smooth, mix in the eggs, sour cream, and vanilla. Pour all of the filling into the springform pan. Smooth the top with a spatula, then gently place the pan in the water bath in the oven and bake for 70 minutes or until the top is light brown. After 70 minutes, turn the oven heat off and let the cheesecake sit in the closed oven for another 20 minutes. Remove the cheesecake from the oven and let it cool, then cover and chill for at least 4 hours in the refrigerator.

5 To serve the cheesecake, remove it from the springform pan and cut into 12 slices. Slice the stem end off the strawberries, then dip each strawberry into the glaze (it helps to pierce the strawberry with a skewer to dip it into the glaze). Place a slice of cheesecake on a serving plate. Place two glazed strawberries on top of each slice of cheesecake and one strawberry on the plate. Add a dollop of whipped cream on top of each slice of cheesecake and a dollop of whipped cream on the plate, if desired.

THE CHEESECAKE FACTORY VANILLA BEAN CHEESECAKE

🏅 First-Time Hack

⟩ Active Prep: 30 min.
Inactive Prep: 5 hrs.

M🌡 Difficulty: Medium

👥 Yield: 12 servings

The secret to a super-creamy cheesecake that's not cracked on top—just like those you get at The Cheesecake Factory—is baking the cheesecake in a water bath. You will need a 10-inch springform cake pan for this recipe and another pan that is larger than the springform pan to hold some water for the cheesecake to sit in while it bakes. This cheesecake has vanilla bean seeds throughout every layer, so you will need three vanilla bean pods. Those vanilla beans can be pricey at around 5 bucks per pod, but you're cloning a cheesecake that at the restaurant costs around 50 bucks for a whole 10-inch cake. Even when you figure in the other ingredients, you're still gonna pay less by making your own home knockoff. And any leftovers will freeze well for a month or two.

CRUST
11 ounces (1 box) Nilla wafers
½ cup (1 stick) unsalted butter, **melted**

VANILLA BEAN CHEESECAKE FILLING
24 ounces (3 8-ounce pkgs.) Philadelphia cream cheese, **softened**
1 cup granulated sugar

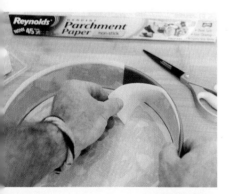

3 large eggs
⅓ cup sour cream
2 teaspoons vanilla extract
Seeds scraped from 1½ vanilla beans

VANILLA BEAN MOUSSE
8 ounces (1 pkg.) Philadelphia cream cheese, softened
2 large egg yolks
¾ cup granulated sugar
1½ teaspoons unflavored gelatin
2 tablespoons water
2¼ cups heavy cream
2 teaspoons vanilla extract
Seeds scraped from 1 vanilla bean

VANILLA BEAN WHIPPED CREAM
½ teaspoon unflavored gelatin
2 teaspoons water
1¼ cups heavy cream
¼ cup granulated sugar
½ teaspoon vanilla extract
Seeds scraped from ½ of a vanilla bean

OPTIONAL
Extra creamy canned whipped cream

❶ Line the bottom and sides of a 10-inch springform cake pan with parchment paper. Lightly butter the pan to make the paper stick. Wrap a sheet of aluminum foil around the outside of the springform pan so that the water cannot get into the pan when it is submerged in the water bath in the oven.

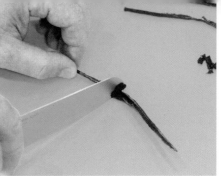

2 Make the crust by pulverizing the cookies into crumbs using a food processor or blender, or crushing them by hand in a bag with a kitchen mallet. Mix the melted butter with the Nilla wafer crumbs and press the mixture into the bottom of the lined pan. Place the pan in your freezer until you are ready to fill it.

3 Preheat the oven to 350 degrees F. Fill a pan that is larger than the springform pan with ½ inch of water and place it in the center of the oven.

4 Make the cheesecake filling by combining the cream cheese with the sugar in a large bowl with an electric mixer on high speed. When the mixture is smooth add the eggs, sour cream, and vanilla. Slice the vanilla beans in half and use the edge of a knife to scrape out the seeds. Add the seeds to the cream cheese and mix well with an electric mixer until smooth, about 1 minute. Pour all of the filling into the springform pan. Smooth the top with a spatula, then gently place the pan in the water bath in the oven and bake for 70 minutes or until the top is light brown.

5 Cool the cheesecake, then set it in your refrigerator while you make the vanilla bean mousse.

6 Make the vanilla bean mousse by placing a saucepan that is half full of water over medium heat. Use an electric mixer to whip together the cream cheese, egg yolks, and sugar in a metal bowl. Place this bowl over the pan of hot water, stirring often, until the sugar is dissolved and the mixture is hot, about 5 minutes. Place the hot bowl into another bowl filled with ice to cool it down while you whip the cream. Combine the gelatin with the water in a small bowl and quickly pour the mixture (before it solidifies) into the cream in a medium bowl and stir it. Add the vanilla extract and vanilla bean seeds and whip the cream with an electric mixer on high speed until stiff peaks form. Fold the whipped cream in several batches into the cooled cream cheese/egg yolk mixture. Spread it over the top of the cheesecake. Chill for 3 hours.

7 After the cheesecake has cooled for 3 hours, make the whipped cream by

combining the gelatin with the water in a small bowl and quickly pouring it into the cream along with the sugar, vanilla, and vanilla bean seeds in a large bowl. Whip with an electric mixer until the cream forms stiff peaks, then spread the whipped cream over the top of the cheesecake. Allow the cake to set for another hour, then remove the cheesecake from the springform pan and slice it into 12 portions to serve.

CHICK-FIL-A CHICKEN SANDWICH

 Improved Hack

 Active Prep: 20 min.
Inactive Prep: 2 hrs.

M Difficulty: Medium

Yield: 4 sandwiches

Pickle juice, huh? I think not. While researching this recipe I came across several unusual formulas on the Internet that claim the secret to the great taste of the chicken fillet in this sandwich comes from marinating it in pickle juice. I can only guess that this odd hack originated when someone sampled the fillet removed from a sandwich and detected the distinct taste of pickles, most likely because there are pickles stacked on the sandwich directly under the chicken so the pickle flavor had transferred to the fillet. But we don't need to do any guesswork to disqualify the ingredient. This widespread pickle juice theory is easily debunked by simply checking out the list of ingredients posted on the Chick-fil-A website. Not a speck of pickle juice in there, nor any other unusual ingredients. I did discover that marinating the chicken before breading *is* a big part of the secret to its flavor and juiciness. In this case, though, we'll just be using a common brine containing salt, sugar, and MSG, a natural flavor enhancer.

I first cloned this signature sandwich from the growing chain way back in the '90s, but over the years I have learned new secrets for making fantastic fried chicken fillets that look and taste exactly like those you'll find at the famous food chains. In addition to the 2-hour brining process, another big change to this recipe includes adding baking powder to the breading to make it perfectly crispy and a beautiful golden brown color. Thanks to these changes and a few other tweaks, this is probably the best chicken breading secret formula that I have come up with, and it makes a far better clone for this famous chicken sandwich than any recipe you will find—with or without pickle juice.

BRINE
4 teaspoons salt
1 tablespoon granulated sugar
1½ teaspoons MSG (such as Accent seasoning)
2 cups water
1 teaspoon paprika
¼ teaspoon onion powder
¼ teaspoon garlic powder
¼ teaspoon white pepper

4 small skinless chicken breast fillets or 2 large skinless chicken breast fillets
4 to 8 cups peanut oil
1 large egg, beaten
1 cup milk

BREADING
1 cup all-purpose flour
2 tablespoons powdered sugar
1 teaspoon salt
1 teaspoon MSG
1 teaspoon baking powder
½ teaspoon paprika
½ teaspoon ground white pepper
¼ teaspoon garlic powder
¼ teaspoon onion powder

¼ cup margarine, melted
4 plain white hamburger buns
8 dill pickle hamburger slices

1 Make the brine for the chicken by dissolving the salt, sugar, and MSG in the water in a medium bowl. Add the other ingredients.

2 If using large chicken breasts, slice them in half. Cover the chicken breast fillets with plastic wrap and pound them to between ¼ inch and ½ inch thick using a kitchen mallet, then place them into the bowl of brine and marinate for 2 hours in your refrigerator.

3 When the chicken has "brinerated" for 2 hours, remove it from the brine and rinse off each fillet. Blot them dry with paper towels.

4 Preheat the oil in a deep fryer or a large saucepan (the oil should be at least 3 to 4 inches deep) to 325 degrees F.

5 Combine the beaten egg with the milk in a medium bowl. Combine all of the breading ingredients in a shallow bowl or pie pan.

6 Bread each chicken fillet by first adding a light coating of the dry ingredients.

Submerge the fillet into the egg/milk mixture, let some of the liquid drip off, then place it back into the dry blend. Gently coat the fillet with the egg/milk one more time, then bring it back over to the dry stuff for a final breading. Let the fillets sit for a bit in the dry ingredients so that the breading sticks to the chicken. Arrange all of the coated fillets on a small baking sheet or a plate and let them sit for 5 minutes before frying so that the breading sticks to the chicken.

7 Gently drop each fillet (if your fryer is big enough you can cook two at a time) into the hot oil and fry for 5 to 7 minutes or until the chicken is golden brown. Drain the fillets on a plate lined with paper towels.

8 As the fillets are frying, preheat a skillet over medium heat. Brush a little of the melted margarine on the faces of the hamburger buns and place them face-down in the hot pan until light brown.

⑨ Build each sandwich by placing two pickle slices on the face of the heel (bottom bun). Place a chicken fillet on top of the pickles and then top off the sandwich with the crown (top bun).

TIDBITS In 2012 KFC closed 77 units and Chick-fil-A opened 77 units. That made Chick-fil-A the No. 1 highest-grossing chicken chain in the U.S. for the first time ever, according to *QSR Magazine*.

MSG is monosodium glutamate, an amino salt. It can usually be found where herbs and spices are stocked in your market. Accent Flavor Enhancer is one popular brand.

CHILI'S CALIFORNIA GRILLED CHICKEN FLATBREAD

🏅 First-Time Hack

➤ Active Prep: 45 min.
Inactive Prep: 1 hr. 30 min.

M🌡 Difficulty: Medium

👥 Yield: 2 flatbreads

When Chili's recently retrofitted their kitchens with new equipment, including a conveyer oven, the chain introduced a line of flatbread pizzas that were not only a big hit with customers, but this new dish also went on to win the Menu Masters 2014 New Menu Item Award from *Nation's Restaurant News*. For my hack of the very popular California Grilled Chicken Flatbread you first must make a couple of 16-inch-long flatbreads from scratch—and don't worry, it's not that hard to do. The flatbreads are topped with an easy-to-make roasted garlic aioli, pico de gallo, and grilled chicken. Once these components are made, you assemble the flatbreads and bake them for about 10 minutes. There's no need to make the tomato-based sauce from scratch since I found that Ragu traditional pasta sauce is a close enough match to what Chili's uses to top its flatbreads and it's one of the most widely available and inexpensive sauces in stores.

FLATBREAD
7 ounces (1⅓ cups) all-purpose flour
1 teaspoon granulated sugar
½ teaspoon salt
¼ teaspoon fast-rising yeast
1 tablespoon extra virgin olive oil
½ cup warm water (105 to 110 degrees F)

ROASTED GARLIC AIOLI
4 large garlic cloves (see Tidbits)
1 teaspoon extra virgin olive oil
½ cup mayonnaise
1 tablespoon milk
½ teaspoon lime juice
Pinch of salt

PICO DE GALLO
½ cup diced Roma tomato (1 large tomato)
2 tablespoons diced red onion
1 tablespoon diced jalapeño (½ of a jalapeño)
½ teaspoon lime juice
Pinch of salt

1 skinless chicken breast fillet
2 teaspoons extra virgin olive oil
Salt
Ground black pepper

6 tablespoons **Ragu traditional pasta sauce**
1 cup shredded **mozzarella cheese**
1 cup shredded **Monterey Jack cheese**
2 slices cooked **thick-sliced bacon,**
   crumbled or chopped
2 teaspoons grated **Parmesan cheese**
8 avocado slices **(½ of an avocado)**
2 teaspoons chopped **cilantro**

1 Combine the flour, sugar, salt, and yeast in a medium bowl. Make a well in the flour and add the oil and water and mix by hand until you can pick up the dough, then knead it with your hands for 5 minutes. If the dough is tacky, add a little more flour. Cover the dough and let it stand in a warm spot for 1 hour.

2 While the dough rises, make the garlic aioli by first roasting some garlic. Preheat your oven to 350 degrees F and rub 4 large peeled garlic cloves with 1 teaspoon of oil. Arrange the garlic in an oven-safe dish or on a small baking pan and roast them in the oven for 10 minutes, then flip the cloves over

and roast for another 10 minutes. They should be starting to turn brown. Cool, then smash the garlic with the flat side of a chef's knife and finely mince. Combine the minced roasted garlic with the other aioli ingredients, then set it aside until needed.

3 Make the pico de gallo by combining all of the ingredients in a small bowl and set aside.

4 After the dough has been sitting for 1 hour, preheat your oven to 450 degrees F.

5 Roll the dough out to slightly more than 16 inches long by 10 inches high on a well-floured surface. You are going to trim the dough to 16 x 10 inches with straight edges so you want some extra dough to trim off. It will be very thin. I find that a pizza wheel works great to trim the dough. Once you have a 16 x 10-inch rectangle, slice through the middle, creating two 16 x 5-inch portions. Carefully place the dough portions on parchment paper on an 18 x 13-inch sheet pan. Brush with extra virgin olive oil and use a

73

fork to poke several holes in the dough to prevent bubbles from forming. Bake for 6 to 8 minutes or until the top is just beginning to brown. Use a fork to pop any bubbles that begin to form. Remove the flatbreads from the oven and cool. When cool, seal the flatbreads in plastic wrap if you're not using them right away. They will last for a couple of days.

6 Preheat your grill to high heat to cook the chicken. Flatten the chicken breast with a kitchen mallet, then rub it with some oil and sprinkle with salt and pepper. Grill for 4 to 5 minutes per side until done. You can also cook the chicken using a grill pan on your stovetop preheated over medium heat. Slice the chicken into bite-size pieces when it's done.

7 When you are ready to bake your flatbreads, preheat the oven to 450 degrees F. With the flatbreads on the 18 x 13-inch sheet pan, spread 3 tablespoons of pasta sauce on each. Combine the shredded cheeses and cover each flatbread with cheese. Divide the chicken and arrange the pieces on the cheese,

then sprinkle each one with the crumbled bacon. Bake the flatbreads for 10 to 12 minutes or until the cheese begins to brown on top and the flatbread is darkening around the edges.

8 When the flatbreads come out of the oven, sprinkle each one with about 1 teaspoon of Parmesan cheese. Drizzle garlic aioli over the top of each one (a squirt bottle works well for this) and sprinkle some pico de gallo over each flatbread. Arrange 4 avocado slices on each flatbread, then finish each with a sprinkle of chopped cilantro. Use a pizza wheel to slice the flatbreads into four even portions, then sliced diagonally through each of those pieces making eight triangular slices for each flatbread.

TIDBITS You want enough garlic so that you will have 1 tablespoon of minced garlic after it's roasted. Rather than roasting your own garlic, you can use 1 tablespoon of bottled roasted garlic, which is found in many stores.

CHILI'S CHIPOTLE CHICKEN FLATBREAD

  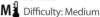

First-Time Hack

Active Prep: 45 min.
Inactive Prep: 1 hr. 30 min.

M Difficulty: Medium

Yield: 2 flatbreads

If you like your grub with a little kick to it, this is the flatbread for you. Chili-rubbed chicken tops this four-cheese flatbread that's drizzled with a flavorful chipotle pesto. All of the components to replicate Chili's popular spicy flatbread pizza are here, including a thin flatbread crust made from scratch. Since the amount of dough produced with this recipe is small, I found mixing and kneading the dough by hand to be the best method. This recipe makes two flatbreads, which is enough to serve four people.

FLATBREAD
7 ounces (1⅓ cups) all-purpose flour
1 teaspoon granulated sugar
½ teaspoon salt
¼ teaspoon fast-rising yeast
1 tablespoon extra virgin olive oil
½ cup warm water (105 to 110 degrees F)

CHIPOTLE PESTO
½ cup extra virgin olive oil
⅓ cup grated Parmesan cheese
¼ cup pine nuts
3 tablespoons pureed canned chipotle peppers (see Tidbits)
1 tablespoon white vinegar
2 cloves garlic
¼ teaspoon salt
¼ teaspoon dried basil
⅛ teaspoon ground black pepper

PICO DE GALLO
½ cup diced Roma tomato (1 large tomato)
2 tablespoons diced red onion
1 tablespoon diced jalapeño (½ of a jalapeño)
½ teaspoon lime juice
Pinch of salt

1 skinless chicken breast fillet
2 teaspoons extra virgin olive oil
Salt
Ground black pepper
Chili powder

6 tablespoons Ragu traditional pasta sauce
⅔ cup shredded mozzarella cheese
⅔ cup shredded Monterey Jack cheese
⅔ cup shredded medium cheddar cheese
2 teaspoons grated Parmesan cheese
2 teaspoons chopped cilantro

1 Combine the flour, sugar, salt, and yeast in a medium bowl. Make a well in the flour and add the oil and water and mix by hand until you can pick up the dough, then knead it with your hands for 5 minutes. If the dough is tacky, add a little more flour. Cover the dough and let it stand in a warm spot for 1 hour.

2 While the dough rises, make the chipotle pesto by combining all of the ingredients in a blender and blending on high speed for 10 to 15 seconds or until the nuts are ground up. Set aside.

3 Make the pico de gallo by combining all of the ingredients in a small bowl and set aside.

4 After the dough has been sitting for 1 hour, preheat your oven to 450 degrees F.

5 Roll the dough out to slightly more than 16 inches long by 10 inches wide on a well-floured surface. You will trim the dough to 16 x 10 inches so you want some extra dough to trim off. The dough will be thin. A pizza wheel works great for trimming the dough. Once you have a 16 x 10-inch rectangle, slice lengthwise through the middle, making two 16 x 5-inch-long rectangles. Carefully place

the dough portions on parchment paper on an 18 x 13-inch sheet pan. Brush the top with extra virgin olive oil and use a fork to poke several holes in the dough to prevent bubbles from forming. Bake for 6 to 8 minutes or until the top is just beginning to brown. Use a fork to pop any bubbles that begin to form. Remove the flatbreads from the oven and cool. When cool, seal the flatbreads in plastic wrap if you're not using them right away and they will last for a couple of days.

6 Preheat your grill to high heat to cook the chicken. Flatten a chicken breast with a kitchen mallet, then rub it with some oil and sprinkle with salt and pepper. Grill for 4 to 5 minutes per side until done. Just before removing the chicken from the grill, sprinkle it with a little chili powder. Remove the chicken from the grill and slice it into bite-size pieces. You can also cook the chicken using a grill pan on your stovetop preheated over medium heat.

7 When you are ready to bake your flatbreads, preheat the oven to 450 degrees F. Spread 3 tablespoons of tomato sauce on each of the flatbreads on the 18 x 13-inch

sheet pan. Combine the shredded cheeses and cover each flatbread with cheese. Divide the chicken and arrange the pieces on the cheese. Bake the flatbreads for 10 to 12 minutes or until the cheese begins to brown on top and the flatbread is darkening around the edges.

8 When the flatbreads come out of the oven, sprinkle each one with about 1 teaspoon of Parmesan cheese. Drizzle chipotle pesto over the top of each one (a squirt bottle works well for this) and sprinkle some pico de gallo over each flatbread, followed by a little chopped cilantro. Use a pizza wheel to slice the flatbreads into four even portions, then slice diagonally through each of those pieces, making eight triangular slices for each flatbread.

TIDBITS Make the chipotle pepper puree by pouring a small can of chipotle peppers with all of the adobo sauce plus ⅓ cup of water into a blender and blending on high speed for 15 seconds or until smooth.

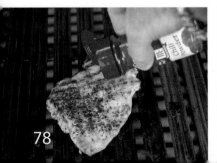

CHILI'S GRILLED BABY BACK RIBS

👍 Improved Hack

🕐 Active Prep: 20 min.
Inactive Prep: 4 hrs.

M🌡 Difficulty: Medium

👥 Yield: 4 full racks

When I hacked this recipe on my TV show *Top Secret Recipe* I learned that the only way to make ribs taste just like the famous original version from Chili's is to smoke them with pecan wood chips. I had access to the development kitchen at Chili's corporate headquarters in Dallas where I discovered that the chain uses a special commercial smoker made by Convotherm that is preprogrammed to first smoke the ribs and then steam them until tender. To simulate the steam function in a home smoker, you will need to spray the ribs with a little water every half hour in the second half of the cooking process.

It's also important to use the right kind of ribs if you want the perfect clone. Get well-trimmed baby backs that aren't too thick. Chili's ribs are trimmed pretty close to the bone to ensure even smoking and grilling. I also learned on the show that the chain wraps up the hot ribs in plastic wrap and foil immediately after they are smoked and before they are finished on the grill to help make them extra tender. You can skip this step if you're rushed, but if you have the time to work it in, the meat will fall off the bone on the way to your mouth.

CLUE — CONVOTHERM OVEN

If you don't have a smoker, you can still use the seasoning and sauce recipes here and turn out some great ribs. You can give the ribs their great smoky flavor using a smoking box found on some grills or by folding pecan wood chips into a pouch made from foil and cutting a couple of slices into the top of the foil so that the smoke can come out. Place the pouch over low heat to one side of your closed grill. Occasionally spray the ribs with water to keep them from drying out and smoke them for 2 to 4 hours, depending on how hot your grill is, then grill and baste them following this recipe.

RIB SEASONING

2¼ teaspoons **garlic powder**
2 teaspoons **salt**
1¼ teaspoons **coarse ground black pepper**
1 teaspoon **granulated sugar**

½ teaspoon **onion powder**
⅛ teaspoon **citric acid**
⅛ teaspoon **ground thyme**

4 racks trimmed **baby back ribs**

SAUCE
1 cup ketchup
1 cup water
3 tablespoons light brown sugar
3 tablespoons apple cider vinegar
2½ teaspoons yellow mustard
1 teaspoon hickory liquid smoke
½ teaspoon plus ⅛ teaspoon salt
⅛ teaspoon onion powder
⅛ teaspoon garlic powder
⅛ teaspoon ground black pepper
Pinch of citric acid

YOU WILL ALSO NEED
Smoker
Small pecan wood chips
Sprayer bottle of water

1 Preheat a smoker to 225 degrees F.

2 Combine the seasoning ingredients in a small bowl then pour it into a shaker and shake generously over the ribs.

3 Place the ribs in your smoker with ¼ cup to ½ cup of small pecan wood chips and a pan or metal bowl of water. Smoke for 4 hours (open the vent for the first 2 hours). After 2 hours, add more water to the pan if necessary, mist the ribs with water, and close the vent. Spray the ribs with water every half hour from now on until done.

4 While the ribs are smoking, make the sauce by combining all of the ingredients in a saucepan over low heat. Heat for 2 hours, uncovered, stirring occasionally, until thick. Cover and remove from the heat until the ribs are done.

5 When the ribs are done smoking, wrap them in plastic wrap, then aluminum foil, and put them in your refrigerator for a couple of hours, or until you plan to serve them. This will give your ribs a similar tenderness and flavor to the real thing. However, if you want to serve the ribs sooner, skip to the next step.

6 When you are ready to serve the ribs, preheat a barbecue grill to high heat.

7 When the grill is heated, place the ribs, bony side-down, on the hot grill. Baste the top of the ribs with sauce and grill for 2 minutes. Flip the ribs and baste the bottom of each rack with sauce and grill for 2 minutes. Turn them sooner if the sauce begins to burn. Flip the ribs over onto the bony side again and give each a final baste with the sauce. Cook for 2 more minutes and serve.

TIDBITS If you want even better smoky flavor in your ribs, try using apple or cherry wood chips in your smoker, rather than pecan chips.

81

CHILI'S MOLTEN CHOCOLATE CAKE

👍 Improved Hack

⏱ Active Prep: 20 min.
Inactive Prep: 3 hrs. 30 min.

M 🌡 Difficulty: Medium

👥 Yield: 4 servings

My first recipe for Chili's mega-popular chocolate cake with the hot fudge center was a shortcut technique relying on a box of cake mix for the cake baked in a jumbo muffin tin with bottled fudge for the molten middle. It's an easy recipe that makes a great dessert, but it's not a perfect clone. This time around I've whipped up a hack from scratch to exactly match the taste, shape, and texture of the original you find at the restaurant chain. My first recipe called for making the cake in a jumbo muffin pan since that is a more common pan, but if you want molten cakes that resemble the Chili's version, find yourself four 5½-inch fluted brioche pans. You can still use a jumbo muffin pan for this recipe if you don't have brioche pans available; in that case you'll just have a couple more smaller cakes. Plan to make this dessert several hours or a day or two ahead of time since the fudge-filled cakes will need to set up in the fridge for at least a couple of hours. When you're ready to serve, all it takes is a quick zap in the microwave to heat up the fudgy middle.

CAKE

1 cup hot water
1½ ounces (½ cup) unsweetened cocoa
7 ounces (1⅓ cups) all-purpose flour
1 teaspoon baking soda
½ teaspoon baking powder
½ teaspoon salt
1½ cups granulated sugar
¼ cup (½ stick) unsalted butter, **softened**
¼ cup vegetable oil
2 large eggs
1½ teaspoons vanilla extract

FUDGE

¾ cup heavy cream
6 tablespoons unsalted butter
4 ounces bittersweet chocolate
⅓ cup granulated sugar
Pinch of salt
½ teaspoon vanilla extract

Caramel topping (Hershey's in a jar is best)
4 scoops of vanilla ice cream
Smucker's Chocolate Magic Shell topping

1 Preheat the oven to 350 degrees F.

2 Stir the hot water into the cocoa in a medium bowl and let it sit to cool.

3 In another medium bowl, combine the flour, baking soda, baking powder, and salt.

4 Use an electric mixer on high speed to combine the sugar with the butter and oil in a large bowl. Add the eggs and vanilla and mix until smooth and creamy.

5 Mix the dry mixture into the wet mixture, then add the chocolate. Mix until combined, then pour the batter into four 5½-inch fluted brioche pans that have been sprayed with nonstick cooking spray. You can also use a jumbo muffin pan, filling each of 6 cups about three-quarters full. Bake for 26 to 32 minutes or until a toothpick stuck into the center of a cake comes out clean. Let the cakes cool for 1 hour. It's easiest to get the cakes out of the brioche pans if you chill the cakes in the refrigerator for about an hour, then heat up the outside of each pan on your stovetop over high heat for about 5 seconds. The cakes will then slide out without falling apart.

6 While the cakes cool, make the fudge by combining the cream, butter, chocolate, sugar, and salt in a small saucepan over medium/low heat. Stir often as the chocolate melts. Cook until the mixture begins to bubble around the edge, then continue cooking for 5 minutes. Turn off the heat, stir in the vanilla, and let the fudge cool uncovered for 30 minutes.

7 When the cakes are out of the pans, slice the domed top off of each one so that they will sit flat when inverted. Turn all of the cakes over and use a knife to make a circular slice about three-quarters of the way down into the cake. Use a teaspoon to scoop out the cake, making a well. Fill each well to the top with fudge, then chill all of the cakes for at least 2 hours or overnight.

8 When you are ready to make the dessert, load some caramel sauce into a squirt bottle and drizzle it onto your serving plate. Microwave a cake, with the fudge well facing up, for 30 to 40 seconds on high on another plate, or until the fudge just begins to soften. Immediately slide the cake onto the plate drizzled with caramel sauce. Add a scoop of ice cream on top of the cake. Squeeze Magic Shell topping over the ice cream and serve.

CHIPOTLE MEXICAN GRILL BLACK BEANS

 First-Time Hack

 Active Prep: 15 min.
Inactive Prep: 25 hrs.

E Difficulty: Easy

Yield: 8 servings

With over 1,400 units and counting, Chipotle Mexican Grill is one of the top ten fastest-growing chains in the country and the biggest Mexican food chain behind Taco Bell. But unlike the typical fast-food model, servers at Chipotle build you a custom burrito or bowl with your choice of the meats, sides, and sauces on display in front of you. With this new recipe and the two that follow, you can now build your own burritos or bowls at home that taste just like those from the chain. Or maybe you just want a good side of mildly spicy black beans to go along with another dish you have in mind.

I tried everything I could think of to speed up the process for cloning the great black beans served at Chipotle Mexican Grill, but the only way to duplicate the slightly al dente texture of the chain's dish is to use dry beans, and dry beans must rehydrate in water for 24 hours before they're ready for the saucepan. The chipotle chili–flavored cooking liquid is the secret to making these beans taste great. Use canned chipotle chilies here, but before you chop them, rinse away the adobo sauce they usually come packed in. You can use store-bought ground cumin in this recipe, but if you want ground cumin that tastes just like what Chipotle uses, you'll want to toast whole cumin seeds over medium/low heat for 10 minutes (as described in the recipe on page 88), then grind the seeds to powder in a coffee/spice grinder. This technique will make your beans taste best . . . and, as a bonus, your kitchen will smell great.

1 **pound** dry black beans
2 **cups** water
¼ **cup chopped** yellow onion
1 **tablespoon chopped** canned chipotle chilies (rinsed)
2 **tablespoons** vegetable oil
1 **tablespoon** lime juice
2 **cloves** garlic
1½ **teaspoons** salt
1 **teaspoon** dried oregano
1 **teaspoon** ground cumin
½ **teaspoon** ground black pepper
2 **bay leaves**

❶ Pour the beans into a colander and sort through them for anything that shouldn't be in there like tiny rocks or unicorn teeth. Rinse the beans thoroughly, then pour them into a bowl and cover with water (about 8 cups). Let the beans soak for 24 hours.

❷ The next day, when you are ready to make the beans, combine all of the ingredients except the bay leaves and black beans in a blender. Blend on high speed for 30 seconds or just until tiny bits of chilies are visible.

3 Drain the water from the beans and pour them into a 3-quart saucepan. Pour the chipotle cooking liquid into the pot, add the bay leaves, cover, and bring the beans to a boil over medium heat. When the beans are bubbling, reduce the heat to low and let the beans cook for 1 hour or until tender but slightly al dente.

CHIPOTLE MEXICAN GRILL CILANTRO-LIME BROWN RICE

First-Time Hack

Active Prep: 5 min.
Inactive Prep: 1 hr.

Difficulty: Easy

Yield: 8 servings

It seems to me that many rice recipes call for too much water. Even recipes printed right there on the package of rice often have it wrong. So here is the secret formula for perfect brown rice. But not just any brown rice. This is cilantro-lime brown rice just like the stuff you get at America's second-largest Mexican chain. Use it as a side for any dish or on burritos just like they do at Chipotle Mexican Grill.

3¾ cups **water**
2 cups **uncooked brown rice**
2 tablespoons **unsalted butter**
1 teaspoon **salt**
¼ cup minced **fresh cilantro**
4 teaspoons **lime juice**

❶ Combine the water, rice, butter, and salt in a 3-quart saucepan over high heat.

❷ When the liquid begins to boil, reduce the heat to low and cover the saucepan. Cook for 45 minutes, then turn off the heat and let the rice sit, covered, for 10 to 15 minutes or until tender.

❸ Stir in the cilantro and lime juice.

CHIPOTLE MEXICAN GRILL ADOBO-MARINATED GRILLED CHICKEN AND STEAK

  First-Time Hack

Active Prep: 20 min.
Inactive Prep: 16 to 24 hrs.

E Difficulty: Easy

Yield: 2 to 4 servings

The marinated and grilled chicken and steak at Chipotle Mexican Grill are the star ingredients for most burritos and burrito bowls served there every day. Looking over ingredient statements, it appears the chicken and beef are marinated in the same secret adobo sauce—overnight, according to servers there. Obviously getting the flavor of the adobo marinade is the most important hacking job here, but it's also important to use the right chicken and cow parts. Chipotle uses only dark meat chicken, so grab yourself some skinless thigh fillets if it's the chicken you're cooking up. If you decide to go with the beef, grab a pound and a half of New York strips. Chipotle uses toasted cumin seeds to make a more flavorful ground cumin for this recipe, so I have included that technique in the first step (you can also substitute with bottled ground cumin if you like). You'll need a coffee/spice grinder or mortar and pestle to grind the cumin seeds once they're toasted—you'll know the seeds are done when your kitchen fills with the toasty aroma. Start this recipe a day ahead so you can give your chicken or steak 16 to 24 hours to soak in the marinade.

ADOBO MARINADE
1½ teaspoons cumin seeds
1½ cups water
¼ cup chopped canned chipotle chilies (rinsed)
2 cloves garlic
¼ cup vegetable oil
1½ teaspoons salt
½ teaspoon ground black pepper
½ teaspoon dried oregano

1½ pounds skinless chicken thigh fillets or
  1½ pounds New York strip steak

❶ Toast the cumin seeds in a small sauté pan over medium/low heat for 5 to 7 minutes or until you can easily smell the cumin. Remove the pan from the heat immediately if the

seeds begin to smoke. Use a coffee bean grinder or spice grinder to grind the cumin until it is a fine powder.

② Add the water, chilies, and garlic to a blender and blend on high speed for 10 to 15 seconds or until the garlic and chilies are pureed. Add the other adobo ingredients, including the ground cumin, and blend just until combined—about 5 seconds.

③ If you are preparing steak—and your steaks are on the thick side—slice the steak through the middle to make 2 thinner steaks. Add the chicken or steak to the marinade in a large bowl. Cover and chill for 16 to 24 hours.

④ When you are ready to prepare your chicken or steak, preheat your barbecue grill to high heat. You can also cook the chicken on an indoor grill pan on your stove over medium heat. Cook the chicken for 4 to 5 minutes per side or until done, and steak for 2 to 3 minutes per side, or until done.

⑤ Allow the chicken or steak to sit for 3 minutes, then dice. Use immediately to make burritos, tacos, bowls, and salads.

CINNABON CLASSIC CINNAMON ROLL

  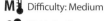

👍 Improved Hack

🕐 Active Prep: 45 min.
Inactive Prep:
7 hrs. 20 min.

Ⓜ️ Difficulty: Medium

👥 Yield: 6 rolls

I made several discoveries on episode 2 of my CMT show *Top Secret Recipe* that helped me improve significantly on the recipe for a clone of these great cinnamon rolls that I first hacked many years ago. After interviewing the creator of the Cinnabon roll, Jerilyn Brusseau (aka "Cinnamom"), at her home in Seattle and visiting Cinnabon headquarters in Atlanta, I was able to sleuth out some important clues that make this recipe the closest clone formula you'll find. I learned about the unique gooey properties of a specific cinnamon found in Indonesia (Korintje cinnamon, which Cinnabon calls "Makara"), and how to give the rolls their signature golden color (buttermilk and baking soda). I also discovered that the dough must rise in your refrigerator for at least 5 hours and that adding some xanthan gum to the filling will keep the filling from leaking down into the pan as the rolls bake (find powdered xanthan gum online or at a specialty store such as Whole Foods).

Cinnabon master chefs allowed me to step into the development kitchen at Cinnabon headquarters for an up-close demonstration of the rolling and slicing techniques, so the instructions I have laid out for you here come straight from the inside and will give you beautiful rolls that look and taste just like those you get at the mall. In fact, if you follow these instructions carefully, being sure to weigh the ingredients rather than measure by volume, everyone will be shocked that the delicious finished product came out of your very own kitchen.

ROLLS

24 ounces (5¼ cups) unbleached all-purpose
   flour
2½ ounces (5 tablespoons) granulated sugar
¾ teaspoon salt
¾ teaspoon rapid-rise yeast

⅛ teaspoon baking soda
2 large eggs
1 cup water
1 tablespoon buttermilk
2½ ounces (5 tablespoons) margarine

FILLING (SCHMEAR)

½ cup (1 stick) **margarine, softened**
14 ounces (2½ cups packed) **dark brown sugar**
2 tablespoons **Indonesian Korintje cinnamon**
1 tablespoon **xanthan gum**

FROSTING

¾ cup (1½ sticks) **unsalted butter**
4 ounces (½ cup) **cream cheese**
½ teaspoon **vanilla extract**
¼ teaspoon plus ⅛ teaspoon **salt**
2 drops **lemon extract**
7¼ ounces (2 cups) **powdered sugar**

❶ Combine the flour, sugar, salt, yeast, and baking soda in a large bowl. Mix until combined.

❷ Beat the eggs in a separate bowl. Whisk in the water and buttermilk. Combine this wet mixture with the flour mixture, then add the margarine and beat with an electric mixer (stand mixer with a paddle works best) until all of the dry ingredients are moist. Use a kneading hook to knead the dough for 15 minutes or knead by hand. Wrap the dough in plastic and place it in your refrigerator for 5 to 6 hours (or as long as overnight) until the dough doubles in size.

❸ Remove the plastic and press the dough out onto a lightly floured surface.

Flatten the dough with your hands for a bit, then use a rolling pin to shape the dough into a 20-inch-long by 17-inch-wide rectangle. Use your hands to stretch the dough as necessary to the proper dimensions.

❹ Use a spatula to spread 1 stick of softened margarine over the dough, but leave the bottom 1 inch of dough uncoated with margarine.

❺ Combine the brown sugar, cinnamon, and xanthan gum in a medium bowl. Pour the cinnamon/sugar onto the margarine and use your hands to spread it to the edges, leaving the bottom 1 inch uncovered with cinnamon. Run a rolling pin over the filling to flatten it into the margarine.

6 Roll the dough tightly starting at the top. Stretch the dough a little as you roll it down, so that you have 5½ to 6 rotations by the time you get to the bottom. Brush a little water over the bottom 1-inch uncoated strip of dough and complete the rolling. Mark the approximate middle of the dough roll, then use a ruler to make 3 marks every 2½ inches to the left of the middle mark, and 3 marks every 2½ inches to the right of the middle mark. Use a serrated knife to cut at each mark to make 6 rolls (the ends can be tossed).

7 Place the rolls evenly spaced out on parchment paper in a 9 x 13-inch baking pan. Place the pan in your unheated oven along with a large saucepan of boiling water to proof the rolls. The rolls should proof for about 1 to 2 hours or until nearly full size in the pan. Reheat the water in the pan to boiling after the first hour if the rolls are not nearing full size.

8 When the rolls have proofed to almost full size, preheat a convection oven to 325 degrees F (350 F if not convection). Bake for 16 to 20 minutes or until light brown and the rolls register around 170 degrees F to 175 degrees F in the middle. Spin the pan around 180 degrees approximately halfway through the baking.

9 While the rolls bake, whip the butter, cream cheese, vanilla, salt, and lemon extract for 10 minutes on high speed with an electric mixer until fluffy. Add the powdered sugar, then mix again (slowly at first, then on high speed) for 30 seconds.

10 When the rolls come out of the oven, immediately top each with a generous coating of frosting.

CRACKER BARREL HASHBROWN CASSEROLE

👍 Improved Hack

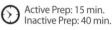
⟩ Active Prep: 15 min.
Inactive Prep: 40 min.

E 🌡 Difficulty: Easy

👥 Yield: 9 servings

When I first cloned Cracker Barrel's most popular menu item back in 1997, the chain had only 260 restaurants, located mostly in southern states. Today that number has exploded to more than 620 stores in all but eight U.S. states and the chain is more popular than ever. Cracker Barrel's menu will present you with some tough decisions when you're hankerin' for a good southern-style meal. Regardless of which entrée you choose, you'll probably want one of your side dish choices to be the chain's most popular signature dish: the hashbrown casserole. My first clone version of this recipe tasted great, but I've now tweaked the technique so that you first make a cheese sauce that includes a little cream of chicken soup stirred into the potatoes before baking. It's a technique you won't find anywhere else and it makes a finished product that's a dead ringer for the original.

8 ounces (about 3 cups) shredded Colby cheese
½ cup Campbell's cream of chicken soup
½ cup water
¼ cup (½ stick) unsalted butter
2 tablespoons bacon fat (from cooking 4 slices of bacon)
1 teaspoon salt
1 teaspoon ground black pepper
⅓ cup diced onion
1 30-ounce pkg. Ore-Ida frozen shredded hash browns

1 Preheat the oven to 375 degrees F.

2 Make a sauce by combining the cheese, soup, water, butter, bacon fat, salt, and pepper in a medium microwave-safe bowl. Microwave for 2 minutes on high, stirring after 1 minute. The cheese and butter should be melted. Mix the ingredients together with an electric mixer on high speed until the sauce is smooth. Mix in the onion.

3 Pour the frozen hash browns into a large microwave-safe bowl and microwave on high for 3 minutes, stirring halfway through, so that the hash browns are mostly defrosted and the chunks are broken up. They will still be cold in spots.

4 Stir the cheese mixture into the hash browns, then pour everything into an 8 x 8-inch baking dish or one of comparable size.

5 Bake for 30 to 40 minutes or until the casserole is hot all the way through and just beginning to brown on top.

CRACKER BARREL CHICKEN FRIED STEAK

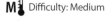

First-Time Hack

Active Prep: 20 min.
Inactive Prep: 10 min.

Difficulty: Medium

Yield: 4 servings

The restaurant and gift store chain that was founded in 1969 to attract highway travelers in the South now has stores in forty-two states, but the closest one to my home in Las Vegas is located over two hours away in St. George, Utah. With a cooler packed up in the back of my car, I drove out of Nevada, through a corner of Arizona, and into Utah to taste the epitome of southern food—the best chicken fried steak on the planet, smothered in milky white Sawmill Gravy. I cleared my plate, ordered another one to go with gravy on the side, and headed back with grub in tow to work up this original clone of one of Cracker Barrel's most popular guilty pleasures.

SAWMILL GRAVY

1 ounce breakfast sausage
1½ tablespoons bacon fat (from cooking
   3 slices of bacon)
2 tablespoons all-purpose flour
2 cups whole milk
½ teaspoon salt
½ teaspoon coarse ground black pepper

CHICKEN FRIED STEAK

1½ cups all-purpose flour
2 teaspoons salt
2 teaspoons paprika
1½ teaspoons ground black pepper
1 teaspoon rubbed sage
½ teaspoon garlic powder
½ teaspoon onion powder
3 large eggs, beaten
1 cup whole milk
4 5-ounce cube steaks
Vegetable oil

1 Cook the sausage in the bacon fat in a medium saucepan over medium heat until done or you can see no more pink. Crumble the sausage into small bits as it cooks. A potato masher works great for this.

2 Stir in the flour and cook until the flour becomes tan in color, about 2 minutes. Add the milk, salt, and pepper and cook over medium heat, stirring often, until the gravy thickens, about 5 minutes. Turn off the heat and cover.

3 Make the steaks by combining the flour, salt, paprika, pepper, sage, garlic powder, and onion powder in a shallow

bowl or pie pan. Combine the eggs and the milk in another shallow bowl.

4 Heat up about a ½ inch of oil in a large skillet over medium heat. The oil is hot enough when a pinch of flour dropped into it bubbles rapidly.

5 Bread the steaks one at a time by first coating one with the flour mixture. Dredge the steak in the wet mixture, then drop it

back into the flour, coating thoroughly. Repeat the process one more time, dipping the steak into the egg/milk mixture, then back into the flour. Set the steak aside on a plate and repeat with the remaining steaks.

6 When the oil is hot, pan-fry the steaks for 4 to 5 minutes per side or until golden brown. Drain on a rack or paper towel–lined plate after frying, then serve with sawmill gravy spooned over the top.

DIPPIN' DOTS BANANA SPLIT ICE CREAM

First-Time Hack

Active Prep: 20 min.
Inactive Prep: 1 hr. 10 min.

H Difficulty: Hard

Yield: 8+ servings

When shooting episode 5 of *Top Secret Recipe* at the Dippin' Dots manufacturing plant in Paducah, Kentucky, I saw large tanks of liquid nitrogen spitting out cases and cases of Dippin' Dots beaded ice cream, but it was hard to tell exactly how the ice cream beads were being formed in the -346 degrees F liquid. Even more puzzling was trying to figure out how I was going to duplicate the process in my little food truck without the help of all the expensive equipment.

It wasn't until Dippin' Dots creator Curt Jones handed me a Styrofoam cup that I began to put the puzzle together: I discovered that holes poked into the bottom of the cup with a needle would allow the ice cream base to dribble into the liquid nitrogen, making perfect little beads of ice cream that were indistinguishable from the real thing.

This recipe can be used to make the very popular banana split flavor of Dippin' Dots that is made with beads of vanilla, chocolate, strawberry, and banana ice cream, or you can chose to make only a single flavor. You will need approximately two liters of liquid nitrogen to convert each flavor of ice cream base into Dippin' Dots. You'll also need some dry ice in a cooler to store the dots as

they are being made. After the dry ice has evaporated in a day or two, you can store the ice cream in your freezer. Just be sure to be careful with the liquid nitrogen—I suggest wearing protective gloves and eyewear to avoid injury. And don't put the ice cream into your mouth immediately after it comes out of the nitrogen since it's much too cold and will instantly stick to your tongue, causing a painful loss of taste buds (it happened to me and my tongue gushed blood!). I recommend waiting about 10 minutes to taste your finished version of "The Ice Cream of the Future" to keep all buds intact.

VANILLA

1½ **cups whole milk**
1 **cup heavy cream**
¾ **cup fat-free half-and-half**

½ **cup granulated sugar**
⅛ **teaspoon salt**
1½ **teaspoons vanilla extract**

STRAWBERRY

1½ cups whole milk
1 cup heavy cream
¾ cup fat-free half-and-half
½ cup granulated sugar
⅛ teaspoon salt
2 teaspoons strawberry extract
10 drops red food coloring

BANANA

1½ cups whole milk
1 cup heavy cream
¾ cup fat-free half-and-half
½ cup granulated sugar
⅛ teaspoon salt
1 teaspoon banana extract
10 drops yellow food coloring

CHOCOLATE

1½ cups whole milk
1 cup heavy cream
¾ cup fat-free half-and-half
6 tablespoons granulated sugar
⅛ teaspoon salt
½ cup Hershey's chocolate syrup

ALSO REQUIRED

5 to 10 liters of liquid nitrogen
1 large Styrofoam cup
1 sewing needle
Large metal cocktail shaker
Dry ice for storing
Ice chest

❶ Make the ice cream base by combining the milk, cream, fat-free half-and-half, sugar, and salt as required for the flavor of your choice in a medium saucepan over medium/low heat. Stir often as the mixture heats, then remove the pan from the heat as soon as the sugar is dissolved. Add the flavorings and colorings (if required) to the pan, then pour the ice cream base into a sealed container and chill in your refrigerator (or freezer for a quicker chill) until cold. Repeat with the other flavors, if you are making more than one.

❷ To make beads of ice cream, poke 16 to 20 evenly spaced holes in the bottom of a large Styrofoam cup with a needle. Put on your gloves and protective eyewear before handling the liquid nitrogen. Fill a metal cocktail shaker about three-quarters full with liquid nitrogen. Hold the Styrofoam cup 4 to 5 inches above the liquid nitrogen and fill the cup with the ice cream base flavor of your choice.

Let the ice cream base dribble into the liquid nitrogen. When around a quarter to a third of the cup has emptied, pour the liquid nitrogen out of the shaker into a large metal bowl or another metal shaker, but don't pour out the ice cream beads. Shake the shaker vigorously back and forth to free any beads that may have stuck together, then pour the beads into a container, seal it up, and place it in an ice chest with dry ice.

❸ Repeat the process with each flavor of ice cream until you have used up all of the liquid nitrogen. You may not use up all of the ice cream base.

❹ Combine equal parts of each flavor to create a banana split–flavored ice cream mix. When the dry ice has evaporated, store the ice cream beads in your freezer.

DOMINO'S LARGE CHEESE PIZZA

 First-Time Hack

 Active Prep: 30 min.
Inactive Prep: 48 hrs.

 Difficulty: Medium

 Yield: 2 large pizzas

The culinary development team at Domino's spent two years of trial-and-error testing to create a new version of the chain's original signature crust. The end result was a more flavorful crust with a top secret garlic spread brushed on after the pizza baked. While hacking Domino's new pizza for my TV show, I discovered several secrets that will help you make a great home clone of this world-famous pie.

First, you'll want to track down high-gluten flour, either online or at a restaurant supply outlet (I found some at Smart & Final). If you can't locate high-gluten flour, use 25 ounces (5⅓ cups) of bread flour. Also, you'll want to plan ahead for this recipe since the best way to make commercial-quality dough is to let it rise very slowly in the refrigerator—two days works great. If you don't have that much time, at least let the dough rise overnight. And if you want the bottom of the crust to look just like the chain's version, find a 14-inch perforated or mesh pizza pan while you're online or at a restaurant supply store getting that high-gluten flour. These pans make a huge difference in the finished product.

This recipe was developed for the taste-test judges' table using information discovered on episode 4 of *Top Secret Recipe* on CMT. Before the judging of this pizza, I struck a deal with Domino's CEO Patrick Doyle that, considering the difficulty of this recipe, if I could fool just one judge, it would be a victory for me—and that's exactly what happened. This recipe hack is a winner.

This makes two large plain cheese pizzas, but feel free to add any toppings of your choice before baking.

DOUGH

3 tablespoons granulated sugar
1 teaspoon active dry yeast
16 ounces (2 cups) room temperature bottled water

13 ounces (2¾ cups) bread flour
12 ounces (2⅔ cups) high-gluten flour
2 teaspoons salt
3 tablespoons vegetable oil
1 cup cornmeal for stretching the dough

SAUCE

1 cup canned crushed tomatoes
2 cups tomato puree
4 teaspoons granulated sugar
1 teaspoon vegetable oil
¾ teaspoon salt
¼ teaspoon ground black pepper
¼ teaspoon garlic powder
¼ teaspoon ground oregano
¼ teaspoon dried basil
¼ teaspoon dried marjoram
⅛ teaspoon ground cayenne pepper

6 cups shredded mozzarella-provolone
cheese blend **(or combine 4 cups shredded
mozzarella with 2 cups shredded
provolone)**

GARLIC OIL SPREAD (FOR CRUST)

½ cup (1 stick) margarine
¼ teaspoon dried parsley **(slightly crushed)**
⅓ cup grated Parmesan cheese
¼ teaspoon garlic powder
⅛ teaspoon salt

1 Dissolve the sugar and yeast in the water.

2 Combine the flours and salt in a stand mixer using a paddle, or by hand.

3 When yeast solution begins to foam, pour it into the flour along with the oil. Use a dough hook to mix until all of the ingredients come together, or mix by hand. Knead with a dough hook or by hand for 5 minutes. Place the dough in a plastic bag and then in your refrigerator for 2 days.

4 Make the sauce by pureeing the crushed tomatoes in a blender until smooth, then combine all of the ingredients in a small saucepan over medium heat. When the mixture begins to bubble, reduce the heat to low and simmer, covered, for 1 hour, stirring occasionally. Remove the sauce from the heat and cool, then chill it in a covered container until you make your pizza.

5 When you are ready to make the pizza, preheat a convection oven to 450 degrees F (or conventional oven to 475 degrees F).

6 Divide the dough in half. Form half of the dough into a dough ball on a well-floured surface. Sprinkle cornmeal on a clean flat surface and begin to stretch out the dough using your hands until you have stretched it enough to fit on a 14-inch pizza screen. Lay the dough on the screen and stretch it to the edge of the screen, forming a perfect circle.

7 Spoon a thin layer of sauce over the pizza dough, leaving about a 1-inch margin at the edge.

8 Sprinkle about 3 cups of the shredded cheese blend over the sauce. Don't worry if some falls onto the edge of the dough.

9 Bake the pizza for 8 to 9 minutes or until the cheese and crust begin to brown.

10 While the pizza bakes, make the garlic oil spread by melting the margarine in a microwave oven or in a small saucepan over low heat. Use a mortar and pestle (or your fingers and a small bowl) to crush the dried parsley into smaller bits. Remove the melted margarine from the heat and add the Parmesan cheese, parsley, garlic powder, and salt.

11 When the pizza is done, remove it from the oven and brush the crust with garlic oil spread. Use a pizza wheel to cut the pizza into 8 slices. Repeat the process for the second large pizza.

EL POLLO LOCO FIRE-GRILLED CHICKEN

 Improved Hack

 Active Prep: 15 min.
Inactive Prep: 50 hrs.

 E Difficulty: Easy

Yield: 4 servings

This 400-unit West Coast Mexican-style grilled chicken chain was built on a family's secret recipe for chicken marinade containing fruit juices, herbs, and spices. At El Pollo Loco restaurant the chickens are butterflied, marinated, then slowly cooked until done over a low open flame. My first version of this recipe did not allow for enough marinating time, and it wasn't until recently that I discovered that the chickens in the restaurant are marinated in a vacuum tumbler, which, because of the vacuum pressure and convection, will thoroughly marinate a whole chicken in about 25 minutes. These tumblers are pretty spiffy contraptions and can be purchased for home use, but they cost hundreds of dollars. I'm not buying one right now and I wouldn't expect you to, so we must marinate the old-fashioned way . . . with patience.

I marinated several chickens at various lengths of time without using a tumbler and with different formulations of marinade. After a couple of weeks of testing, I discovered the perfect marinating time with this improved formula to be 48 hours—so plan your meal accordingly. The chicken takes around 2 hours to slow-grill, so if you like to eat dinner at six p.m., start marinating the chicken two days before at four p.m. It's important to grill the chicken over a medium/low flame so that the skin does not burn. Since all grills are different, this may take some experimenting to get just the right temperature setting for your grill. Ideally you want the chicken to be nicely browned in spots when done but not badly charred. If the chicken begins to burn, flip it over and reduce the temperature.

1 whole roaster chicken (4 to 5 pounds)

MARINADE
4 cups water
⅓ cup vegetable oil
½ cup orange juice
½ cup pineapple juice
2 tablespoons lime juice
2 tablespoons lemon juice
2 tablespoons salt
1 tablespoon garlic powder
2 teaspoons onion powder
1½ teaspoons ground black pepper
1 teaspoon ground oregano
1 teaspoon ground thyme
1 teaspoon ground coriander
¼ teaspoon or 20 drops yellow food coloring

ON THE SIDE (OPTIONAL)
Flour or corn tortillas
Black beans or pinto beans
Rice
Salsa

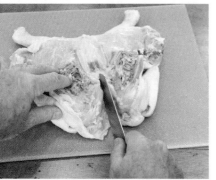

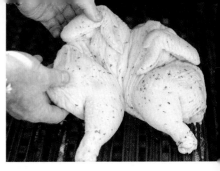

❶ First butterfly the chicken with a pair of kitchen shears by cutting all the way down both sides of the backbone. Cut through the small rib bones and not through the backbone, but cut close to the backbone, so that you don't lose too much meat. Once you have sliced down both sides of the backbone, remove it from the chicken. Position the chicken so that the drumsticks are pointing away from you and use a paring knife to slice through the white cartilage at the top of the breastbone. Bend the carcass of the chicken back at the cut and the breastbone will pop out. Run your fingers down both sides of the breastbone to pull it away from the meat, then pull it out. Remove any excess fat found inside the carcass, and your chicken is ready for marinating.

❷ Make the marinade by combining all of the ingredients in a large bowl.

❸ Place the chicken in a 3½- to 4-quart container with a lid and pour the marinade over the top. Cover and marinate for 48 hours in the refrigerator. Move the chicken around in the marinade a couple of times while it marinates.

❹ When you are ready to cook the chicken, preheat your grill to medium/low heat. Place the chicken, starting skin-side up, on the grill and cook for 2 hours or until the internal temperature in the breast is 165 degrees F. If the chicken is showing signs of charring after 30 minutes, turn down the heat a bit. If, after the first 30 minutes, you are getting no light browning at all, turn up the heat. Flip the chicken over after 1 hour and continue for the final hour.

❺ Use a large knife to separate the chicken into 8 pieces: 2 drumsticks, 2 wings, 2 thighs, and 2 breasts. Serve with tortillas and your choice of beans, rice, and salsa.

FRITO-LAY CRACKER JACK

👍 Improved Hack

🕐 Active Prep: 20 min.
Inactive Prep: 6 min.

M🌡 Difficulty: Medium

👥 Yield: 8 cups

All clone recipes for Cracker Jack that I know about—including my previous version—call for butter, which makes the candy coating more like toffee than the caramel-flavored coating on the 122-year-old American snack. So, this time around I have eliminated the butter and replaced it with just a little bit of margarine, which contains the vegetable oil and lecithin found in real Cracker Jack. I have also tweaked the formula to use a more convenient amount of popcorn (1 bag of microwave popcorn rather than 1½ bags), and I found that I was able to eliminate the molasses since there is enough in the dark brown sugar to give the candy-coated popcorn only a subtle molasses flavor more like the original.

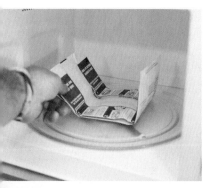

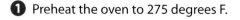

8 cups **natural (not butter flavor) microwave popcorn (from 1 bag)**
⅓ cup **Spanish peanuts**
7 ounces (1 cup packed) **dark brown sugar**
⅓ cup **light corn syrup**
1 tablespoon **margarine**
¼ teaspoon **salt**

❶ Preheat the oven to 275 degrees F.

❷ Combine the popped popcorn with the peanuts in a large metal (or other oven-safe) mixing bowl and place the bowl in the preheated oven. Make sure it sits in there for at least 15 minutes to get hot.

❸ Combine the brown sugar, corn syrup, margarine, and salt in a medium saucepan over medium heat and heat to 290 degrees F, or just under the hard crack stage. You should use a candy thermometer to monitor the temperature, but you can also test the caramel candy by dribbling a little into cold water once it begins to darken in color. If the candy in the cold water is hard when cool, then it has reached the right temperature.

4 Drizzle the caramel over the popcorn, then hold the bowl with a towel or potholder and stir the popcorn until it is well coated with the candy. If you have trouble coating the popcorn, place the bowl back in the oven for 10 minutes and stir again. Pour the coated popcorn and peanuts onto wax paper or a silicone mat. Break up the popcorn and peanuts as it cools.

FUDGSICLE ORIGINAL FUDGE BARS

- First-Time Hack
- Active Prep: 10 min. Inactive Prep: 6 hrs.
- Difficulty: Easy
- Yield: 8 bars

Re-creating this popular frozen ice pop is more than just mixing sugar and cocoa into skim milk and freezing it with a stick in the middle. In addition to the great chocolaty taste, a Fudgsicle clone wouldn't be right if it didn't have the same creamy—and not at all icy—texture of the original. So just how do we hack that? We'll use a little gelatin in the mix plus a secret ingredient that will help to prevent the formation of ice crystals when the bars are frozen. Fat-free half-and-half, which is made with skim milk (as are Fudgsicles), also contains the same natural thickener found in the original ice pops. Mix these ingredients together in a saucepan over medium heat until the sugar is dissolved and pour the creamy mixture into an ice pop mold. When the pops are semisolid, add the sticks. A few hours later you'll have seven or eight perfect fudge pops with the same taste and texture as the chocolaty original.

2 cups fat-free half-and-half
¼ cup unsweetened cocoa
¼ cup granulated sugar
¼ cup light corn syrup
2 teaspoons shortening
2 teaspoons (1 pkg.) unflavored gelatin
Pinch of salt

YOU WILL ALSO NEED
Ice pop maker
8 ice pop sticks

❶ Whisk the ingredients together in a medium saucepan. Place the pan over medium heat and cook until the mixture is hot and the sugar has dissolved.

❷ Remove the pan from the heat, cover it, and let it cool for about 15 minutes. Place the pan in your refrigerator until the mixture is cold—about 2 hours.

❸ Whisk the mixture again once it is cold, then carefully pour it into 7 or 8 molds of the ice pop maker. Add the lid but do not add the sticks yet. Place the ice pops in your freezer for 2 hours.

④ After 2 hours you can insert the sticks about halfway down into each of the bars. Continue to freeze for 4 more hours or overnight.

⑤ When the bars are frozen solid, remove them from the molds by setting the molds out for 6 to 8 minutes. Carefully remove the bars from the molds, being sure not to pull too hard if the bars are not loose, or you may pull a stick out. Place each bar into a small plastic bag or wrap with plastic wrap and store the bars in the freezer until ready to eat.

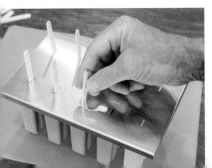

GATORADE ORANGE SPORTS DRINK

  First-Time Hack

 Prep Time: 5 min.

 E Difficulty: Easy

Yield: 64 ounces

Researchers at University of Florida's College of Medicine developed Gatorade in 1965 when the head coach of the Florida Gators football team requested a specially designed drink that could replace lost fluids during hot weather games. With players pounding the new sports drink, the Gators went on to take their first Orange Bowl victory in 1967 against the Georgia Tech Yellow Jackets. When the head coach of the Yellow Jackets was asked why his team lost, he said, "We didn't have Gatorade. That made the difference." Later that year, Gatorade became the official drink of the NFL.

The secret to making Gatorade at home is not just about getting the flavor right but also about locating a simple source of the drink's important supplemental ingredients, potassium and dextrose. Potassium (along with salt) replaces electrolytes that are lost when you sweat to ensure proper functioning of your brain and organs. I discovered that a good source of potassium is Morton's salt substitute, which is made with potassium chloride. Most supermarkets should have it stocked near the salt. Dextrose, on the other hand, is a natural sugar that absorbs quickly into your body to restore muscles' glycogen lost during physical activity. Bodybuilders and athletes use it during and after games and workouts to speed up recovery and stimulate muscle growth. Luckily, I was able to find the perfect product that added just the right amount of dextrose to 64 ounces of water and that also came in the perfect orange flavor: Willy Wonka Pixy Stix. Find the large 1-ounce size in the giant plastic straw, and grab two. I found them online for 50 cents each.

Dump everything here into a 64-ounce pitcher of water, stir to dissolve, and in just a few minutes you'll have the same taste and energy benefits of one of the two original flavors of Gatorade, but at about half the price.

2 quarts (8 cups) water
7 tablespoons granulated sugar
2 1-ounce (⅓ cup total) orange-flavored Willy Wonka Pixy Stix
½ teaspoon citric acid (aka sour salt)
¼ teaspoon orange-flavored unsweetened Kool-Aid powder
¼ teaspoon unflavored gelatin
⅛ teaspoon salt
⅛ teaspoon Morton's salt substitute (potassium chloride)

Combine everything in a 2-quart pitcher and stir until all of the solid ingredients have dissolved. Serve cold.

TIDBITS The orange-flavored version of Gatorade was one of just two flavors sold for almost twenty years. The other was lemon-lime. The University of Florida receives 20 percent of Gatorade sales every year, which totals around $12 million annually.

GIRL SCOUT COOKIES SAMOAS/CARAMEL deLITES

First-Time Hack

Active Prep: 2 hrs.
Inactive Prep: 5 hrs.

Difficulty: Hard

Yield: 55 cookies

This recipe isn't easy. The process involves baking shortbread cookies, coating them with caramel, sprinkling freshly toasted coconut onto the caramel, dipping the bottom of the cookies into chocolate, and then adding a chocolate drizzle over the top. It takes time to make each one, but the technique I'm revealing here does produce a delicious cookie that will satisfy anyone who loves Samoas, which is the #2 most popular Girl Scout Cookie (Thin Mints are #1). This may be the recipe to make when you have the ability to recruit some joyous and enthusiastic kitchen helpers.

COOKIES
½ **cup vegetable shortening**
3 **tablespoons** unsalted butter, **softened**
½ **cup granulated sugar**
1½ **teaspoons vanilla extract**
½ **teaspoon salt**
10 **ounces (2 cups) all-purpose flour**
1 **teaspoon baking powder**
¼ **cup milk**

COCONUT/CARAMEL
11 **ounces (3 cups) sweetened coconut flakes**
80 **unwrapped Kraft caramels (2 9½ ounce bags)**
⅓ **cup evaporated milk**
2 **tablespoons water**
½ **teaspoon salt**

2 12-**ounce bags** Ghirardelli dark melting wafers
   (**or other chocolate candy melts**)

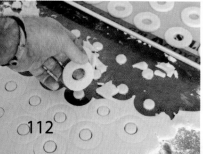

❶ Cream together the shortening, butter, and sugar in a large bowl with a mixer on high speed for 1 minute. Add the vanilla and salt and mix for another minute. Mix the baking powder into the flour in a medium bowl and add it to the wet ingredients along with the milk. Mix well by hand until the dough can be formed into a ball. Cover the dough with plastic wrap and chill it for 1 hour.

2 After 1 hour, preheat the oven to 325 degrees F.

3 Roll the dough out on a flat, floured surface to about ¼ inch to ⅛ inch thick. Use a 2-inch biscuit cutter or round cookie cutter to punch out rounds of the cookie dough. Use a small lid that is about ¾ inch across, like one from a bottle of vanilla extract, to cut holes in the center of each cookie.

4 Place all of the cookie dough rings ½ inch apart on parchment paper– or Silpat pad–lined baking sheets and bake for 12 to 16 minutes. The cookies will be lightly browned on the bottom when done. Allow the cookies to cool completely before coating.

5 Set the oven temperature to 300 degrees F.

6 While the cookies are cooling, toast the coconut by spreading it out on a baking sheet. Pop the coconut into the oven for 15 to 20 minutes or until browned. Stir the coconut every 5 minutes as it toasts. Once the coconut is cool, use a food processor (or a blender in several batches) to chop the toasted coconut into bits about the size of rice.

7 Combine the caramels with the evaporated milk, water, and salt in medium saucepan over medium/low heat. Stir often until the caramels are completely melted, about 15 minutes.

8 Dip each of the cookies into the caramel one-at-a-time. Use the tip of a butter knife in the hole of the cookie to fish it out of the caramel and place it onto wax paper or parchment paper. Sprinkle the tops of the cookies with toasted coconut while the caramel is warm so that it sticks.

9 Give each cookie a minute to cool a bit then pick each one up and roll the edges around in the coconut so that the sides of the cookie are coated with toasted coconut. Place the cookie back onto the pan to cool. Allow the caramel-coated cookies to cool for 1 to 2 hours.

10 When the cookies have cooled, melt the dark chocolate in a bowl in the microwave on high for 1 minute or until it is soft. Hold each cookie flat by the edges, dip the bottom of each cookie into the chocolate, and place the cookie onto fresh sheets of wax paper.

11 When all of the cookies have been dipped, reheat the chocolate for 30 seconds in the microwave on high, then load the chocolate into a squirt bottle. Use a sweeping motion to make chocolate stripes across all of the cookies. Each cookie should have 4 stripes if you want them to look exactly like the real cookies. Let the cookies set up for several hours and then store them in a covered container in a cool spot.

GIRL SCOUT COOKIES TREFOILS/SHORTBREAD COOKIES

👍 Improved Hack

🕐 Active Prep: 30 min.
Inactive Prep: 90 min.

E🌡 Difficulty: Easy

👥 Yield: 50 servings

Because Girl Scout Cookies are produced at two different bakeries, many of the cookies have two names, such as the Peanut Butter Patties/Tagalongs, the Samoas/Caramel deLites, and this very popular shortbread cookie, also called Trefoils. A trefoil is a design of overlapping rings that makes up the symbol of the Girl Scouts and you've seen it at least a million times. You can duplicate this shape on your homemade Trefoils by making four indentations on the round punched-out dough using the sides of your fingers. Or you can choose to simply leave them round. Either way, they will have a taste reminiscent of the famous little boxed shortbread cookies sold every March. You can use parchment paper to line your baking sheet, but if you've got a silicone baking mat, use it. It's nonstick, but it also helps prevent the bottoms of the cookies from over-browning.

½ **cup shortening**
3 **tablespoons unsalted butter, softened**
½ **cup plus 1 tablespoon granulated sugar**
1½ **teaspoons vanilla extract**
½ **teaspoon salt**
1 **teaspoon baking powder**
10 **ounces (2 cups) all-purpose flour**
¼ **cup milk**

❶ Cream together the shortening, butter, and sugar in a large bowl with a mixer on high speed for 1 minute. Add the vanilla and salt and mix for another minute. Mix the baking powder into the flour in a medium bowl and add it to the wet ingredients along with the milk. Mix well by hand until the dough can be formed into a ball. Cover the dough with plastic wrap and chill it for 1 hour.

❷ After 1 hour, preheat the oven to 325 degrees F.

❸ Roll the dough out on a flat, floured surface to between ⅛ and ¼ inch thick. Use a 2-inch biscuit cutter or round cookie cutter to punch out rounds of the cookie dough.

4 Place all of the cookie dough rounds ½ inch apart on parchment paper– or Silpat pad–lined baking sheets. Use the sides of the tips of your index fingers to make four indentations in the edges of each cookie.

5 Bake the cookies for 12 to 16 minutes. The cookies will be just very lightly browned on the bottom when done.

HOSTESS CUPCAKES

First-Time Hack

Active Prep: 90 min.
Inactive Prep: 20 min.

H Difficulty: Hard

Yield: 12 cupcakes

One of the first recipes I cloned over twenty-five years ago was the Hostess Twinkie, but it wasn't until just recently that I got around to knocking off the brand's iconic chocolate cupcake with the seven white icing swirls on top. The crème filling recipe here is the same as in the Twinkie, but the cake, chocolate frosting, and white icing are all brand-new scratch recipes. Place small rounds of parchment paper into the cups of a 12-cup muffin pan for easy removal of the cupcakes and you'll need a piping bag or pastry gun with a medium tip to fill the cupcakes and a small tip to add the seven loops of white icing on top.

CAKE
1 cup hot water
2 ounces (²/₃ cup) unsweetened cocoa
6 ounces (1 cup plus 3 tablespoons) all-purpose flour
¾ teaspoon baking soda
¾ teaspoon salt
2 large eggs
1½ cups granulated sugar
1 teaspoon vanilla extract
6 tablespoons vegetable oil

CRÈME FILLING
2 teaspoons vanilla extract
½ teaspoon water
⅛ teaspoon salt

1 7-ounce jar marshmallow crème
½ cup shortening
2 ounces (½ cup) powdered sugar

CHOCOLATE FROSTING
½ cup (1 stick) unsalted butter, melted
4 ounces (1 cup) powdered sugar
1 ounce (⅓ cup) unsweetened cocoa
2 tablespoons heavy cream
⅛ teaspoon salt

WHITE ICING
4½ ounces (1½ cups) powdered sugar
2 tablespoons shortening
1 tablespoon plus 1 teaspoon milk
½ teaspoon vanilla extract

1 Preheat the oven to 350 degrees F.

2 Spray 12 cups of a standard-size muffin pan with nonstick cooking spray and add a circle of parchment paper to the bottom of each cup.

117

3 Make the cakes by pouring the hot water over the cocoa in a medium bowl. Use a whisk to combine until smooth, then set the cocoa aside to cool.

4 Combine the flour, baking soda, and salt in another medium bowl.

5 Use an electric mixer on medium speed to mix the eggs with the sugar and vanilla in a large bowl for 1 minute. Mix in the oil.

6 Add the flour mixture to the wet ingredients and mix well with an electric mixer on high speed until smooth. Add the cocoa and mix well. Pour ⅓ cup of batter into each cup (fill about three-quarters up) and bake for 18 to 22 minutes or until cooked through. Cool.

7 While the cupcakes cool, make the crème filling by combining the vanilla, water, and salt in a small bowl. Stir until most of the salt is dissolved. Mix the marshmallow crème, shortening, and powdered sugar together in a large bowl using an electric mixer on high speed. Add the vanilla/salt solution and mix for 1 minute. Set aside.

8 Make the frosting by combining the melted butter, powdered sugar, cocoa, cream, and salt in a medium bowl with an electric mixer on high speed. Let it sit to cool until it is a medium consistency—not too runny, not too thick—that will stick to the cupcakes when they are dipped into it.

9 Make the white icing by combining all of the ingredients with an electric mixer in a medium bowl for 1 minute.

10 When the cupcakes are cool, load the filling into a piping bag or pastry gun with a medium round tip, and the icing into a piping bag or pastry gun with a small round tip.

11 Slice the top off of each cupcake so that they are flat on top, then use the blunt end of a skewer or the tip of a chopstick to poke down through the top of each cupcake and swirl it around inside to make some space for the filling. Pipe some filling into the center of each cupcake.

12 Dip the filled cupcakes upside-down into the chocolate frosting so that just the tops

are frosted. Set the cupcakes aside to cool for about 10 minutes, then give each cupcake a second coat. Use a knife to smooth out the frosting if needed. If the frosting becomes too thick, microwave it on high for 15 seconds to loosen it up.

13 When the frosting on top of the cupcakes is cool, pipe a line of 7 loops onto the top of each cupcake.

HOSTESS TWINKIE

👍 Improved Hack
🕐 Active Prep: 45 min.
Inactive Prep: 1 hr. 20 min.
M🌡 Difficulty: Medium
👥 Yield: 16 snack cakes

When Hostess closed its doors in November 2012, many thought they would never again see the spongy, crème-filled snack cake they grew up with. But on July 15, 2013, the Twinkie was resurrected by a group of investors known for reviving old brands, and the iconic treat was back on store shelves in boxes that said, "The sweetest comeback in the history of ever." I am actually writing this recipe on Twinkie comeback day.

The Hostess Twinkie is one of the first recipes I hacked back in the late '80s. In my original recipe the sponge cake was made by combining a box of pound cake mix with beaten egg whites to lighten it up. It was an easy solution, but perhaps not the best way to replicate the light, spongy texture and the distinct flavor of the original cake. When I went back into the lab this time around to improve my twenty-year-old recipe, I decided that the cake must be made from scratch. But I wanted the recipe to stay simple, so I came up with a way to make delicious sponge cake without separating

the eggs. You're going to have to beat the eggs for a while so a stand mixer helps here, but you can still make the recipe just fine with a handheld mixer.

I also found that the only way to make cloned Twinkies that look like real Twinkies is to find a canoe cake pan—otherwise known as a "Twinkie pan"—that makes cakes that are the same size as Twinkies. After the Twinkie disappeared in 2012, these pans became easier to find both online and in brick-and-mortar cooking stores. If you don't have a canoe cake pan, you can make Twinkie cake pans from scratch using aluminum foil and a spice bottle. I've laid out those steps in Tidbits for you, along with an optional way to make the recipe using real butter instead of butter flavoring.

CAKE

4 large eggs
1⅔ cups granulated sugar
¾ cup whole milk
½ cup vegetable oil
2 teaspoons vanilla extract
1 teaspoon butter flavoring
10 ounces (2 cups) cake flour
1½ teaspoons baking powder
1½ teaspoons salt

FILLING

¼ teaspoon salt
2 teaspoons vanilla extract
½ teaspoon water
1 7-ounce jar marshmallow crème
½ cup shortening
2 ounces (½ cup) powdered sugar

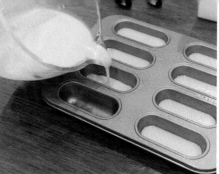

1 Preheat the oven to 325 degrees F.

2 Beat the eggs with the sugar in a large bowl with an electric mixer on high speed for 5 minutes. It is best to use a stand mixer—if you have one—with a paddle attachment, but a handheld mixer will also work.

3 Add the milk, oil, vanilla, and butter flavoring and mix on low speed until the ingredients are combined.

4 Add the flour, baking powder, and salt and mix on low speed just until the batter is smooth, with no lumps. Cover the batter and let it sit for 30 minutes, then mix it up again on low speed for 20 seconds.

5 Grease canoe cake pans (Twinkie pans) with shortening, butter, or nonstick cooking spray. Fill each cup a third to halfway full with batter, then bake the cakes for 20 to 24 minutes or until the tops begin to turn light brown.

6 Cool the cakes for 5 minutes before removing them from the pan. Use a teaspoon to gently lift them out of the pan. Fill the cakes when they have completely cooled

7 To make the filling, combine the salt with the vanilla and water in a small bowl and stir until much of the salt dissolves.

8 Combine the marshmallow crème, shortening, powdered sugar, and vanilla/salt in a large bowl and mix well with an electric mixer—using the whisk attachment—on high speed until fluffy.

9 Load the filling into a pastry bag or pastry gun with a medium round tip. Inject the filling into the bottom (flat side) of each cake in three places. Swirl the tip around a bit as you press it into the cake to make a cavity for the filling. Store the cakes in a sealed container at room temperature for several days or freeze to keep them for a couple of months.

TIDBITS If you can't find a canoe cake pan or don't feel like buying one, you can also make clone Twinkie cake pans using a little technique I came up with years ago calling for aluminum foil and a standard spice bottle. These will make cakes that are bigger than real Twinkies, but they will still have the basic shape.

Rip off a 1-foot-long piece of aluminum foil and fold it in half, then fold it in half again. Wrap this around a spice bottle, being sure to leave the top open so you can take the spice bottle out and later pour the batter in. Make ten of these and place them in a 9 x 13-inch baking pan, with the openings facing up. Spray the insides with nonstick cooking spray, fill each halfway with batter, and bake following the instructions in the recipe.

If you'd like to make a version of these cakes with real butter instead of using the imitation stuff, just eliminate the imitation butter flavoring, add ¼ cup of melted butter to the batter when adding in the oil, and reduce the oil to ¼ cup.

HOUSTON'S CHICAGO-STYLE SPINACH DIP

Improved Hack

Active Prep: 10 min.
Inactive Prep: 5 min.

Difficulty: Easy

Yield: 4 to 6 servings

This is one of the best spinach dips out there so it needs a proper clone. While the hack I created several years ago was good, it just wasn't as creamy as the real thing, plus it was missing a few key ingredients such as Tabasco, lemon juice, and sugar. I've also tweaked the cooking method here so that you get a creamier sauce (by making a roux), and the spinach is brighter green in the finished product (no more overcooking). According to servers at the restaurant, Houston's uses Parmigiano-Reggiano in the dip. It's an especially tasty Parmesan cheese from a specific region in Italy, but I recently discovered that here in the U.S. regulations for cheese labeling are not as strict as in Europe. The Parmigiano-Reggiano you buy at your market may in fact be a locally made imitation. The good news is the recipe works just as well with any Parmesan cheese you find. So go ahead and use the cheaper stuff. It works just fine here and still makes a crazy good dip.

1 10-ounce box **frozen chopped spinach, thawed**
¾ cup diced **canned artichoke hearts (not marinated)**
2 tablespoons **light olive oil**
2 tablespoons **minced onion**
2 teaspoons **minced garlic (2 cloves)**
2 tablespoons **all-purpose flour**
¾ cup **heavy cream**
¼ cup **chicken broth**
⅓ cup **grated Parmigiano-Reggiano cheese**
2 tablespoons **sour cream**

1 teaspoon **lemon juice**
½ teaspoon **granulated sugar**
¼ teaspoon **salt**
¼ teaspoon **Tabasco pepper sauce**
½ cup shredded **Monterey Jack cheese**

ON THE SIDE
Tortilla chips or strips
Sour cream
Salsa

❶ Squeeze the liquid out of the thawed spinach and combine it with the artichoke hearts in a medium bowl. Cover the bowl with plastic wrap and microwave on high for 5 minutes. Keep the bowl covered and set it aside until needed.

❷ While the spinach and artichoke hearts are in the microwave, heat up the olive oil in a medium saucepan over medium heat. Add the onion and garlic and sauté for 1 minute, but do not let the garlic brown.

❸ Whisk in the flour and cook for 1 minute.

4 Whisk in the cream, then add the chicken broth. Cook for 1 to 2 minutes or until the sauce bubbles and thickens.

5 Stir in the spinach and artichoke hearts mixture. Add the Parmigiano-Reggiano cheese, sour cream, lemon juice, sugar, salt, and Tabasco. Continue cooking for 2 minutes—stirring often—or until the mixture is hot.

6 When the dip is hot, spoon it into a serving dish. Sprinkle the Monterey Jack cheese over the top and serve with tortilla chips, plus sour cream and salsa on the side.

IHOP
NEW YORK
CHEESECAKE PANCAKES

- First-Time Hack
- Active Prep: 15 min.
  Inactive Prep: 15 min.
- Difficulty: Easy
- Yield: 8 pancakes

More like dessert than breakfast, this delicious IHOP creation is now one of the top picks from the casual chain's original pancake choices. These pancakes are made by sprinkling little cheesecake bits into IHOP's original buttermilk pancake batter as it cooks. There's no need to make a whole cheesecake just to dice it up into tiny bits for pancakes, so I've got a shortcut: just chop up a frozen Sara Lee New York Style Cheesecake and toss the pieces in a mixture of graham cracker crumbs and sugar. To make the perfect amount of cheesecake bits you'll need three slices of the frozen cake if the cake were sliced into eight equal portions, or three-eighths of the cake. And keep the cheesecake frozen when you slice it—it's much easier to cut and coat that way. Top off your stacks with canned strawberry pie filling and some whipped cream squirted on top and you'll have a perfect clone that tastes just like the chain's popular original creation.

½ **cup graham cracker crumbs**
1 **tablespoon granulated sugar**
3 **slices frozen Sara Lee New York Style**
   Cheesecake (⅜ of the cake), not defrosted

½ **teaspoon salt**
1½ **cups buttermilk**
1 **large egg**
2 **tablespoons unsalted butter, melted**

PANCAKE BATTER
6 **ounces (1¼ cups) all-purpose flour**
3 **tablespoons granulated sugar**
1½ **teaspoons baking soda**

ON TOP
1 **can (21 ounces) strawberry pie filling**
Canned whipped cream

1 Combine the graham cracker crumbs with the sugar in a medium bowl. Cut 3 slices from the frozen (not thawed) cheesecake, each one-eighth of the cake. Cut the crust off the bottom of each slice and discard it. Dice the remaining cheesecake portions and toss them in the graham cracker crumbs until coated. Put this bowl in the freezer until you are ready to cook the pancakes.

2 To make the pancake batter, combine the flour with the sugar, baking soda, and salt in a large bowl.

3 Add the buttermilk, egg, and melted butter to the bowl and mix on high speed with an electric mixer for 1 minute or until the batter is smooth. Let the batter sit for 5 minutes before using it.

4 Preheat a large nonstick skillet or griddle over medium heat. Spray with nonstick cooking spray.

5 Pour ⅓-cup portions onto the hot pan or griddle. Immediately drop a small handful of cheesecake bits into each of the pancakes. Cook the pancakes for 1½ to 2 minutes per side or until golden brown.

6 Serve a stack of pancakes with strawberry pie filling spooned over the top and finished off with a pile of whipped cream.

TOP SECRET RECIPES
VERSION OF

IHOP ORIGINAL BUTTERMILK PANCAKES

 Improved Hack

 Active Prep: 5 min.
Inactive Prep: 15 min.

 Difficulty: Easy

 Yield: 8 pancakes

My first version of this recipe called for ¼ cup of oil, which I now think is excessive. As a result the pancakes are too moist, even gummy if you don't cook them enough. This time around I've reduced the fat and replaced the oil with melted butter to make the finished product even more flavorful and fluffy. If you liked my first recipe, then you'll want to try this new one. It's got just one little change, but it makes a world of difference.

6 ounces (1¼ cups) all-purpose flour
3 tablespoons granulated sugar
1½ teaspoons baking soda
½ teaspoon salt
1½ cups buttermilk
1 large egg

2 tablespoons unsalted butter, melted

ON THE SIDE
Softened butter
Maple syrup

1 Combine the flour with the sugar, baking soda, and salt in a large bowl.

2 Add the buttermilk, egg, and melted butter and mix on high speed with an electric mixer for 1 minute or until the batter is smooth. Let the batter sit for 5 minutes before using it.

3 Preheat a large nonstick skillet or griddle over medium heat. Spray with nonstick cooking spray.

4 Pour ⅓-cup portions onto the hot pan or griddle. Cook the pancakes for 1½ to 2 minutes per side or until golden brown. Serve with butter and maple syrup on the side.

IKEA SWEDISH MEATBALLS

 First-Time Hack

 Active Prep: 20 min.
Inactive Prep: 20 min.

 Difficulty: Medium

 Yield: 30 meatballs

I know IKEA is a giant global furniture chain, but before researching these great little balls of meat I wasn't aware that IKEA is also one of the world's largest food retailers. At the very top of the list of the most popular menu items at the stores' cafeteria-style IKEA Restaurant & Bistro are the Swedish Meatballs, which are consumed at a rate of 150 million each year. The meatballs are moist and delicious and come smothered in a cream sauce and served with a side of lingonberry jam. But if you don't feel like working your way through the giant rat maze of furniture that is the ingenious layout of each store to get to a plate of these meatballs, you can now make them at home with very little effort. The secret is to use ground beef that is 20 percent fat and a food processor to puree all of the ingredients. If you don't have a food processor, a blender will work to puree the onions, which you can add to the rest of the ingredients and mix thoroughly with your hands. I found that a

1¼-inch cookie scooper is the best way to form the balls, but you can also form the balls with a teaspoon measure and your hands—keep your hands thoroughly moistened with water to prevent the meat mixture from sticking to them.

MEATBALLS
⅓ cup chopped onion
1 large egg
1 egg white
⅓ cup beef broth
2 tablespoons water
½ pound ground beef
    (20 percent fat)
½ pound ground pork
½ cup plain bread crumbs
1 teaspoon salt
½ teaspoon white pepper
⅛ teaspoon allspice

CREAM SAUCE
1¼ cups beef broth
⅓ cup heavy cream
4 teaspoons cornstarch
1 tablespoon apple juice
¼ teaspoon salt
⅛ teaspoon garlic powder
⅛ teaspoon onion powder
⅛ teaspoon white pepper
1 bay leaf

2 teaspoons vegetable oil

ON THE SIDE (OPTIONAL)
Lingonberry preserves

1 Combine the onion, egg, egg white, beef broth, and water in a food processor or blender and mix on high speed for 15 seconds or until the onion is completely pulverized. If using a blender, pour

this mixture into a large bowl and combine it with the ground meats, bread crumbs, and seasoning. Mix thoroughly with your hands. If using a food processor, add the ground meats, bread crumbs, and seasoning to the food processor and mix on high speed for 30 seconds or until all of the ingredients are combined and the meat has a smooth consistency.

2 Preheat your oven to 350 degrees F.

3 Use a ⅓-ounce cookie scooper (or a teaspoon measure) moistened with water to form balls that are about 1¼ inches in diameter. Moisten your fingers with water to make forming the balls easier. Place the balls on a nonstick baking sheet or a baking sheet lined with parchment paper or a silicone baking mat and bake for 20 to 25 minutes or until the meatballs are just lightly browned.

Turn the meatballs over halfway through the cooking time.

4 While the meatballs are baking, make the sauce by whisking all of the ingredients, except the bay leaf, into a small saucepan over medium heat. When the mixture begins to bubble, add the bay leaf, then reduce the heat and simmer for 6 to 7 minutes or until thick. Discard the bay leaf.

5 Just before you are ready to serve the meatballs, brown them in a sauté pan over medium heat with a couple of teaspoons of vegetable oil. Serve the meatballs with the cream sauce poured over the top along with a small side of lingonberry preserves, if desired.

TIDBITS You can freeze the meatballs after they have baked. To reheat, add 2 teaspoons of oil to a sauté pan over medium heat. Cook the meatballs in the pan, stirring often, until browned and hot all the way through.

JACK IN THE BOX
BEEF TACO

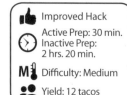

👍 Improved Hack

⏱ Active Prep: 30 min.
Inactive Prep:
2 hrs. 20 min.

M🌡 Difficulty: Medium

👥 Yield: 12 tacos

Eating one of these tacos today still reminds me of the bagfuls we'd grind through on a hot summer day at the beach when I was a kid. The Jack in the Box at Warner Avenue and Pacific Coast Highway in Huntington Beach, California, was right on the sand, and a bike ride away from the house I grew up in, so that's where my friends and I set up camp for a day of body surfing and cheap fast food. Today the recipe is the same as it was since the first Jack in the Box opened way back in 1950: finely ground spiced beef, melted American cheese, shredded lettuce, and tangy taco sauce all wedged into a deep-fried corn tortilla. Properly hacking this decades-old recipe requires a perfect formula for the ground beef, which is the heart and soul of the taco. The chain incorporates vegetable proteins and soy grits into the beef, but those ingredients are not something you're likely to find at your corner market. So I've developed a clone recipe that includes a little all-purpose flour and cornmeal in the mix to give the beef a similar texture to the original. A food processor is used here to

puree the ground beef with those ingredients along with all the spices.

To seal the tortilla around the beef (so oil doesn't get in while the tacos are frying), I came up with a method that calls for placing a bowl upside down on the egg-washed edge of the tacos until they are frozen shut. With a new taco-sealing trick and the better beef filling formula, this clone is a huge improvement on the original recipe I created for my first book over twenty years ago.

Just know before you get started that you will need a food processor for this recipe and six bowls with a 4¾-inch diameter, or bowls that are just slightly smaller in diameter than the corn tortillas you are using. If you don't have a food processor, you can still make the recipe using your hands, but the beef won't have quite the same smooth consistency as the original.

8 ounces ground beef (20 percent fat)
½ cup water
2 tablespoons all-purpose flour
1 tablespoon cornmeal
1½ teaspoons chili powder
1 teaspoon ketchup

½ **teaspoon** Worcestershire sauce
½ **teaspoon** salt
¼ **teaspoon** garlic powder
¼ **teaspoon** onion powder
⅛ **teaspoon** MSG (such as Accent seasoning)
12 corn tortillas (Mission brand works well)
4 to 12 cups canola oil
1 large egg, beaten
6 slices American cheese, cut diagonally into
   12 halves
½ **cup** Ortega medium original taco sauce
2 cups thinly sliced iceberg lettuce

1 Combine the ground beef, water, flour, cornmeal, chili powder, ketchup, Worcestershire sauce, salt, garlic powder, onion powder, and MSG in a bowl and mix well with your hands to combine all of the spices into the beef. Put the beef into a food processor and puree for about 1 minute until smooth.

2 Dump the pureed beef mixture into a sauté pan and heat over medium heat while stirring until the meat is thoroughly cooked, 5 to 10 minutes.

3 Preassemble each taco by first heating up about 1 tablespoon of oil in a clean sauté pan over low heat. Place a corn tortilla in the oiled sauté pan for 30 seconds or so (do not flip it over), or until hot, and then remove it from the pan and place it oiled-side-down on a plate. This process will make the tortilla more pliable so that it does not crack when folded over the meat. Spread a heaping tablespoon of the beef mixture off-center onto the non-oiled side of the tortilla. Brush a little beaten egg around the edge of the half of the tortilla with the beef on it, fold the tortilla over the beef, then move the taco to a rimmed baking sheet lined with wax paper and invert a small bowl with a 4¾-inch diameter onto the folded taco to keep it sealed around the edge. Repeat the filling process with the next taco and position it next to the first one so that the bottoms are touching, then replace the bowl to hold both tacos closed. Repeat the process with all of the tacos, then place the baking sheet in your freezer for 2 to 3 hours or until the tacos are completely frozen.

4 When the tacos are frozen, preheat the oil in a deep fryer or a deep saucepan to 350 degrees F.

131

5 Fry two tacos at a time for 2 to 3 minutes or until they are just beginning to turn light brown around the edges. Drain the tacos on a rack or paper towels for about 20 to 30 seconds or until cool enough to handle.

6 Carefully open each taco just wide enough to place a triangular slice of cheese inside. Pour in about 2 teaspoons of taco sauce and finish off each taco by pushing in some sliced lettuce.

KFC
COLE SLAW

👍 Improved Hack

🕐 Active Prep: 20 min.
Inactive Prep: 4 hrs.

E 🌡 Difficulty: Easy

👥 Yield: 6 cups

When creating the first version of this recipe over twenty-five years ago, I did not have easy access to fast-food chains' ingredients lists, which are so simple to locate these days online.

If the Internet had existed back then, I would have discovered that there is no dairy ingredient in KFC's famous cole slaw, and I would likely not have included buttermilk and milk as ingredients in that first recipe. I would have also discovered that the chain uses a blend of vinegars in the cole slaw dressing rather than just white vinegar, as I used in my first recipe. Now, with just a few adjustments, you can make an even better clone of this world-famous cole slaw—with even fewer ingredients. This popular recipe is now tastier and easier! Just be sure to chop your cabbage into very small pieces before you combine it with the dressing and let the cole slaw sit for at least 4 hours (overnight is even better) before you eat it.

¾ cup mayonnaise
6 tablespoons granulated sugar
5 teaspoons white vinegar
2 teaspoons apple cider vinegar
2 teaspoons lemon juice
⅛ teaspoon salt

8 cups (1 head) finely chopped green cabbage
¼ cup shredded and chopped carrot (about ½ carrot)
2 tablespoons minced white onion

❶ Whisk together the mayonnaise, sugar, vinegars, lemon juice, and salt in a large bowl.

❷ Stir the cabbage, carrot, and onion into the dressing.

❸ Cover and chill for at least 4 hours.

KFC GRILLED CHICKEN

First-Time Hack

Active Prep: 15 min.
Inactive Prep: 2 hrs. 40 min.

Difficulty: Easy

Yield: 4 servings

It took chefs several years to develop what would eventually become KFC's most clucked-about new product launch. Oprah Winfrey featured the chicken on her talk show and gave away so many coupons for free grilled chicken meals that some customers waited in lines for over an hour and half, and several stores ran out and had to offer rain checks. Company spokesperson Laurie Schalow told the Associated Press that KFC has never seen such a huge response to any promotion. "It's unprecedented in our more than fifty years," she said. "It beats anything we've ever done."

When I heard about the commotion over this new secret recipe, I obtained a sample of the proprietary seasoning blend and got right to work. After days of nibbling through what amounted to a small flock of hens, I'm happy to bring you this perfected clone version of the fast-food recipe so that you can now reproduce it in your own kitchen. The secret preparation process requires that you marinate (brine) your chicken for a couple of hours in a salt and MSG solution. After the chicken has brined, it's brushed with liquid smoke–flavored oil that will not only make the seasoning stick to the chicken but will give the chicken a smoky flavor and ensure that it doesn't stick to the pan. I duplicated the cooking process using an oven-safe grill pan, searing the chicken first on the stovetop to add the grill marks, then cooking the chicken through in the oven. If you don't have a grill pan or a grill plate, you can sear the chicken in any large oven-safe sauté pan. If you have a convection function on your oven you should definitely use it, but the recipe will still work in a standard oven with the temperature set just a little bit higher. After baking the chicken for 20 minutes on each side, you're ready to dive into your own eight-piece bucket of delicious indoor grilled chicken that's as tasty as the fried stuff, but without a lot of the fat and calories.

MARINADE
¼ **cup salt**
2 **tablespoons granulated sugar**
2 **teaspoons MSG**
8 **cups water**

1 **whole roaster chicken (4 to 5 pounds), cut into 8 pieces**

BRUSH WITH
¼ **cup vegetable oil**
¼ **teaspoon liquid smoke**
¼ **teaspoon soy sauce**

SEASONING
4 **teaspoons all-purpose flour**
1½ **teaspoons chicken bouillon powder (Knorr brand is best)**
½ **teaspoon beef bouillon powder (Knorr brand is best)**
½ **teaspoon salt**
½ **teaspoon coarse ground black pepper**
½ **teaspoon crushed dried rosemary**
½ **teaspoon dried basil**
¼ **teaspoon dried oregano**
¼ **teaspoon garlic powder**

1 Dissolve the salt, sugar, and MSG in the water to make the marinade (brine). Add the chicken, cover, and chill for exactly 2 hours.

2 When the chicken has marinated, rinse each piece of chicken with water and blot dry. Whisk together the oil, liquid smoke, and soy sauce in a small bowl. Brush the oil over one side of each piece of chicken.

3 Combine all of the ingredients for the seasoning in a small bowl. Sprinkle the seasoning over the oiled side of each piece of chicken, then flip each piece, brush with oil again, and sprinkle on more seasoning.

4 Preheat your oven to 350 degrees F, or 325 degrees F if you have a convection oven. Brush some of the leftover oil solution onto an oven-safe grill pan or grill plate. Set the pan over medium heat, and when the oil begins to smoke, place the chicken skin-side down on the pan. Cook the chicken for 2 to 3 minutes or until the skin begins to brown and grill marks form on the chicken, then flip the chicken and cook it for another 1 to 2 minutes. Pop the grill pan in the oven for 20 minutes, then flip each piece of chicken and bake for another 20 minutes or until the surface of the chicken is golden brown and the chicken is cooked through.

TIDBITS If you can't find the chicken and beef bouillon powder for this recipe, you can use bouillon cubes in a pinch. Just crush the cubes into fine powder before measuring.

For a better coating of the spice blend, use an empty shaker bottle to shake the seasoning on each piece of chicken.

KFC
ORIGINAL RECIPE
FRIED CHICKEN

👍 Improved Hack

⟳ Active Prep: 30 min.
Inactive Prep:
3 hrs. 30 min.

M🌡 Difficulty: Medium

👥 Yield: 4 servings

One of the most protected,

discussed, and sought-after secret recipes in the food world is KFC's Original Recipe Fried Chicken. Long ago I published my first hack of this famous formula, but the recipe, which was based on research from *Big Secrets* author William Poundstone, includes only salt, pepper, MSG, and flour in the breading, and not the blend of eleven herbs and spices we have all heard about. The fried chicken made with my first recipe is good in a pinch, but it really needs several more ingredients to be a true clone. That is why, over twenty years later, I was happy to get another crack at the secret when we shot the pilot episode for my CMT series *Top Secret Recipe*. In the show I visited KFC headquarters, talked to friends of Harlan Sanders, who had seen the actual recipe, and even checked out the Corbin, Kentucky, kitchen where Harland Sanders first developed his chicken recipe. During that four-day shoot I was able to gather enough clues about the secret eleven herbs and spices to craft this new recipe—one that I believe is the closest match to the Colonel's secret fried chicken that anyone has ever revealed.

On the show I learned that the chicken must be brined, so give yourself 3 hours to marinate the chicken in a salt solution. That will keep the chicken moist and fill it with flavor. Also, you want to use parts from small chickens. The best way to get small chicken pieces is to cut up the chicken yourself. Find a 4- to 5-pound roaster and get hacking. There are plenty of instructional

videos on the Internet that will show you how to properly slice up your clucker if you don't know how.

The real KFC Chicken is cooked in a specially designed pressure fryer, but consumer models are hard to come by, so I have designed this recipe to work in a standard deep fryer. You could also heat up the oil on the stovetop in a deep pan with a thermometer attached, but a deep fryer makes it much easier to regulate and control the temperature, which will fluctuate quite a bit when the cold chicken is dropped in.

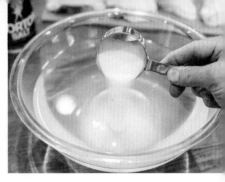

BRINE
⅓ cup salt
1 tablespoon MSG (such as Accent seasoning)
8 cups water

1 whole roaster chicken (4 to 5 pounds), cut into 8 pieces
6 to 12 cups vegetable oil

BREADING
9 ounces (1¾ cups) all-purpose flour
1 tablespoon plus 1 teaspoon salt
1 tablespoon MSG
2 teaspoons granulated sugar
2 teaspoons ground tellicherry pepper
½ teaspoon ground white pepper
½ teaspoon paprika
½ teaspoon ground savory
½ teaspoon ground sage
¼ teaspoon ground ginger
¼ teaspoon ground marjoram
¼ teaspoon onion powder
⅛ teaspoon garlic powder
⅛ teaspoon ground cayenne pepper

DREDGE
4 large eggs
2 cups skim milk

1 To make the brine, dissolve the salt and MSG in the water. Add the chicken pieces and marinate for 3 hours. Remove the chicken from the brine, rinse with water, and blot dry.

2 Heat the oil in a deep fryer to 300 degrees F.

3 Make the breading by combining all of the ingredients in a large bowl.

4 In a separate bowl, beat the eggs and then stir in the milk.

5 When the oil is hot, dip each piece of chicken in the egg and milk mixture and then press into the breading. Toss each chicken piece in the breading until well coated. Let the chicken sit for 5 minutes in the breading, gently tossing every minute or two to ensure a good coating. Gently shake off the excess breading and fry 2 to 4 pieces at a time (or whatever your fryer can hold) for 16 to 20 minutes or until the chicken is golden brown. Drain the fried chicken on a rack for at least 5 minutes before serving.

TIDBITS If you want to keep the chicken warm until every piece is cooked so that you can serve it all at once, place the fried pieces on a rack on a baking sheet and keep them in your oven set to 200 degrees F.

LEGAL SEA FOODS NEW ENGLAND CLAM CHOWDER

 First-Time Hack

 Active Prep: 30 min.
Inactive Prep: 1 hr. 30 min.

 Difficulty: Medium

Yield: 9 cups

This phenomenal clam chowder, made with lots of fresh littleneck clams, was chosen to represent the state of Massachusetts at the first inauguration of Ronald Reagan in 1981—just a year after first being served at the restaurant—and has been served at every presidential inauguration since. I think it's the best clam chowder you'll get at any casual restaurant chain in America, and that makes it a perfect clone candidate for this book. I was able to glean only minimal information from servers at the Legal Sea Foods location in Philly where I first tasted this fantastic chowder. Fortunately, the company has an online seafood store where I could order a quart of the soup—for a whopping 45 bucks with shipping!—which provided me with an ingredients list on the package to aid in the hacking. The restaurant has its own cookbook, which provided a few more clues, but the recipe there does not produce a soup that is anything like the version in the restaurant. Many of the ingredients I found on the label of the restaurant version are not listed in the cookbook recipe.

The real soup includes a little salt pork, which I have replaced here with bacon since such a small amount is used. For the best flavor you'll want to use fish or seafood stock, which I found at Walmart, but you can substitute with chicken broth if seafood stock is unavailable. This recipe makes over 2 quarts of the soup and will cost you a fraction of what I paid for just a single quart through the company's website.

8 pounds **littleneck clams**
2 cups **water**
2 teaspoons minced **garlic (2 cloves)**
1 slice uncooked bacon, **finely chopped**
¼ cup (½ stick) **unsalted butter**
2 cups minced **white onion (1 medium onion)**
3 tablespoons **all-purpose flour**

1 tablespoon **cornstarch**
2 cups **fish stock or seafood stock**
3 cups diced peeled **russet potato (1 large potato)**
2 cups **heavy cream**
½ teaspoon **coarse ground black pepper**
½ teaspoon **Worcestershire sauce**
¼ teaspoon **Tabasco pepper sauce**

❶ Cover the clams with cold water in a large bowl and let them sit for 20 to 30 minutes so that they spit out any sand. Repeat the process until no more sand is coming out of the clams. Three times should do it.

❷ Pour 2 cups of water into a large soup pot, add the garlic and clams, and bring to a boil. Cover the pot, reduce the heat to a simmer, and steam the clams for 8 to 10 minutes until they all open. Remove the clams from the pot, then strain the liquid to remove the garlic and any detached clam meat, and save the liquid (clam juice).

3 When the clams have cooled, remove them from their shells and chop them up. Set aside. You will have around 2 cups of clams.

4 Rinse out the pot, then add the bacon to the pan and cook it over medium/low heat until crispy, about 10 minutes. Remove the bacon from the fat and set the bits aside. Add the butter to the pan. When the butter has melted, add the onions and cook until beginning to turn translucent, about 10 minutes.

5 Stir the flour into the onions and cook for another 5 minutes, stirring often. Dissolve the cornstarch into the seafood stock, then pour it into the onions along with 4 cups of the clam juice. Raise the heat to high.

6 When the soup comes to a boil, add the potatoes and cook for 15 minutes or until they begin to get tender. Reduce the heat to medium/low, then add the cream, black pepper, Worcestershire, Tabasco, and bacon bits. Bring the soup to a low simmer and cook for another 15 minutes or until it thickens. Just before serving, add the clams and turn off the heat.

TIDBITS Depending on how salty your clams are, you may want to add a bit of salt to the soup. Even better, add about a tablespoon of Better than Bouillon concentrated clam base to punch up the flavor.

LEGAL SEA FOODS
LEGAL'S SIGNATURE
CRAB CAKES

First-Time Hack

Active Prep: 20 min.
Inactive Prep: 12 min.

Difficulty: Easy

Yield: 6 crab cakes

This 31-unit Boston-based seafood chain got its name from "Legal Cash Market," the grocery store that founder George Berkowitz's father, Harry, opened in Cambridge, Massachusetts, in 1904. In 1950 George opened a fish market next door to his dad's store and called it "Legal Sea Foods," and eighteen years later it expanded into a thriving restaurant business. In 1986 NBC's *Today* named Legal Sea Foods "The Best Seafood Restaurant in America." One of the signature dishes at the chain is Legal's Signature Crab Cakes, which are filled with big chunks of lump crab and served with a top secret mustard dipping sauce. These delicious baked crab cakes are simple to prepare, as is the sauce, both of which I have hacked here for the first time.

MUSTARD SAUCE
½ cup mayonnaise
1 tablespoon Grey Poupon Dijon mustard
2 teaspoons bottled prepared horseradish
¾ teaspoon Worcestershire sauce
¼ teaspoon granulated sugar

CRAB CAKES
¼ cup mayonnaise
1 large egg
1½ teaspoons Old Bay seasoning
1 teaspoon Grey Poupon Dijon mustard
1 teaspoon Worcestershire sauce
5 saltine crackers, crumbled
1 pound jumbo lump crab
2 tablespoons unsalted butter, **melted**

1 Preheat the oven to 475 degrees F.

2 Make the mustard sauce by combining all of the ingredients in a small bowl. Set aside.

3 Make the crab cakes by whisking together the mayonnaise, egg, Old Bay, mustard, and Worcestershire sauce in a large bowl. Stir in the crackers (which have been crumbled in a small bag with a mallet or rolling pin). Gently fold in the crab, being careful not to break up the chunks.

4 Measure ½-cup portions of the crab onto a nonstick baking pan or a pan lined with a nonstick pad. Form the crab into cakes and then brush each cake with melted butter.

5 Bake the crab cakes for 12 to 16 minutes or until they are beginning to brown on top. Serve with the mustard sauce on the side or use a squeeze bottle to add a drizzle of the sauce on the plate before adding the crab cakes.

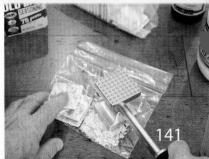

LOFTHOUSE FROSTED COOKIES

 First-Time Hack

Active Prep: 15 min.
 Inactive Prep:
2 hrs. 30 min.

E Difficulty: Easy

Yield: 28 cookies

When the Lofthouse frosted cookies were first produced from a handed-down family recipe in a makeshift bakery in the back of a Utah garage in 1994, it's likely the ingredients were different than they are in the mass-produced product found in markets across the country today. To maintain a long shelf-life, it is common for baked goods to be manufactured with nondairy substitutes, so butter is often replaced with hydrogenated oil and butter flavoring (otherwise known as margarine), and various vegetable gums and preservatives are added to improve the texture and stabilize the product.

Rather than using ingredients such as artificial flavoring, lecithin, cellulose gum, or carrageenan in this recipe, as you will see on the label of the store product, we will use real butter, fresh eggs, and vanilla extract in our clone—perhaps just as the family who created the recipe did back in the day. The big difference is that you have to be sure to eat the cookies within a few days to get that freshly baked taste and texture. Or you may want to freeze them. Cake flour is used here rather than all-purpose flour to duplicate the tender, cakey texture of the original; and sour cream is used to add in the dairy needed without overliquefying the dough (as milk would). An added benefit of sour cream is the high acidity, which activates the leavening power of the baking soda. The dough is still going to be much thinner and tackier than typical cookie dough, so chilling it for a couple of hours before portioning it out onto a baking sheet is a must to make it easier to shape.

COOKIES
½ cup (1 stick) unsalted butter, softened
¾ cup plus 2 tablespoons granulated sugar
1 large egg
1 egg white
1¼ teaspoons vanilla extract
¾ cup sour cream
¼ teaspoon salt
14 ounces (3 cups) cake flour
½ teaspoon baking soda
½ teaspoon baking powder

FROSTING
16 ounces (4 cups) powdered sugar
¼ cup (½ stick) unsalted butter
¼ cup shortening
¼ cup whole milk
¼ teaspoon vanilla extract
¼ teaspoon plus ⅛ teaspoon salt

OPTIONAL
20 drops food coloring (red, blue, yellow, or green)

Decorative candy sprinkles

1 Make the cookies by combining the butter and granulated sugar in a large bowl with an electric mixer on high speed. Add the egg, egg white, and vanilla and mix until smooth. Add the sour cream and salt and mix well.

2 In a medium bowl mix together the cake flour, baking soda, and baking powder.

3 Pour the dry mixture into the wet mixture and mix well by hand. Cover the bowl and chill for at least 2 hours or overnight.

4 When you are ready to make the cookies, preheat your oven to 300 degrees F.

5 Scoop out 1-ounce portions of dough (slightly smaller than a golf ball) and roll them into balls in the palms of your hands. Fill a small cup with water and use it to moisten your fingertips as you press each dough ball onto parchment paper, nonstick aluminum foil, or a silicone baking mat. Form the dough into a circle that is about 2½ inches in diameter. Leave about half an inch of space between the cookies.

6 Bake the cookies for 14 to 16 minutes or

until the dough has puffed up and is firm. You don't want the cookies to brown. Cool.

7 While the cookies are baking, make the frosting by combining the powdered sugar, butter, shortening, milk, vanilla, salt, and food coloring (if you want colored frosting).

8 When the cookies have completely cooled, make a circle of frosting on top of each cookie with an icing knife or butter knife.

9 To add the sprinkles, pour a small amount onto a small plate and invert each cookie onto the sprinkles. Press down so that the sprinkles stick and the frosting is flattened to look more like the original cookies. Repeat with each cookie. Cover the cookies to keep them fresh for several days, or you can freeze them for a couple of months.

LONG JOHN SILVER'S TARTAR SAUCE

   First-Time Hack

Active Prep: 5 min.
Inactive Prep: 30 min.

E Difficulty: Easy

Yield: ½ cup

I figure if I'm going to include a clone in this book for Long John Silver's Battered Fish (page 146), then I should also include something for you to dip it in. No need to go out and buy tartar sauce when it's so easy to make a perfect copy at home that tastes better than any bottled stuff you will find in grocery stores. Just measure, stir, and chill.

½ cup mayonnaise
1 tablespoon sweet pickle relish
1 teaspoon granulated sugar
½ teaspoon white vinegar
¼ teaspoon dehydrated minced onion
⅛ teaspoon salt
⅛ teaspoon onion powder
Pinch of dry ground mustard

1 Combine all of the ingredients in a small bowl.

2 Stir well, then cover and chill for 30 minutes before using. Stir again before using.

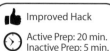

Improved Hack

Active Prep: 20 min.
Inactive Prep: 5 min.

E Difficulty: Easy

Yield: 2 servings

LONG JOHN SILVER'S BATTERED FISH

Time for a better batter. My first version was good, but with this formula you will create a spot-on copy of the famous fish served at more than 900 Long John Silver's restaurants across the country. The secrets I missed the first time around include the addition of cornstarch, corn flour, and a little baking powder for the light, crispy texture and golden brown color. Also, I called for cod fillets in my first recipe—which work great as a substitute—but the chain actually uses Alaskan pollack fillets, which you can usually find frozen in your supermarket. If you like the famous battered fish from Long John Silver's, you're really going to love this new hack.

6 to 8 cups **vegetable oil**
½ **cup plus 4 ounces (¾ cup) all-purpose flour**
2 tablespoons **cornstarch**
1 tablespoon **yellow corn flour (masa)**
1½ teaspoons **salt**
1½ teaspoons **baking powder**
½ teaspoon **ground black pepper**
¼ teaspoon **MSG (such as Accent seasoning)**
¼ teaspoon **paprika**
¼ teaspoon **garlic powder**
1 cup plus 2 tablespoons **water**
4 2½- to 3-ounce **pollack fillets (or cod)**

❶ Preheat the oil in a large saucepan with a thermometer attached to 350 degrees F.

❷ Measure ½ cup of flour onto a plate. Combine the remaining 4 ounces (¾ cup) flour with the remaining dry ingredients in a medium bowl. Add the water and whisk aggressively, yet happily, until the batter is smooth and no lumps remain.

❸ Coat all of the pollack fillets with the flour on the plate. Let the fillets sit for about 5 minutes so that the flour sticks.

❹ When you are ready to fry the fish, dip each fillet in the batter, let a little of the batter drip off, then carefully drop the fillet in the oil. After 3 to 4 minutes, flip the fish over in the oil so that it cooks evenly on both sides until golden brown. Drain on a rack or a paper towel–lined plate.

MARIE CALLENDER'S FAMOUS GOLDEN CORNBREAD

 Improved Hack

Active Prep: 15 min.
Inactive Prep: 50 min.

E Difficulty: Easy

Yield: 9 slices

I love cornbread and Marie Callender's has one of the best of any casual restaurant chain. I first cloned the chain's Golden Cornbread many years ago and that recipe has received great reviews on our website, but I felt it could be even better. So, back into the underground lab I went to tinker with my seventeen-year-old formula, and I am now proud to present the new, improved version of the best cornbread on the planet. You'll find that this recipe produces much thicker, cakier, and more delicious cornbread that is virtually indistinguishable from the real thing. Even the honey butter formula has been improved. This time around, whip the butter on high speed for at least 8 minutes to make it fluffier. Since it takes some time to fluff up the butter, it's best to use a stand mixer if you've got one, although a handheld mixer will still work.

11 ounces (about 2 cups) all-purpose flour
6 ounces (1 cup) yellow cornmeal
6 ounces (1 cup) granulated sugar
2½ teaspoons baking powder
¾ teaspoon salt
2 large eggs

1½ cups whole milk
½ cup canola oil

HONEY BUTTER
1 cup (2 sticks) unsalted butter, softened
¼ teaspoon salt
6 tablespoons honey

1 Preheat the oven to 325 degrees F.

2 Combine the flour, cornmeal, sugar, baking powder, and salt in a large bowl.

❸ Whisk the eggs until beaten in a medium bowl, then mix in the milk and oil.

❹ Pour the wet ingredients into the bowl of the dry ingredients and mix well with an electric mixer on medium speed.

❺ Pour the batter into an 8 x 8-inch baking pan that has been greased with shortening or nonstick cooking spray. Bake for 50 to 55 minutes or until the top of the cornbread is light brown. Cool and slice into 9 servings.

❻ Make the honey butter by whipping the butter and salt with an electric mixer on high speed for 6 to 8 minutes or until fluffy (a stand mixer works best for this). Add the honey and mix again for 20 to 30 seconds. Serve the honey butter on the side with each slice of cornbread.

MARIE CALLENDER'S BANANA CREAM PIE

 Improved Hack
Active Prep: 30 min.
Inactive Prep: 5 hrs. 45 min.
Difficulty: Medium
Yield: 8 slices

The knockoff for this restaurant chain's number one best-selling pie just got better. Marie Callender's amazing pies start with a fantastic crust—it's thick, it's flaky, it's tender, and it perfectly complements the sweet, creamy filling. That is why for this re-hack I spent most of the time perfecting the shell. Once that was complete, I moved on to the filling, which, after much trial and error, better fills the shell and holds its shape better when sliced with the addition of gelatin to the formula (and there's now a little gelatin in the whipped cream to stabilize it as well). I also discovered that it is best to use the disposable 8¾-inch foil pie pans found in most supermarkets rather than the more common 9-inch glass or metal pans, which are slightly too big to make a decent clone. Add in a few other tweaks, such as more banana and the addition of toasted sliced almonds, and you will have before you the best-ever banana cream pie with the best piecrust recipe I've had the pleasure to hack. I should mention that to properly bake a nice-looking pie shell without any bubbling or warping, you will need some piecrust weights or a 1-pound bag of dried beans to pour into the crust before baking.

CRUST
12 ounces (2½ cups) all-purpose flour
2 tablespoons granulated sugar
¼ teaspoon plus ⅛ teaspoon salt
¾ cup cold shortening
¼ cup (½ stick) cold unsalted butter
¼ cup very cold water
1 egg yolk, beaten

WHIPPED CREAM
½ teaspoon unflavored gelatin
2 teaspoons water
1 cup heavy cream
¼ cup powdered sugar
1 teaspoon vanilla extract

FILLING
4 ounces (½ cup plus 1 tablespoon) granulated sugar
1 ounce (¼ cup) cornstarch
1½ teaspoons unflavored gelatin
¼ teaspoon salt
3 cups whole milk
4 egg yolks, beaten
2 teaspoons vanilla extract
3 medium bananas (or 2 large bananas), sliced

1 tablespoon sliced almonds

YOU WILL ALSO NEED
Piecrust weights or 1 pound dry beans
A pastry bag

1 Make the dough for the crust by combining the flour, sugar, and salt in a large bowl. Use a fork or pastry cutter to cut the cold shortening and butter into the dry ingredients until the texture is

149

crumbly and only small pea-size bits of butter and shortening remain.

2 Combine the cold water and egg yolk in a small bowl. Add this to the crust mixture and work it in with a large mixing spoon until the dough comes together. Use your hands to form the dough into a 6-inch-wide disk, but take care not to overwork the dough or your crust might become too tough. Wrap the dough in plastic, and place it in your refrigerator for 1 hour, or for up to 2 days.

3 Make the whipped cream by combining the gelatin with the water in a small bowl. Quickly add it to the heavy cream along with the sugar and vanilla and beat the mixture just until the cream forms stiff peaks, then cover and chill it until later.

4 When you're ready to make the piecrust, preheat the oven to 350 degrees F. Gently roll out the cold dough on a floured surface until it is slightly larger than the pie pan. Place the dough into an 8¾-inch disposable foil pie pan and press down until it fits snugly in the pan. Make the edge of the dough flat and flush with the edge of the pan by tearing away any excess. Fill any gaps, holes, or tears with excess pieces of dough. Even after this

repair process you should have a little extra dough left over.

5 Press a square piece of foil down into the dough and over the edge, then top with the pie weights or pour in a full bag (16 ounces) of dry beans to keep the dough from bubbling as it bakes. Bake for 30 minutes, then remove the foil and weights and bake the pie shell for another 15 minutes or until the dough is just beginning to turn light brown around the edges and the dough in the middle is no longer moist and springy. Cool.

6 Make the filling by mixing together the sugar, cornstarch, gelatin, and salt in a 2-quart saucepan. Whisk in the milk, then heat over medium heat, stirring often for 6 to 8 minutes or until the mixture thickens and begins to bubble. Remove from the heat. Do not cover.

7 Spoon a little of the hot milk mixture into the egg yolks in a small bowl to temper them so that they don't cook, then pour the yolk mixture into the pan and stir immediately. Stir in the vanilla. Pour a little of the custard filling into the baked pie shell until it is about halfway full. Top the custard with the sliced

bananas, then pour the remaining custard over the top of the bananas. Cover and chill for at least 4 hours or until the filling has firmed up.

8 When you are ready to serve the pie, spoon the whipped cream into a pastry bag or gun with a decorative tip. Pipe the whipped cream around edge of the pie and add several dollops of whipped cream in the middle.

9 Toast the sliced almonds in a small skillet over medium heat for a couple of minutes or just until golden brown, then sprinkle them over the whipped cream.

10 Use a very sharp knife to carefully cut the pie into 8 slices and serve.

MAUNA LOA
KONA COFFEE
GLAZED MACADAMIAS

👍 Improved Hack

🕐 Prep Time: 30 min.

M🌡 Difficulty: Medium

👥 Yield: 4 cups

It's not difficult to make these delicious candy-coated macadamia nuts at home, but you will need a couple of basic tools if you want the best clone of the original: a candy thermometer and a nonstick baking sheet or a baking sheet lined with a silicone nonstick mat. After spending some more time with this formula in the underground lab, I found that my first version of this recipe could be substantially improved upon. The brown sugar has been eliminated (since there is no molasses flavor in the original), and the salt, butter, and vanilla measurements have been systematically tweaked. I have also adjusted the final target temperature of the candy down a bit so that you are less likely to scorch it. That's exactly what happened to a couple of my batches, and I want to be sure it doesn't happen to you. (Because when it does, it makes your house really stink for, like, five hours.) Use Kona coffee here for the best clone, but you can certainly use any coffee available and it's pretty likely that no one will complain. Just be sure to brew it double-strength.

12 ounces (3 cups) dry-roasted macadamia nuts
½ cup double-strength Kona coffee
½ cup granulated sugar
½ cup light corn syrup
⅓ cup unsalted butter
¼ teaspoon plus ⅛ teaspoon salt
1 teaspoon vanilla extract

❶ Preheat your oven to 225 degrees F.

❷ Pour the nuts onto a baking sheet and place in the oven until they are needed.

❸ Brew the coffee with twice the grounds recommended by your coffee machine so that it is double-strength. Combine the coffee, sugar, corn syrup, butter, and salt in a 2- or 3-quart saucepan. Place the pan over medium-low heat and attach a candy thermometer.

The candy should eventually reach a steady simmer. If it begins to boil rapidly, reduce the heat. Slowly heat the candy until it reaches 275 degrees F, then immediately add the vanilla and turn off the heat.

❹ Pour the warm nuts into the candy and stir gently until they are coated. Be careful not to overstir or they will begin to fall apart

since macadamias are so soft. Pour the candied nuts back onto the warm baking sheet (if not a nonstick pan, line the pan with a silicone mat) and separate the nuts as much as possible while they are still hot.

❺ When the nuts have cooled completely, break them up into bite-size pieces and store them in a covered container in a dry spot.

153

McDONALD'S McCAFÉ BLUEBERRY POMEGRANATE SMOOTHIE

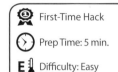

🏅 First-Time Hack

⏱ Prep Time: 5 min.

E 🌡 Difficulty: Easy

👥 Yield: 1 med. drink

McDonald's introduced the blueberry pomegranate smoothie for its McCafé line of drinks in the spring of 2013 and the new flavor became a quick hit. The name of the drink mentions only two fruits but the drink is actually made with more than just blueberries and pomegranate juice. According to the ingredients list provided by McDonald's, pineapple juice, apple juice, and raspberries are also on the team, added in there to help improve the flavor. Because they're in the real thing, I've included those juices here, with apple raspberry juice added in super-sweet concentrated form to help offset the tartness of the pomegranate juice.

1 cup ice
½ cup frozen blueberries
½ cup frozen apple raspberry juice concentrate
¼ cup pomegranate juice
¼ cup pineapple juice
¼ cup vanilla yogurt

❶ Combine all of the ingredients in a blender and blend on high speed for 30 seconds or until the ice is crushed and the drink is smooth.

❷ Pour into a 16-ounce glass and add a straw.

McDONALD'S PREMIUM SWEET CHILI CHICKEN McWRAP

First-Time Hack

Active Prep: 15 min.
Inactive Prep: 15 min.

E 🌡 Difficulty: Easy

Yield: 4 wraps

Although seemingly simple in design, McDonald's award-winning Premium McWraps are the culinary creation of a global team of company chefs. The basic design of the McWraps, including the special packaging that makes them easy to eat on the go, was developed by teams in Austria and Poland while the sweet chili sauce was developed by McDonald's chefs in Australia. A duplicate of that sauce is included here, as well as the delicious yogurt-based creamy garlic sauce that is spread on the wraps. For the chicken, you save time by using precooked frozen grilled chicken fillets. I found that the chicken breast fillets from Nature Raised tasted the closest to what McDonald's uses, with those from Tyson coming in a close second. This recipe is easy to prepare and will not require a team of chefs to help you make it at home.

SWEET CHILI SAUCE
⅓ **cup white vinegar**
2 **tablespoons water**
2 **teaspoons cornstarch**
⅔ **cup granulated sugar**
4 **teaspoons chili sauce (sambal)**
½ **teaspoon salt**
½ **teaspoon garlic powder**

CREAMY GARLIC SAUCE
¼ **cup mayonnaise**
3 **tablespoons plain low-fat yogurt**
1¼ **teaspoons lime juice**
¼ **teaspoon granulated sugar**
¼ **teaspoon garlic powder**

4 **frozen grilled chicken fillets (Nature Raised or Tyson is best)**
4 **10-inch flour tortillas**
4 **cups thinly sliced iceberg lettuce**
2 **cups 50/50 mixed lettuce greens (or Spring mix)**
8 **slices English cucumber**

1 Make the sweet chili sauce by combining the vinegar and water in a small bowl. Dissolve the cornstarch in the water and vinegar, then pour the mixture into a small saucepan over medium heat and add the remaining ingredients. Bring the mixture to a boil but reduce the heat if it begins to boil over. Simmer for 3 minutes, then turn off the heat. When the sauce is cool, store it in a covered container until needed.

2 Make the creamy garlic sauce by combining all of the ingredients in a small bowl. Cover and chill until needed.

3 When you are ready to make the wraps, cook the chicken breast fillets following the directions on the package (bake at 375 degrees F for 18 to 20 minutes).

4 Heat the tortillas in a tortilla warmer or wrapped in a moist towel in your microwave oven on high for 40 seconds.

5 Build each wrap by spreading 1 heaping tablespoon of creamy garlic sauce onto a tortilla, followed by 1 tablespoon of sweet chili sauce. Arrange approximately 1 cup of sliced iceberg lettuce down the center of the tortilla, followed by a small handful of the mixed greens. Place 2 cucumber slices on top of the lettuce, then slice a chicken breast into 4 strips and arrange the chicken on the greens. Fold up the bottom of the tortilla, then fold over the left side of the tortilla. Fold the right side over the left side, leaving the top open, and serve. Repeat for the remaining wraps.

McDONALD'S BIG MAC

👍 Improved Hack

🕐 Active Prep: 20 min.
Inactive Prep: 1 hr.

M🌡 Difficulty: Medium

👥 Yield: 4 burgers

In a cooking demonstration posted to YouTube in the summer of 2012, McDonald's Canada, Inc., executive chef Dan Coudreaut shows us exactly how a Big Mac is made. Well, not exactly. He does make it clear that the recipe he is demonstrating in his home kitchen isn't made with the exact same stuff McDonald's uses. He says the ingredients in the Big Mac are "similar" to the type of items you "could buy at your local grocery store." And Dan doesn't give us any measurements. Oh what a tease you are, Dan. So, while this video did provide many clues as to how I could improve my twenty-five-year-old clone recipe for a Big Mac, there was still plenty of work to do. One thing I had to figure out was how to easily form the patties into the perfect size each time without having to track down a specialty baking ring. As I was looking at other objects that could do the trick, I noticed that a large tuna can is the perfect size to shape the patty—and even better, we don't need to open the can to use it! Just press the ground beef onto the top of the can to form perfect circles. In addition to this tip, the special sauce formula has been entirely re-hacked for the best Big Mac sauce clone ever published.

SAUCE
⅔ cup mayonnaise
⅓ cup sweet pickle relish
2 teaspoons yellow mustard
¾ teaspoon white vinegar
½ teaspoon paprika
¼ teaspoon garlic powder
¼ teaspoon onion powder

14 ounces ground beef (20 percent fat)
4 sesame seed hamburger buns, plus 4 additional heels (bottom bun)
Salt
Ground black pepper
4 teaspoons finely minced white onion
1 cup coarsely chopped iceberg lettuce
4 slices American cheese
8 to 12 dill pickle hamburger slices

YOU WILL ALSO NEED
1 12-ounce can of tuna (or other can with 4-inch diameter)

1 Mix together the sauce ingredients in a small bowl, then cover and chill the sauce until it's needed.

2 Use a kitchen scale to measure out 1¾-ounce portions of the ground beef and form it into balls (or estimate making balls that are slightly bigger than golf balls). Press each ball of ground beef down flat onto the top of a 12-ounce tuna can with a 4-inch diameter. Invert the can to peel away the patties and arrange them on a wax paper–lined sheet pan. Cover the patties and place them in your freezer for 1 hour.

3 Preheat a griddle or large skillet to medium/low heat.

4 Slice a thin layer off the bottom of each of the extra bun heels. These will be your center buns, or clubs.

5 Lightly brown the faces of all of the buns (both sides of the club) on the hot griddle or pan.

6 When the buns are browned, cook the beef patties on the hot griddle or pan for

2 to 3 minutes per side. Lightly sprinkle salt and pepper on each patty as they cook.

7 While the beef is cooking, prepare each sandwich by spreading a couple of teaspoons of sauce on the face of the bottom bun and on one side of the club bun.

8 Sprinkle about a teaspoon of onion on top of the sauce on each bun, followed by about ¼ cup of chopped lettuce.

9 Lay a slice of American cheese on the lettuce on the bottom bun, and 2 to 3 pickles on the lettuce on the club bun.

10 Arrange a beef patty on the cheese, and another one on the pickles, then place the club bun on the bottom bun and top off the sandwich with the crown. Microwave on high for 15 seconds to warm and soften the buns as if the burger had been packed in a box.

TIDBITS The burgers McDonald's uses for Big Macs are called 10-to-1 patties, which means that there are 10 patties in a pound, or 1.6 ounces each. For the purpose of this

recipe I've rounded the weight up to a measurement that is more likely to register on all kitchen scales (1¾ ounces). If your sesame seed buns are large (McDonald's buns are relatively small), you may want to make your patties 2 ounces each and press down on them on the wax paper with your fingers after molding them to make the diameter even larger to fit your buns.

159

McDONALD'S McRIB SANDWICH

🏅 First-Time Hack

⏱ Active Prep: 20 min.
Inactive Prep: 2 hrs.

🌡 Difficulty: Medium

👥 Yield: 4 sandwiches

You'll never again have to go without the guilty pleasure that is the famous boneless pork creation offered for only a limited time each year at your local McDonald's. To make your own McRib Sandwich at home, you'll need a food processor to thoroughly grind up meat that's cut away from the bones of a rack of uncooked pork spareribs. If you trim the meat off carefully, you will still have a useable rack of spareribs to cook up later. Just be sure to include some fat from the ribs into your trimmings—around 15 to 20 percent fat will give your rib patties the texture and taste of the original. The finely ground porky bits in the real McRib sandwich are combined with salt, a little dextrose (sugar), plus water and a few preservatives; and the meat is then pressed into the shape of a small rack of ribs and cooked. Of course your version won't have the same fake bones stamped into the patty—unless you feel like doing some impromptu meat sculpting—but once the pork is formed

into patties and then frozen, it takes just 10 minutes to assemble a McRib Sandwich clone whenever you're ready. Follow these steps exactly and you will be amazed at how similar your home version tastes to the real McCoy McRib.

16 ounces uncooked pork spareribs meat (cut off the bones from 1 rack; include some fat)
3 tablespoons water
1 teaspoon granulated sugar
¾ teaspoon salt
¼ teaspoon hickory liquid smoke flavoring
4 6-inch French sandwich rolls
1 cup Hunt's Original Barbecue Sauce
8 dill pickle hamburger slices
½ cup chopped white onion

❶ Combine the pork, water, sugar, salt, and liquid smoke in a food processor and puree on high speed for 30 to 60 seconds or until completely smooth.

❷ Divide the pureed pork into 4 equal portions that weigh 4 ounces each. Line a baking sheet with wax paper or parchment paper. Using your fingers, form each portion of pork on the lined baking sheet into a rectangle that measures 7 inches by 3 inches.

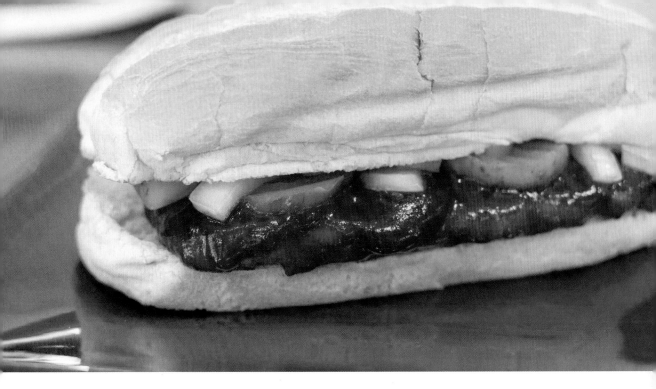

Gently press another sheet of wax paper or parchment paper on top of the pork patties and then pop the whole pan into the freezer for a couple of hours, or until the pork is frozen solid.

3 When you are ready to make your sandwiches, preheat a large skillet or griddle over medium heat. Slice the sandwich rolls all the way through to separate the top and bottom half, then brown the faces of the top and bottom roll halves (crown and heel) in the hot pan.

4 When the faces of the rolls are lightly browned, use the same pan to cook the pork. Cook the pork on one side for 3 to 4 minutes or until browned in spots, then flip each pork patty over and cook for another 3 minutes.

Remove all of the pork patties to a platter to cool just a bit. The barbecue sauce will stick better if the pork cools down for a minute or two.

5 As the pork cools, pour the barbecue sauce into a large shallow bowl. Use tongs to dip each patty into the barbecue sauce until the pork is generously covered with sauce. Place the pork onto the heel of a sandwich roll, then arrange two pickle slices on the pork. Arrange about 2 tablespoons of chopped onion on the pork, and then top off each sandwich with the crown of the roll.

6 Just before serving, zap each sandwich in your microwave for 15 seconds on the highest setting. This will warm the bread as if it had been wrapped in paper just like the original.

161

McDONALD'S BAKED APPLE PIE

 First-Time Hack

 Active Prep: 45 min.
Inactive Prep: 1 hr. 45 min.

M Difficulty: Medium

Yield: 8 to 10 pies

When McDonald's introduced fast-food apple pies to America in 1968, they were originally deep fried, but in 1992 the chain replaced the fried pies on the standard menu with a healthier baked version (although you can still find the original fried pies at a few U.S. locations and at McDonald's restaurants overseas). The secret to a perfect clone of the famous pastry is a great crust, which is best made from scratch, but the filling can be quickly duplicated with canned apple pie filling that has been chopped up, and then perked up with a little bit of ground cinnamon. If you're the nostalgic type and would like to re-create the original fried version from yesteryear, pop on down to the Tidbits for an easy recipe variation that should bring back some tasty memories.

CRUST
10 ounces (2 cups) all-purpose flour
3 tablespoons granulated sugar
1 teaspoon salt
½ cup shortening
¼ cup (½ stick) unsalted butter
½ cup water

FILLING
1 21-ounce can (2 cups) apple pie filling
¼ teaspoon ground cinnamon

1 large egg, beaten

TOPPING
Ground cinnamon in a shaker bottle

1 Make the crust by combining the flour with the sugar and salt in a medium bowl. Add the shortening, butter, and water and stir well until the ingredients come together into a ball. Use your hands to form the ball, then cover and chill for 1 hour.

2 Prepare the filling by chopping the apples into smaller bits about the size of a dime. You can use a knife, or use a food processor by pouring the entire contents of the can into the processor and pulsing briefly. Stir in the cinnamon.

3 When the dough has chilled, roll it out on a clean floured surface until it is between 1/16 and 1/8 inch thick. Slice the dough into rectangles that are 5 inches wide by 2½ inches tall.

4 To build each pie, brush beaten egg around the edge of a piece

of dough. Spoon about 2 tablespoons of filling into the middle of the dough and then press another piece down on top, being sure to firmly seal the edges. When all of the pies are made, let them chill in your refrigerator for 20 to 30 minutes.

5 When you are ready to bake the pies, preheat your oven to 425 degrees F.

6 Lightly shake ground cinnamon over the top of each pie, then use a kitchen brush to brush most of the cinnamon off the crust, leaving just a little bit behind for color. Use a sharp, lightly oiled paring knife to make 4 1-inch slices in the top of each pie, then

place the pies on parchment paper on a baking sheet (or on a nonstick baking mat) and bake for 16 to 18 minutes or until done.

TIDBITS To make a clone of the original fried apple pies, follow all of the instructions through step 4, but freeze the pies for 2 hours instead of chilling them in the refrigerator. You won't be making slices in the pies or sprinkling them with cinnamon for this version. Instead, when the pies are frozen, preheat 4 to 6 cups of shortening to 325 degrees F in a deep fryer or in a pan on your stovetop, and fry a couple of pies at a time for 5 to 6 minutes or until golden brown.

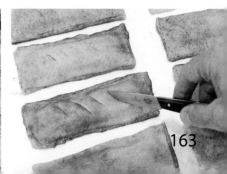

THE MELTING POT CHEDDAR CHEESE FONDUE

🏅 First-Time Hack

🕐 Prep Time: 20 min.

E🌡 Difficulty: Easy

👥 Yield: 4 to 6 servings

This 140-unit chain is America's go-to restaurant for great fondue since 1975. The four-course menu includes a salad, a broth fondue entrée with a variety of meats and vegetables, and a selection of chocolate fondues for dessert. But the dining experience starts with a delicious cheese fondue served with various sliced breads, apples, and vegetables for dipping. The most popular of the cheese fondues is this one made with medium cheddar and just a little Emmentaler Swiss cheese melted into beer and combined with garlic and spices. Talking with a manager at my local Melting Pot, I learned that the chain uses Milwaukee's Best or Colt 45 in the fondue, so make sure you use a mild (and cheap) lager beer. He told me that the mild flavor of these beers doesn't overpower the cheese. Use a traditional fondue pot intended for cheese/chocolate fondue.

10 ounces (3¼ cups) shredded medium cheddar cheese
2 ounces (¾ cup) shredded Emmentaler Swiss cheese
3 tablespoons all-purpose flour
6 ounces (¾ cup) Milwaukee's Best or other mild lager beer
2 teaspoons minced garlic
½ teaspoon dry mustard
1 teaspoon Worcestershire sauce
¼ teaspoon ground black pepper

FOR DIPPING
Cubed bread (**French bread, rosemary bread, or Outback Steakhouse Honey Wheat Bushman Bread**—see recipe on page 183)
Chopped **red and green apples**
Chopped **broccoli**
Chopped **cauliflower**
Sliced **baby carrots**

❶ Combine the cheeses in a medium bowl, then toss the cheese with the flour.

❷ Pour the beer into a fondue pot (double-boiler style used for cheese and chocolate) that is preheating on your stove over a burner set to medium. Make sure there is water in the bottom pan beneath the pot.

❸ When the beer is hot and steaming, stir in the garlic and dry mustard and cook for a couple of minutes.

4 Add a handful of cheese to the beer and use a fork to stir the cheese until it is mostly melted. Add more cheese and stir until it's melted, then add the rest and stir with the fork until it is completely melted and a smooth consistency.

5 Stir in the Worcestershire sauce and the pepper. Serve immediately with bite-size slices of bread, apples, and vegetables on the side for dipping.

THE MELTING POT TRADITIONAL SWISS CHEESE FONDUE

🏅 First-Time Hack

⏱ Prep Time: 20 min.

E🌡 Difficulty: Easy

👥 Yield: 4 to 6 servings

The cheddar cheese fondue may be the chain's most popular cheese fondue selection at this forty-year-old niche chain, but I've always been a fan of the more traditional Swiss cheese version. Emmentaler and Gruyère cheeses are the stars here, melted into a very dry wine such as Chablis—the cheaper, the better. An inexpensive Chablis will not upstage the flavorful cheeses, and that's exactly what you want. It's a great dish to serve for a small get-together, maybe paired up with a nice white wine to drink. I'm all for that.

You'll need a double boiler–style fondue pot (the kind for cheese and chocolate fondue) to prepare this very easy recipe that makes a great appetizer for a cheese-loving group of four to six.

6 ounces (2 cups) shredded **Emmentaler Swiss cheese**
6 ounces (2 cups) shredded **Gruyère cheese**
3 tablespoons **all-purpose flour**
6 ounces (¾ cup) **Chablis wine**
2 teaspoons minced **garlic**
2 tablespoons **fresh lemon juice (1 lemon)**
2 tablespoons **kirschwasser cherry brandy**
¼ teaspoon **ground black pepper**
⅛ teaspoon **nutmeg**

FOR DIPPING
Cubed bread (French bread, rosemary bread, or Outback Steakhouse Honey Wheat Bushman Bread (recipe on page 183)
Chopped red and green apples
Chopped broccoli
Chopped cauliflower
Sliced baby carrots

1 Combine the cheeses in a medium bowl, then toss the cheese with the flour.

2 Pour the wine into a fondue pot (double-boiler style) that is preheating on your stove over a burner set to medium. Make sure there is water in the bottom pan beneath the pot. Heat the wine for 5 minutes until very hot and steaming.

3 Stir in the garlic and lemon juice once the wine is hot. Cook for a couple of minutes.

4 Add a handful of cheese to the wine and use a fork to stir the cheese until it is mostly melted. Add more cheese and stir until melted, then add the rest and stir with the fork until the mixture is completely melted and a smooth consistency.

5 Add the kirschwasser around the inside edge of the pot or bowl. Give it a couple of minutes to burn off, then use the fork to slowly bring the brandy into the middle of the mixture and stir to combine.

6 Stir in the pepper and nutmeg. If your cheese is not very salty, you may need to add a little salt to taste. Serve immediately with bite-size slices of bread, apples, and vegetables on the side for dipping.

MRS. FIELDS CHOCOLATE CHIP COOKIES

 Improved Hack

 Active Prep: 15 min.
Inactive Prep: 1 hr. 20 min.

E Difficulty: Easy

Yield: 20 cookies

I jumped at the chance to get another crack at hacking one of America's most famous chocolate chip cookies when I was faced with the challenge for my show, *Top Secret Recipe*. After all, this was the very first recipe I cloned over twenty-five years ago, and I've learned many new tricks for replicating famous foodstuffs since then. Getting the chance to improve on my old secret recipe with new information was a golden opportunity to craft the best Mrs. Fields Chocolate Chip Cookie clone recipe ever revealed. So I hopped on a plane and headed to Salt Lake City to meet with the man you see standing next to me here in the bottom photo, Tim Casey, president and CEO of Mrs. Fields Cookies.

Tim showed me around the flavoring labs and test kitchens of Mrs. Fields HQ. I watched cookie dough being mixed, noting the oven temperature and length of time the cookies were baked. I was also able to discover one important trick I missed in my first recipe: after the dough was portioned out onto baking sheets, it was frozen. This way, when the cookies were baked, they came out crispy on the edges and soft and gooey in the middle. It made a huge difference!

The company was understandably vague on the specifics of the proprietary vanilla and chocolate chips they use in the cookies, but I discovered through taste tests that Madagascar vanilla extract and high-quality chocolate chips such as those made by Guittard (or even Ghirardelli) are the way to go.

Mission accomplished! What follows is my much-improved re-hack of the classic recipe that started it all, and perhaps one of the best chocolate chip cookies to ever come out of your oven.

1 cup (2 sticks) **unsalted butter, softened**
5 ounces (¾ cup packed) **dark brown sugar**
5 ounces (¾ cup) **granulated sugar**
1½ teaspoons **salt**
2 large **eggs**
2 teaspoons **Madagascar vanilla extract**

14 ounces (2¾ cups) **all-purpose bleached flour**
1¼ teaspoons **baking soda**
½ teaspoon **baking powder**
1 12-ounce bag (about 2 cups) premium **semisweet chocolate chips**

1 Combine the butter with the sugars and salt in a large bowl using an electric mixer on high speed until it's the consistency of peanut butter.

2 Add the eggs and vanilla and mix well.

3 In a separate large bowl, combine the flour with the baking soda and baking powder. Pour this dry mix into the wet stuff and mix until combined. Mix in the chocolate chips.

4 Use an ice cream scoop (or ¼ cup measure) to scoop out ¼ cup portions 2 to 3 inches apart on a parchment paper–lined cookie sheet.

5 Place a 2½-inch ring mold (or biscuit cutter, or empty 2½-inch diameter can with the ends cut out) over each portion of dough and press down on the dough with your fingers so that it is formed into a disk. Remove the mold while holding the dough down with the fingers of your other hand. Place the dough disks into your freezer for 1 hour or until the dough is frozen.

6 Preheat a convection oven to 300 degrees F (or a conventional oven to 325 degrees F).

7 When you are ready to make the cookies, flip over each of the frozen dough pucks onto the parchment paper–lined baking sheet (so that the smooth side of the pucks is on top) and bake for 16 to 20 minutes or until a couple of the cookies show slight browning around the edges. If using a conventional oven, rotate the sheet of cookies halfway through the cooking time.

8 When you take the cookies out of the oven, immediately slide the parchment paper with the cookies on it off of the baking sheet onto your countertop to prevent further cooking. Allow the cookies to cool there for 5 to 10 minutes before handling.

NORDSTROM ROMA TOMATO BASIL SOUP

  First-Time Hack

  Active Prep: 20 min.
Inactive Prep: 1 hr.

E🌡 Difficulty: Easy

👥 Yield: 8 cups

Before, during, or after a shopping trip at Nordstrom, you may have indulged in a hot bowl of this signature soup that many say is the best tomato basil soup they've ever had. It's creamy, it's tomato-y, and it's slightly sweet with the perfect balance of basil in the mix. Now you can make a clone version yourself at home with very little effort using canned tomatoes, dried basil, and fresh carrots and onions. I've even included the hacked recipe here for the crispy Parmesan toasts that are served on the side. If you're a fan of great tomato soup, you gotta give this one a try.

3 tablespoons extra virgin olive oil
10 ounces (about 2 cups) peeled and chopped carrots
5 ounces (about 1¼ cups) chopped yellow sweet onion
2 teaspoons dried basil
2 28-ounce cans whole peeled plum tomatoes
4 cups chicken broth
1 cup water
1 6-ounce can tomato paste
1 teaspoon salt
½ teaspoon ground black pepper
1 cup heavy cream

PARMESAN TOASTS
1 French baguette
½ cup (1 stick) unsalted butter, melted
¼ teaspoon salt
1 teaspoon dried parsley
Pinch of garlic powder
⅓ cup grated Parmesan cheese

1 Heat the oil in a saucepan or soup pot (that will hold at least 4 quarts) over medium heat. Add the carrots and onion and cook for 10 minutes or until the carrots begin to soften. Stir occasionally. After 10 minutes, stir in the basil.

2 Add the remaining ingredients, but not the cream, and

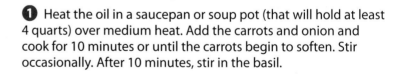

bring the soup to a boil. Reduce the heat and simmer, uncovered, for 1 hour.

❸ While the soup simmers, make the Parmesan toasts by preheating your oven to 375 degrees F. Slice the baguette at an extreme angle into ¼-inch slices. Combine the melted butter with the salt, parsley, and garlic powder in a small bowl. Arrange the bread slices on a baking sheet and brush each slice of bread generously with the butter. Sprinkle each slice with Parmesan cheese, then bake in

the oven for 8 to 12 minutes or until golden brown.

❹ When the soup has simmered for 1 hour, use a blender (working in batches) or an immersion blender to blend the soup until smooth.

❺ Add the cream and reheat the soup over medium heat until hot. Serve with 2 to 3 Parmesan toasts on the side.

NUTS 4 NUTS HONEY ROASTED NUTS

👍 Improved Hack

⊙ Prep Time: 10 min.

M 🌡 Difficulty: Medium

👥 Yield: 2 cups

The copper bowls you see in steaming pushcarts around New York City are an important part of the secret recipe for honey-roasted nuts brought to the city from Argentina in 1984. Since copper is such an excellent conductor of heat, the bowls enable the sugar to more evenly and efficiently crystallize on the nuts. Argentinean Alejandro Rad was a honey-roasted nut vendor in the city in the late '80s, and in 1993 he started his own brand of honey roasted nuts—first called Nuts About Nuts. The name was later changed to Nuts 4 Nuts and now around 100 Nuts 4 Nuts pushcarts can be found all around Manhattan.

It was at one of those carts on a cold winter night that I convinced the vendor to let me watch him make a batch of honey roasted peanuts. For fifteen minutes or so I watched as he cooked down the mixture of nuts and syrup in his copper bowl, then grabbed the bowl by its long wooden handle

and tossed the nuts in the air until crystals formed on them. He then put the nuts back over the fire until the sugar melted to a syrup, again forming a candy coating on each peanut.

Certainly a copper bowl with a long handle for tossing the nuts would be the best way to properly re-create this recipe, but those are expensive and hard to find. The good news is you can still re-create these nuts by cooking them in a regular copper bowl (no long handle necessary) or in a stainless steel skillet that isn't nonstick. You will need raw nuts here for this recipe, which can be found online or at stores like Whole Foods. You can also use raw cashews or almonds with this technique, just as the street vendors do.

1 cup **water**
1 tablespoon **honey**
⅔ cup **granulated sugar**
9 ounces (approx. 2 cups) **raw peanuts**

❶ Combine the water, honey, and granulated sugar in a 12-inch stainless steel skillet or copper bowl over medium heat. Stir the mixture as it heats to dissolve the sugar.

② When the sugar is dissolved and the syrup is bubbling, add the nuts. Cook for 6 to 8 minutes, stirring occasionally, until the syrup thickens and reduces and begins to turn a light amber color. Turn off the heat and continue to stir the nuts until the sugar crystallizes.

③ When the nuts are well coated with sugar crystals, put the pan back on the heat. As the sugar begins to melt over the heat and caramelize, continue stirring the nuts until the sugar is light brown and the nuts begin to darken in spots. Pour the nuts out onto wax paper or a nonstick silicone mat to cool. If the pan begins to smoke, your heat is up too high and you should immediately take the pan off the heat and stir the nuts to keep them from burning, then reduce the heat and continue cooking the nuts until they are light brown in color.

First-Time Hack & Improved Hack 👍
Prep Time: 20 min.
Difficulty: Easy
Yield: 4 servings

OLIVE GARDEN
GARDEN FRESH SALAD &
SALAD DRESSING

One of the most popular items at America's largest Italian restaurant chain is the bottomless garden salad tossed with the chain's delicious vinaigrette dressing. I hacked the dressing years ago in my first restaurant clones book, but I've recently discovered a new way to make the dressing, with perfect color and flavor, and it's nothing like any copycat recipe for this dressing that you'll find anywhere else. One of the special ingredients in this new take is Egg Beaters, which adds the same yellow color contributed by annatto as in the Olive Garden original. Egg Beaters also adds flavor with a variety of spices, plus xanthan gum, a vegetable-based gel, to help thicken the mix. And don't worry about using raw Egg Beaters in your dressing since it's made with pasteurized egg whites, so it's completely safe. I've cloned the Olive Garden dressing before, but the Garden Fresh Salad recipe here to go with your dressing is a first-time hack.

SALAD DRESSING
⅓ **cup white wine vinegar**
¼ **cup vegetable oil**
¼ **cup grated Romano cheese**
3 **tablespoons Egg Beaters (original)**
3 **tablespoons light corn syrup**
½ **teaspoon lemon juice**
½ **teaspoon salt**
½ **teaspoon garlic powder**
¼ **teaspoon Italian seasoning herb blend**
¼ **teaspoon dried parsley flakes**
¼ **teaspoon crushed red pepper flakes**

SALAD
8 **cups hand-torn iceberg lettuce**
4 **cups hand-torn romaine lettuce**
½ **cup thinly sliced red cabbage**
12 **Roma tomato slices**
8 **pickled golden pepperoncini peppers**
8 **canned whole jumbo black olives**
2 **red onion slices, separated**

¼ cup shredded carrot
1 cup Italian-style croutons

OPTIONAL
Freshly shredded Parmesan cheese

1 Make the salad dressing by combining all of the ingredients in a medium bowl and mix with an electric mixer on medium speed for 1 minute. Chill the dressing until it's needed.

2 Build the salad by combining all of the salad ingredients, except for the croutons, in a large salad bowl. Add about half of the dressing and toss. Save the rest of the dressing in a covered container in your refrigerator for another salad. Sprinkle the croutons over the top of the salad. Serve the salad with freshly shredded Parmesan cheese on top, if desired.

ORANGE JULIUS ORIGINAL ORANGE JULIUS

👍 Improved Hack

⏲ Prep Time: 5 min.

E🌡 Difficulty: Easy

👥 Yield: 2 small drinks

In my previous clone recipes for the refreshing drink that was invented in the 1920s, I used fresh egg whites or Egg Beaters to give the drink its signature frothy texture. That works, but if you want a clone that's more like the real thing, we need to use the same natural ingredient that is most likely in the scoop of secret powder added to each Orange Julius drink: dried egg whites. I used a brand called Just Whites found in the baking aisle of my supermarket. This all-natural, fat-free powder adds a perfect white froth to your drink when it's blended, just like the original. This new ingredient, plus less water and more ice in the mix, will give you my best Orange Julius clone yet.

1¼ cups **pulp-free orange juice**
½ cup **water**
6 tablespoons **granulated sugar**

1 teaspoon **vanilla extract**
1 tablespoon **dried egg whites**
2½ cups **ice**

1 Combine the orange juice, water, sugar, and vanilla in a blender.

2 Blend on high speed for 30 seconds or until the sugar has dissolved.

3 Add the dried egg whites and ice and blend for 15 to 20 seconds or until the ice is crushed and the drink is frothy. Pour into two 16-ounce glasses and serve with straws.

TIDBITS You can use 2 tablespoons pasteurized egg whites or Egg Beaters if you can't find dried egg whites. Measure it into the blender along with the ice.

THE ORIGINAL PANCAKE HOUSE APPLE PANCAKE

👍 Improved Hack
🕐 Active Prep: 25 min.
Inactive Prep: 1 hr. 30 min.
M🌡 Difficulty: Medium
👥 Yield: Serves 1 to 2

With newly obtained intel I have developed a much better version of the batter for this pancake and the Dutch Baby that follows. Buttermilk now replaces the cream in the previous recipe after I discovered that the chain uses a powdered form of buttermilk in the mix, according to my inside source. It makes for a lighter—and lower-fat—finished product that more closely matches up with the original. There's also the necessary addition of a bit of nutmeg often found in traditional German pancake recipes. After baking, this pancake is inverted onto the plate so that the apples wind up on top of the pancake with the cinnamon and sugar glaze dripping down onto the plate. The secret here is to keep the apples from floating up through the batter when the pancake bakes. We do that by allowing the sautéed apples to cool in the sugar. This way, the sugar hardens and the apples stick to the bottom of the pan when the batter is poured in. After an hour of cooling, you can tip the pan to see if the apples slide. If they do, stick the pan in your refrigerator for 30 minutes and those apples won't budge until the pancake is turned over onto your plate just before serving. Use a 9-inch cast-iron skillet for the best results.

2 small or 1 large Granny Smith apple(s)
3 tablespoons unsalted butter
½ cup (packed) light brown sugar
¾ teaspoon ground cinnamon

3 large eggs, beaten
½ cup whole milk
½ cup buttermilk
3 tablespoons granulated sugar
¼ teaspoon plus ⅛ teaspoon salt
2 pinches of ground nutmeg
3½ ounces (about ⅔ cup) all-purpose flour

GARNISH (OPTIONAL)
Powdered sugar

❶ Peel the apples. Slice the apples into halves and use a melon baller to remove the core from each of the halves. Slice the halves into approximately 10 slices each and set the slices aside.

2 Melt the butter in a 9-inch skillet over medium heat. A cast-iron skillet is best, although you can use any oven-safe 9-inch skillet or sauté pan. Add the brown sugar, cinnamon, and apple slices, stir until the apples are coated, and bring to a simmer. Cook for 5 to 8 minutes, stirring occasionally, until the apples are soft, then use a spoon or spatula to evenly spread out the apple slices. Let the pan sit and cool for 1 hour so that the sugar hardens and the apples don't slide when the pan is picked up and tilted. If the apples slide around when the pan is tilted, put it in the refrigerator for 30 minutes. This will ensure that the apples will stay on the bottom of the pan when the batter is poured on top.

3 Make the batter by combining the beaten eggs with the milk, buttermilk, sugar, salt, and nutmeg in a medium bowl with an electric mixer on high speed for 30 seconds. Add the flour and mix for 1 minute. Let the batter sit for 10 minutes, then mix it again briefly before pouring it into the pan.

4 While the batter is resting, preheat your oven to 450 degrees F.

5 When the oven is hot, pour the batter over the apples and bake for 16 to 20 minutes or until the top of the pancake is beginning to brown. Remove it from the oven and let it cool for 1 minute. Run a spatula or butter knife around the edges to loosen the pancake. Invert a plate on top of the pan, then flip the pan over so that the pancake falls out onto the plate upside down. Serve with an optional dusting of powdered sugar over the top.

THE ORIGINAL PANCAKE HOUSE DUTCH BABY

👍 Improved Hack

🕐 Active Prep: 5 min.
Inactive Prep: 25 min.

E🌡 Difficulty: Easy

👥 Yield: 2 servings

The Dutch Baby is a smaller version of the German pancake that I previously hacked, but with new information I have developed a much better version of the batter for both this recipe and the Original Pancake House Apple Pancake on page 177. Use a 9-inch cast-iron skillet for the best results here. If you've got two skillets, even better, since this recipe yields two pancakes. If you don't have a cast-iron skillet, you can also use a 9-inch oven-safe sauté pan. If you have only one skillet and you want to serve the pancakes at the same time, you can reheat the first one in the microwave for 30 seconds on high when your second pancake comes out of the oven.

3 large eggs, beaten
½ cup whole milk
½ cup buttermilk
3 tablespoons granulated sugar
¼ teaspoon plus ⅛ teaspoon salt
2 pinches ground nutmeg
3½ ounces (about ⅔ cup) all-purpose flour
1 tablespoon unsalted butter

GARNISH
Powdered sugar

ON THE SIDE
Lemon wedges
Butter
Maple syrup (optional)

1 Preheat the oven to 450 degrees F.

2 Combine the eggs, milk, buttermilk, sugar, salt, and nutmeg in a medium bowl with an electric mixer on high speed for 30 seconds. Add the flour and mix for 1 minute. Let the batter sit for 10 minutes, then mix it again briefly before pouring it into the pan.

3 While the batter sits, heat up ½ tablespoon of butter in a 9-inch cast-iron skillet on the stove over low heat. When the butter has melted, pour half of the batter (1 cup) into the cast-iron skillet. Place the skillet in the preheated oven and cook for 14 to 16 minutes or until the pancake is dark brown around the edges. If you have only one pan and are cooking just one pancake at a time, let

179

the pan cool for 5 minutes, then add the remaining ½ tablespoon of butter. When it's melted, pour in the remaining batter and bake as with the first one.

4 Dust the pancakes with powdered sugar before serving and serve with lemon wedges, butter, and maple syrup, if desired, on the side.

THE ORIGINAL PANCAKE HOUSE SOURDOUGH PANCAKES

First-Time Hack

Active Prep: 20 min.
Inactive Prep: 5 days

Difficulty: Easy

Yield: 12 pancakes

For real sourdough pancakes you need real sourdough starter, which is made with wild yeast that you must grow yourself over the course of five days. The simple process starts with water and whole-wheat flour set to rest in a covered bowl in a warm spot in your kitchen. The flour contains nutrients and microorganisms that help the yeast to grow as the solution sits out. Each day you feed the yeast with additional water and unbleached all-purpose flour and after five days the starter is ready to be used in a fresh batch of these spot-on copycat flapjacks with a subtle sourdough tang.

SOURDOUGH STARTER
4 ounces (about ¾ cup) whole-wheat flour
¾ cup plus 1⅓ cups water
12 ounces (about 2 cups) unbleached all-purpose flour

PANCAKES
6 ounces (1⅓ cups) unbleached all-purpose flour
¾ cup plus 2 tablespoons whole milk
1 large egg
2 tablespoons granulated sugar
1 tablespoon vegetable oil
1 teaspoon baking soda
½ teaspoon salt

ON THE SIDE
Butter
Maple syrup

❶ Make the sourdough starter by combining the whole-wheat flour with ¾ cup of water in a medium bowl. Cover the bowl with plastic wrap and set it in a warm place for 24 hours. The next day, stir the sourdough starter, then remove ⅓ cup and discard it. Add ⅓ cup of water and 3 ounces (about ½ cup) of all-purpose flour. Stir well until no dry flour is visible. Cover and place it back in a warm spot for another 24 hours. Repeat the process again for the next 3 days. On the sixth day, stir the starter and measure out ¾ cup for use in this

181

recipe. You can discard the remaining starter or keep feeding it to use later in other sourdough recipes by following the instructions in the Tidbits.

2 Combine ¾ cup of the sourdough starter with the 1⅓ cups flour, the milk, and egg in a large bowl. Mix well with an electric mixer. Add the remaining ingredients and mix well again. Let the batter sit for about 10 minutes.

3 Preheat a nonstick griddle or large skillet over medium heat.

4 Drop ¼-cup portions of batter onto the griddle and cook for 1 to 2 minutes per side or until golden brown. Serve with butter and maple syrup on the side. You can freeze any leftover pancakes for several weeks and heat them up in the microwave for about 1 minute on high.

TIDBITS You can reserve the starter indefinitely for use later in another recipe by keeping it covered in the refrigerator. Each week you must feed it by removing ½ cup of the starter and adding 3 ounces (about ½ cup) of all-purpose flour and ⅓ cup of water.

OUTBACK STEAKHOUSE HONEY WHEAT BUSHMAN BREAD

👍 Improved Hack

🕐 Active Prep: 25 min.
Inactive Prep: 2 hrs. 30 min.

🌡 Difficulty: Medium

👥 Yield: 8 small loaves

Other knockoff recipes for this sweet dark bread, including my own, list ingredients such as cocoa, instant coffee, and molasses. These ingredients add some interesting flavors and a bit of color to the loaves, but I found that the recipe did not require such things to taste as good as the original, and the bread is made dark with caramel coloring just like pumpernickel bread, so no dark ingredients are necessary for color. You can use caramel coloring for this recipe, but if you can't find that I have an improved formula for giving the bread its dark brown color using a combination of red, yellow, and blue food coloring. You can also make the bread without the coloring at all. It won't look the same as the original, but it will still taste great. Just be sure to add a tablespoon of water to the dough if you don't bring any color into the mix.

2 teaspoons granulated sugar
1¼ cups warm water (105 to 110 degrees F)
1 package (2¼ teaspoons) active dry yeast
10 ounces (2 cups) bread flour
8½ ounces (1¾ cups) whole wheat flour
1¾ teaspoons salt
⅓ cup honey
3 tablespoons unsalted butter, **softened**
1 tablespoon water (only if **NOT** using the coloring)

COLORING (OPTIONAL)
1 tablespoon caramel food coloring
OR
1¼ teaspoons red food coloring
1¼ teaspoons yellow food coloring
½ teaspoon blue food coloring

Cornmeal for dusting

① Dissolve the sugar in the warm water, then stir in the yeast. Let the mixture sit for 5 minutes until it becomes foamy on top.

② Combine the flours with the salt in a large bowl. You can mix the bread by hand or use a stand mixer with a kneading hook. Add the

yeast mixture to the flours, along with the honey, butter, and food coloring, or 1 tablespoon of water if you are not adding the coloring.

3 Bring the dough together by hand or with the dough hook of a stand mixer. Once the dough comes together into a ball, knead for 10 minutes. Cover the dough in the bowl and let it rise in a warm spot until doubled in size, 1 to 1½ hours.

4 When the dough has doubled, divide it into 8 even portions. Roll each portion into a

log that is 5½ to 6 inches long. Press the log into the cornmeal that has been poured onto a plate, and place the dough log on a parchment paper–lined baking sheet or a silicone baking mat. Cover the dough and allow it to rise again for 1 hour.

5 About 15 minutes before the dough is done rising, preheat the oven to 350 degrees F.

6 Bake the bread for 25 to 30 minutes or until the outside of the bread has formed a firm crust. Serve with softened butter on the side.

OUTBACK STEAKHOUSE
BLOOMIN' ONION

👍 Improved Hack

🕐 Active Prep: 35 min.
Inactive Prep: 2 hrs.

H🌡 Difficulty: Hard

👥 Yield: 2 to 4 servings

There's the Awesome Blossom, Texas Rose, Texas Tumbleweed, and Onion Mum, but the original "flowering" fried onion that inspired all of these clones found on casual restaurant chain menus everywhere is the Bloomin' Onion from Outback. The signature appetizer created in 1988 by Outback founders Tim Gannon, Chris Sullivan, and Bob Basham starts with a 4½-inch super colossal onion that is sliced to form a blooming flower. The petals are then separated, and the Bloomin' Onion is breaded and fried and served up hot and crispy with a

cup of creamy dipping sauce nestled in the center. Back in the early days the onion was sliced by hand, but with around 15 million Bloomin' Onions sold every year, the chain was forced to accelerate the process with a once-secret slicing contraption referred to by the code name "Gloria." Today Gloria is not really that much of a secret since you can easily find several photos of it online, and can even buy one at a restaurant supply store if you've got 400 bucks to shed. I don't expect anyone to obtain

their own Gloria so I'm going to reveal the top secret manual slicing technique here that I learned straight from the man himself, Tim Gannon (standing next to me here), who appeared on episode 3 of *Top Secret Recipe*.

Super colossal onions are hard to find but you can still make a great clone with the biggest onions available at your supermarket. Try to buy onions that are at least 4 inches across. To create an accurate clone of the dipping sauce, I designed the recipe to yield more than you will need for one Bloomin' Onion serving, but the sauce will last for a month or more in your fridge for future Bloomin' Onion clones, or you can use it as a dip

for vegetables and steamed artichokes, or as a great spicy hamburger spread. Plan ahead for this dish since the onion will open up much better after soaking it in cold water in your refrigerator for a couple of hours or overnight. Yep, that's another secret I reveal for you here, along with how to make a custom onion-corer from an empty tomato paste can.

DIPPING SAUCE
1½ cups mayonnaise
3 tablespoons cream-style horseradish
2 tablespoons whole milk

1 teaspoon Crystal Louisiana hot sauce
1½ teaspoons sweet paprika
1 teaspoon paprika (McCormick brand
   works best)

¼ **teaspoon** garlic powder
¼ **teaspoon** onion powder
⅛ **teaspoon** salt
⅛ **teaspoon** ground black pepper
⅛ **teaspoon** white pepper
⅛ **teaspoon** ground cayenne pepper
⅛ **teaspoon** cumin
⅛ **teaspoon** dried oregano
⅛ **teaspoon** ground savory

1 **colossal** yellow onion (4 to 4½ inches across)
1 **6-ounce** tomato paste can
12 **cups** shortening

BREADING
10 **ounces (2 cups)** all-purpose flour
4 **teaspoons** salt
3 **tablespoons** sweet paprika
1 **tablespoon** paprika
1½ **teaspoons** ground cayenne pepper
1¼ **teaspoons** ground black pepper
1 **teaspoon** garlic powder
1 **teaspoon** onion powder
½ **teaspoon** ground cumin
½ **teaspoon** white pepper
½ **teaspoon** ground savory

4 **large** eggs
4 **cups** whole milk

❶ Mix all of the sauce ingredients together in a small bowl. Cover and chill for 2 hours or overnight. Uncover and stir occasionally.

❷ Cut approximately a quarter off the stem end of the onion. Be sure to leave the root end intact. Peel the skin from the onion, then place the onion on a cutting board with the cut side down.

3 To slice, use your thumb as a guide by placing it at the root of the onion, then slice straight down from your thumb to the bottom. Spin the onion around, and make another cut directly across from the first slice on the opposite side. Next, make a slice between each of the first two slices on both sides so now you have 4 large petals. Make a slice down the middle of each of the 4 petals, so that you now have 8 petals. For the final slicing step, rotate the onion and make 2 slices between each of the 8 cuts. You will now have an onion with 24 total petals, which is exactly the same number as the machine-sliced real thing. Turn the onion over and it will have bloomed. Submerge the onion in a bowl of cold water and place it in your refrigerator for 2 hours, or even overnight, to help open up the onion and separate the petals.

4 When you are ready to prepare your onion, open both ends of the tomato paste can and empty the contents. Rinse the can, then use a file to sharpen the edge of one end of the can. This is your onion coring tool.

5 Preheat the shortening to 350 degrees F in a large deep fryer or Dutch oven.

6 Combine the breading ingredients in a very large bowl. Beat the eggs in a medium bowl, then add the milk.

7 Take the onion out of the water and shake off the water. Put the onion into the breading and cover with the breading, being sure to get the breading down between each petal.

8 Shake off the excess breading, then gently lower the onion into the egg and milk mixture until it is completely moistened. Lift the onion out of the liquid and let the excess drip off. Place the onion back into the breading and thoroughly coat the onion. Let it sit in the breading for a few minutes so that the breading sticks.

9 Turn the onion over, petals down, onto a spider and gently lower it into the oil. Tap on the bottom of the onion with a large wooden spoon to get out any air bubbles and cook it for 2 to 3 minutes or until it's beginning to brown. Flip the onion over and continue to fry it for 2 to 3 minutes or until it's golden brown. Flip the onion over once again with the spider and remove it from the oil. This will allow the oil to drip out from between the "petals" as it comes up. Flip the onion over once again onto a serving plate.

10 Allow the onion to cool for a minute or so, then press the sharpened end of the tomato paste can down through the middle of the onion to core out the center.

11 Pour the dipping sauce into a small sauce cup, place it in the center of the onion, and serve.

OUTBACK STEAKHOUSE KOOKABURRA WINGS

👍 Improved Hack

⊘ Active Prep: 20 min.
Inactive Prep: 3 hrs.

M🌡 Difficulty: Medium

👥 Yield: 10 wings

The brining process that I have added to this improved recipe will help you turn out wings that have flavor all the way through. The updated breading will give the wings the same color and texture as Outback's version. You can make your wings mild, medium, or hot as in the restaurant by adjusting the amount of cayenne pepper added to the sauce. If you love breaded chicken wings like those at Outback, this should be your go-to hack.

BRINE
2 cups water
1 tablespoon salt
2 teaspoons granulated sugar
1 teaspoon paprika
¼ teaspoon onion powder
¼ teaspoon garlic powder

10 chicken wings

BREADING
⅓ cup plain bread crumbs (such as Progresso brand)
4 teaspoons all-purpose flour
1 teaspoon chili powder
¾ teaspoon ground black pepper
½ teaspoon salt
½ teaspoon ground cayenne pepper
¼ teaspoon onion powder
¼ teaspoon garlic powder
¼ teaspoon dried thyme
¼ teaspoon rubbed sage
¼ teaspoon ground cumin

6 to 12 cups vegetable oil

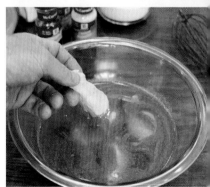

SAUCE
¼ cup (½ stick) unsalted butter
3 tablespoons Frank's RedHot Original Cayenne Pepper
  Sauce
2 tablespoons water
½ teaspoon ground black pepper
Hot: ½ teaspoon ground cayenne pepper
Medium: ¼ teaspoon ground cayenne pepper
Mild: no ground cayenne pepper

ON THE SIDE
Celery sticks
Blue cheese dressing

1. Combine all of the brine ingredients in a medium bowl. Add the wings to the brine, then cover and chill for 3 hours. After 3 hours, rinse the wings and blot dry.

2. Combine all of the breading ingredients in a small bowl. Roll the wings around in the breading until each wing is lightly breaded. Let the wings rest for 10 to 15 minutes while the oil heats.

3. Heat the oil in a large pot or deep fryer to 300 degrees F. Fry the wings in the oil in batches for 8 to 12 minutes (depending on the size of your wings) or until brown and crispy. Remove to a rack or a paper towel–lined plate.

4. Make the sauce by combining all of the ingredients in a small saucepan over medium/low heat. Add the cayenne in the amount specified for hot or medium wings, or no cayenne at all if you like your wings mild. Whisk to combine when the butter has melted and heat just until bubbling, then remove from the heat.

5. Toss the wings in the sauce in a large bowl until coated and serve hot with celery sticks and blue cheese dressing on the side for dipping.

TIDBITS Get the smallest wings you can find for a clone most like the steakhouse's original.

PANERA BREAD BROCCOLI CHEDDAR SOUP

Improved Hack
Active Prep: 15 min.
Inactive Prep: 1 hr.
E Difficulty: Easy
Yield: 6 servings

The most popular soup at Panera Bread deserves a proper clone recipe and this re-hack is a huge improvement over my previous version. The first time around I used Kraft Cheddar Cheese Singles to ensure that the soup was smooth and creamy. The soup was good, but perhaps not as deliciously cheesy as the original. So this time around we'll make a cheese sauce the proper way with a roux, adding half-and-half to it along with the chicken broth, then whisking in the cheese until it's melted smoothly into the soup—without any graininess. The veggies are added to the soup last. When the broccoli is tender, after about 40 minutes, your soup is done. Faster, easier, cheesier, better.

2 tablespoons unsalted butter
2½ tablespoons all-purpose flour
1 cup half-and-half
3 cups chicken broth

12 ounces (6 cups) shredded mild cheddar cheese
8 ounces (3 cups) finely chopped broccoli
½ cup shredded carrot
½ cup diced white onion

1 Heat the butter in a 2½-quart saucepan over medium/low heat until melted. Whisk in the flour. Cook for 3 to 4 minutes or until the flour begins to turn light brown.

2 Whisk the half-and-half into the flour. Stir until the flour is dissolved with no visible lumps. Cook for 2 to 3 minutes or until the half-and-half begins to bubble around the edge of the pan. Pour the

chicken broth into the pan, stir well, and cook for 5 minutes or until the liquid begins to bubble around the edge of the pan. Whisk in the cheese. Continue to whisk thoroughly until the cheese is completely dissolved into the liquid. Cook the soup on a low simmer for 10 minutes. The soup should bubble only a little; do not allow it to reach a rapid boil. Stir often.

❸ Stir in the broccoli, carrot, and onion. Continue to simmer the soup on medium/low for 40 to 45 minutes, stirring occasionally, until the broccoli is tender.

PANERA BREAD ASIAN SESAME CHICKEN SALAD

 First-Time Hack

 Active Prep: 15 min.
Inactive Prep: 4 hrs.

 Difficulty: Medium

 Yield: 4 large salads

This salad and the Fuji Apple Chicken Salad (page 195) are the two most popular salads on Panera's menu. Each of these salads has different toppings and different delicious dressings, but the secret chicken marinade recipe is exactly the same, so regardless of which of the two salad clones you decide to make you'll need some forethought, since the chicken has to marinate for 2 hours, then chill for another 2 hours after it's cooked. This recipe shows you how to make the great crispy wonton strips found on the Panera Bread Asian Sesame Chicken Salad using wonton wrappers, but if you want a shortcut, you can instead use crispy chow mein noodles from the Asian foods section at your market.

CHICKEN MARINADE

½ cup water
½ cup orange juice
¼ cup canola oil
3 tablespoons minced red onion
2 teaspoons crushed dried rosemary
1½ teaspoons lemon pepper
1½ teaspoons salt
½ teaspoon ground black pepper
½ teaspoon crushed red pepper flakes
½ teaspoon dried oregano
½ teaspoon garlic powder
½ teaspoon dried basil
½ teaspoon paprika
¼ teaspoon hickory liquid smoke flavoring

2 6-ounce skinless chicken breast fillets

DRESSING

¼ cup plus 1 tablespoon rice vinegar
3 tablespoons granulated sugar
1½ teaspoons sesame oil
1 teaspoon soy sauce
½ teaspoon Dijon mustard
Pinch of ground oregano
Pinch of salt
⅓ cup canola oil

Vegetable oil or canola oil for frying
8 wonton wrappers
16 cups chopped romaine lettuce
½ cup sliced almonds
¼ cup chopped cilantro

1 Make marinade for the chicken by combining all of the marinade ingredients in a medium bowl. Add the chicken, then cover and marinate for 2 hours in your refrigerator. (See photos on page 195.)

2 When the chicken has finished marinating, remove it from the marinade and place it on a rack with the underside of the chicken breasts facing up. Brush some additional marinade over the top of the chicken and bake it in a 375 degrees F oven for 40 to 45 minutes or until done (internal temperature in the thickest part of the breasts should be 165 degrees). Cool the chicken breasts in a covered container in your refrigerator for several hours, or if you want to rush it, put the chicken in

the freezer for 1 hour, then in your refrigerator for 1 hour. When the chicken breasts are cold, thinly slice each fillet across the width.

❸ Make the dressing by whisking together the vinegar, sugar, sesame oil, soy sauce, mustard, oregano, and salt. Mix until the sugar is dissolved. Add the oil while whisking briskly, then cover and chill the dressing until it's needed.

❹ Make the crispy wontons by heating up some oil in a medium saucepan or deep fryer to 350 degrees F. Slice a stack of 8 wonton wrappers into strips and then slice those strips in half. Fry the sliced wontons in the hot oil for 30 to 45 seconds or until golden brown.

Gently stir the wontons in the oil so that they fry evenly on both sides. Remove the crispy wonton strips from the oil to a paper towel–lined plate.

❺ Build each salad by placing 4 cups of chopped romaine in a large mixing bowl. Toss the lettuce with 3 tablespoons of the dressing, then place the greens on a large plate or in a bowl.

❻ Sprinkle one-quarter of the crispy wonton strips over the lettuce followed by one-quarter of the chicken (half of a chicken breast) on the salad. Top with 2 tablespoons of sliced almonds and 1 tablespoon of cilantro.

PANERA BREAD FUJI APPLE CHICKEN SALAD

First-Time Hack

Active Prep: 15 min.
Inactive Prep: 4 hrs.

M Difficulty: Medium

Yield: 4 large salads

Panera Bread dominates in the U.S. with over 78 percent of all sales in the bakery-café segment. The chain's success is attributed to the great offering of specialty sandwiches, delicious soups, and awesome salads. One of the most popular of those salads is the Fuji Apple Chicken Salad, which includes the chain's citrus–lemon pepper marinated chicken on mixed greens with pecans, gorgonzola, crispy apple chips, and a balsamic apple vinaigrette. For the apple chips you don't need to use apple chips that are specifically Fuji apple chips—any apple chip will work here to make a great clone. I found that Seneca Crispy Apple Chips, the original apple chips, taste the best. This recipe uses the same marinated chicken as in the recipe for Panera Bread Asian Sesame Chicken Salad (page 193), so plan ahead since the chicken must marinate for 2 hours and then chill for another 2 hours after it's cooked.

CHICKEN MARINADE
½ **cup water**
½ **cup orange juice**
¼ **cup canola oil**
3 **tablespoons minced red onion**
2 **teaspoons crushed dried rosemary**
1½ **teaspoons lemon pepper**
1½ **teaspoons salt**
½ **teaspoon ground black pepper**
½ **teaspoon crushed red pepper**
½ **teaspoon dried oregano**
½ **teaspoon garlic powder**
½ **teaspoon dried basil**
½ **teaspoon paprika**
¼ **teaspoon hickory liquid smoke flavoring**

2 **6-ounce skinless chicken breast fillets**

BALSAMIC APPLE VINAIGRETTE
⅓ **cup mayonnaise**
¼ **cup apple juice concentrate**
3 **tablespoons vegetable oil**
1 **teaspoon white balsamic vinegar**

2 **medium tomatoes**
8 **cups chopped romaine lettuce**
8 **cups spring lettuce mix**
1 **medium red onion, sliced into thin rings**
1 **cup gorgonzola cheese**
2 **2½-ounce bags Seneca Crispy Apple Chips (or other brand)**
1⅓ **cups pecan halves**

1 Make the marinade for the chicken by combining all of the marinade ingredients in a medium bowl. Add the chicken, then cover and marinate for 2 hours in your refrigerator.

2 When the chicken has finished marinating, remove it from the marinade and place it on a rack with the underside of the chicken breasts facing up. Brush some additional marinade over the top of the chicken and bake it in a 375 degree F oven for 40 to 45 minutes or until done (internal temperature in

the thickest part of the breasts should be 165 degrees F). Cool the chicken breasts in a covered container in your refrigerator for several hours, or if you want to rush it, put the chicken in the freezer for 1 hour, then in your refrigerator for 1 hour. When the chicken is cold, thinly slice it across the width of each breast.

3 Make the vinaigrette by whisking together all of the ingredients in a medium bowl until thick. Cover and chill until needed.

4 Slice the tomatoes by first slicing off the stem end. Turn the tomatoes onto the sliced end and slice each of them into 8 wedges.

5 To build each salad, combine 2 cups of chopped romaine lettuce with 2 cups of the spring mix in a mixing bowl. Add 4 tomato slices and 8 to 12 red onion rings, then pour 3 tablespoons of dressing over the salad and toss.

6 Arrange the salad on a large plate or in a large bowl, then sprinkle ¼ cup of the gorgonzola on top.

7 Arrange one-quarter of the chicken (half of a chicken breast) on the salad next. Sprinkle 1 cup (½ of a bag) of apple chips on the salad, followed by ⅓ cup of pecans, and serve.

PANERA BREAD
SPINACH & BACON
BAKED EGG SOUFFLÉ

 First-Time Hack

 Active Prep: 10 min.
Inactive Prep: 25 min.

E Difficulty: Easy

Yield: 4 soufflés

Rather than making crescent dough from scratch for the Spinach & Artichoke Baked Egg Soufflé that I cloned several years ago, I used Pillsbury Crescent Butter Flake Dough found in tubes in most markets. However, I have now discovered a better dough that duplicates the flakiness and slight sweetness of the original Panera Bread Baked Egg Soufflés that are so popular in the mornings at this 1,534-unit national sandwich chain. This time around we're cloning the Spinach & Bacon Baked Egg Soufflé, and we're doing it with a better premade dough: Pillsbury Big & Flaky Grands Crescent Dough. Also, I have streamlined the recipe here so that it does not require any precooking of the egg mixture. Just pour the filling into the crescent dough in a 5-inch ramekin, fold the dough over the top, add a piece of bacon on top, and bake.

FILLING

4 slices bacon, cooked
5 large eggs
6 ounces (about 1½ cups) shredded medium cheddar cheese
¼ cup heavy cream
2 tablespoons minced frozen chopped spinach, thawed

¼ teaspoon salt
¼ teaspoon lemon juice
⅛ teaspoon garlic powder
2 drops Tabasco pepper sauce

1 12-ounce tube Pillsbury Big & Flaky Grands Crescent Dough

1 Preheat a convection oven to 350 degrees F (or conventional oven to 375 degrees F).

2 Mince 2 slices of cooked bacon (save the other 2 slices for later), then combine that with the rest of the filling ingredients in a medium bowl and beat with an electric mixer for 1 minute or until the filling begins to thicken.

3 Unroll the crescent dough and separate the dough into

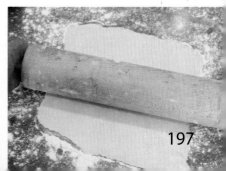

4 portions. Do not tear the dough along the diagonal perforation. Instead, pinch the dough together there, giving you four solid rectangles of dough. Use a rolling pin to roll out the dough on a lightly floured surface, forming it into 4 squares.

4 Butter the inside of four 5-inch ramekins. Line the inside of each ramekin with the dough, being sure to leave the corners hanging over the edge of each ramekin. Pour

even portions of filling into each ramekin (about ½ cup each). Carefully fold the corners over onto the filling and then place a half strip of cooked bacon on top of each.

5 Bake for 25 to 30 minutes or until brown. Let the soufflés cool for 5 to 10 minutes before removing them from the ramekins. You can serve the soufflés right away or keep them warm in a low oven (200 degrees F) until you're ready to serve.

PEPPERIDGE FARM MILANO DARK CHOCOLATE COOKIES

🎖 First-Time Hack

🕐 Active Prep: 35 min.
Inactive Prep: 22 min.

E🌡 Difficulty: Easy

👥 Yield: 25 cookies

The Milano Dark Chocolate Cookie from Pepperidge Farm is the most popular of the "Places" cookies, which are named after various locales where I'd like to go on vacation, including Brussels, Geneva, Tahiti, Maui, and Sausalito. The Milano sandwich cookie was once a nonsandwich cookie called Naples with a layer of dark chocolate on top of one cookie, but when the cookies began to stick together during shipping, another cookie was placed on the chocolate and the Milano was born. The secret in this clone recipe is the combination of all-purpose flour and cake flour to give the cookie its light texture. For the chocolate layer use the dark chocolate melting wafers from Ghirardelli or a dark chocolate intended for candy making and dipping. You'll need a pastry bag or gun with a #12 round tip to form the cookies. And if you have a silicone baking mat, use it here to bake the cookies. If not, a parchment paper–lined baking sheet works well.

½ cup (1 stick) **unsalted butter, softened**
3 ounces (¾ cup) **powdered sugar**
3 **egg whites**
½ teaspoon **vanilla extract**
⅛ teaspoon **salt**
2½ ounces (½ cup plus 2 tablespoons) **all-purpose flour**

2½ ounces (½ cup) **cake flour**
1 teaspoon **baking powder**
1 12-ounce bag **Ghirardelli Dark Melting Wafers (or similar dark dipping chocolate)**

❶ Preheat the oven to 275 degrees F.

❷ Combine the butter with the powdered sugar in a medium bowl with an electric mixer on medium speed. If using a stand mixer, use the paddle attachment. Mix for 1 minute. In a separate bowl, beat the egg whites with a whisk until foamy but still in liquid form, then add to the butter/sugar along with the vanilla and salt. Beat with the mixer for 1 minute.

❸ Combine the flours and baking powder in a medium bowl, then add it to the wet ingredients. Mix until all of the flour is incorporated and the batter is smooth.

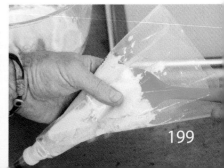

④ Spoon the batter into a pastry bag with a #12 round tip and pipe 2¼-inch-long and ¾-inch-wide tubes of dough 2 inches apart onto a baking sheet lined with a baking mat or parchment paper. The cookies will spread out as they bake, so give them room to grow. Bake for 22 to 26 minutes or until beginning to brown around the edges. Cool.

⑤ Melt the chocolate on high for 30 seconds in your microwave. Stir. Melt the chocolate again if necessary in 15-second intervals until it is completely smooth when stirred. Use a butter knife, frosting knife, or spatula to spread a thin layer of the melted chocolate on the face of one cookie. Place another cookie on top, sandwiching the chocolate in the middle. Repeat with the remaining cookies and chocolate.

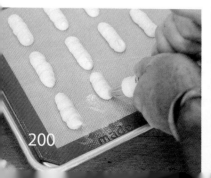

P.F. CHANG'S CHICKEN LETTUCE WRAPS

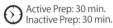

👍 Improved Hack

🕐 Active Prep: 30 min.
Inactive Prep: 30 min.

M🌡 Difficulty: Medium

👥 Yield: 2 to 3 servings

While seeking out information to help make the ultimate hack of these lettuce wraps for *Top Secret Recipe*, I talked to Eric Justice, V.P. of Culinary Development at P.F. Chang's China Bistro (left), who informed me that the restaurant uses a jet cooker stovetop with a high flame to cook food quickly. Jet cookers that blast out powerful 185,000 BTU flames can be found in restaurant supply stores, but I created a clone recipe requiring only the heat provided by most standard home stovetops (a gas flame stove is best).

I also found out that a well-seasoned wok is preferable for this recipe, but it is also possible to produce a close re-creation of these famous lettuce wraps even without one. If you don't have a wok, use a well-seasoned cast-iron skillet and get it nice and hot. You'll also want to track down the right ingredients: black mushroom soy sauce contributes the dark caramel color to the lettuce wrap filling, and it's best to use Lee Kum Kee brand of hoisin sauce and oyster sauce, just as the restaurant does. Heat up your wok (or large skillet) until it smokes and keep the ingredients moving around in the pan so that nothing scorches. This is the recipe that fooled all three judges in a blind taste test on my CMT show.

FILLING
6 to 8 dried shiitake mushrooms (**½ cup finely chopped** when rehydrated)
3 to 4 tablespoons vegetable oil
1 cup coarsely ground white meat chicken (about 1 skinless chicken breast fillet)
¼ teaspoon salt
⅛ teaspoon white pepper
1 tablespoon plus 1 teaspoon minced garlic
1 cup finely chopped canned water chestnuts (1 8-ounce can)
¼ cup chopped green onions (**green part only**)

TABLE SAUCE
2 tablespoons plus 1 teaspoon granulated sugar
½ cup warm water
3 tablespoons soy sauce
1 tablespoon rice wine vinegar
1 tablespoon chopped green onion (**green part only**)

½ to 1 teaspoon Chinese hot mustard paste
1 to 3 teaspoons chili garlic sauce

LETTUCE WRAP SAUCE
1 tablespoon plus ½ teaspoon black mushroom soy sauce
5 tablespoons water
5 teaspoons granulated sugar
1 tablespoon hoisin sauce (Lee Kum Kee is best)
1 tablespoon oyster sauce (Lee Kum Kee is best)
1 tablespoon Shaoxing rice cooking wine
1 teaspoon cornstarch

4 to 6 cups vegetable oil (for frying saifun)
1 to 1½ cups fried saifun bean threads

1 head iceberg lettuce

1 Rehydrate the shiitake mushrooms by filling a medium saucepan about halfway with water and 1 teaspoon of salt. Bring the water to a boil over high heat, then turn off the heat and add the mushrooms. Use a smaller pan or bowl to push down on the mushrooms to make sure they are completely submerged in the water. Let the mushrooms soak for 30 minutes to 1 hour or until they are soft.

2 Make the table sauce for spooning over your lettuce wraps by dissolving the sugar in the water in a small bowl. Add the soy sauce and rice vinegar. Add the chopped green onion and set the sauce aside until you're ready to serve the lettuce wraps. Eventually you will add the Chinese mustard and chili garlic sauce to this special sauce mixture to pour over each of your lettuce wraps. In the restaurant, waiters prepare the sauce at your table the same way based on your desired heat level. We'll get to the specifics of that in step 9.

3 Prepare the lettuce wrap sauce by combining the black soy sauce, 2 tablespoons of the water, the sugar, hoisin sauce, oyster sauce, and cooking wine in a small bowl. Heat for 30 seconds in the microwave on high and stir to dissolve the sugar. Dissolve the cornstarch with the remaining 3 tablespoons of water in a small bowl and add this slurry to the lettuce wrap sauce.

4 Prepare the lettuce cups by slicing the top off a head of lettuce through the middle. Carefully remove the firm outer leaves of lettuce and use kitchen scissors to trim the edges of 6 lettuce leaves so that they are each about 5 inches in diameter.

5 Prepare the saifun bean threads by preheating 4 to 6 cups of oil in a wok or saucepan over high heat to 375 degrees F. When the oil is hot, break up a chunk of saifun and flash fry it for just a second or two until it puffs up, then remove it from the oil and drain on paper towels.

6 Preheat a wok (or cast-iron skillet) with 3 to 4 tablespoons of oil over high heat. When the oil begins to smoke, add the chicken and stir it when it begins to brown. As the chicken cooks, sprinkle it with the salt and white pepper.

7 Add the garlic and let it cook for 20 seconds or until it begins to brown, then add the mushrooms and water chestnuts and cook for a minute or two. Add the lettuce wrap sauce. Continue cooking until the sauce reduces. Add the green onions and remove the wok or skillet from the heat.

8 Arrange a bed of fried saifun rice noodles on a serving plate. Spoon the lettuce wrap filling onto the bean threads and serve with lettuce cups on the side.

9 Prepare the table sauce for spooning onto the lettuce wraps by adding your desired measurement of hot mustard and chili sauce based on preferred spiciness: 1 teaspoon of chili sauce for MILD, ½ teaspoon of mustard paste plus 2 teaspoons of chili sauce for MEDIUM, and 1 teaspoon of mustard paste and 1 tablespoon of chili sauce for HOT. Stir well.

10 To serve, assemble each lettuce wrap by spooning the filling into a lettuce cup, adding the sauce over the top, and eating it like a taco.

203

P.F. CHANG'S OOLONG CHILEAN SEA BASS

👍 Improved Hack

⏲ Active Prep: 10 min.
Inactive Prep:
6 hrs. 30 min.

E 🌡 Difficulty: Easy

👥 Yield: 2 servings

My first attempt at cloning this sea bass soaked in a sweet ginger-soy marinade infused with the flavor of oolong tea included loose oolong tea added to the sauce as it cooks, but I recently found out that is not the way P.F. Chang's makes the dish. Rather than adding loose tea and straining it out before adding the fish, whole tea bags are kept in the marinade along with the fish as it soaks. After you take the fish out of the pan six hours later (and also remove the tea bags), the saucepan goes right on your stove to reduce the marinade within to a warm, flavorful sauce that is spooned over the baked fish before serving.

MARINADE/SAUCE

2 cups water
1 cup (packed) dark brown sugar
⅔ cup soy sauce
6 tablespoons rice vinegar
1 tablespoon fish sauce
2 teaspoons minced ginger
1 teaspoon minced garlic
2 oolong tea bags

2 8-ounce skinless sea bass fillets

GARNISH

1 tablespoon vegetable oil
6 handfuls fresh spinach
1 teaspoon minced garlic

❶ Make the marinade by combining all of the ingredients, except the tea bags, in a medium saucepan over medium/high heat. Bring the mixture to a boil, then reduce the heat and simmer for 5 minutes. Remove from the heat, let the sauce sit for 5 minutes, strain the sauce to remove the ginger and garlic, then pour the sauce back into the saucepan and add the tea bags. When the sauce has cooled for about 30 minutes, add the sea bass, cover, and marinate for 6 hours in the refrigerator.

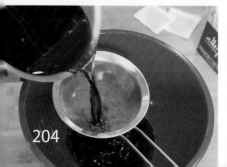

2 When you are ready to prepare the fish, preheat your oven to 425 degrees F.

3 Arrange the fish on a baking sheet that has been lined with aluminum foil and bake for 18 to 22 minutes or until the edges are beginning to turn dark brown. Remove the tea bags from the marinade and place the saucepan over medium heat and bring it to a simmer while the fish cooks. It should thicken up a bit.

4 As the fish is baking, heat up a wok or large skillet over high heat and add the vegetable oil. Add the spinach and garlic and sauté for 30 seconds or just until the spinach is beginning to wilt.

5 When the sea bass is done, split the spinach onto two plates and carefully arrange the sea bass on top of the spinach. Use a spatula so that the fish does not fall apart. Spoon some warm sauce over the fish and serve.

TIDBITS I found my oolong tea bags at Whole Foods.

205

PINKBERRY ORIGINAL FROZEN YOGURT

 First-Time Hack

Active Prep: 5 min.
Inactive Prep: 30 min.

E Difficulty: Easy

Yield: 5 cups

Every recipe I found online claiming to duplicate the tart frozen fat-free yogurt popularized by this 250-unit California-based chain—including one designed by chefs at *Food Network Magazine*—calls for Greek yogurt as the main ingredient when there is no Greek yogurt in the real thing. Plain fat-free yogurt is clearly mentioned in the ingredients statement and a worker at the store confirmed this fact. The tartness in the yogurt comes from citric acid, sometimes called "sour salt," which you can find in many grocery stores or online. To add the hydrocolloid, or gel, found in the real thing, we'll use fat-free half-and-half, which contains natural vegetable gums for a smooth mouth-feel and a less icy texture. This new combination of secret ingredients clones Pinkberry's most popular flavor.

2 cups fat-free plain yogurt
1 cup fat-free half-and-half
1 cup fat-free milk
¾ cup granulated sugar
¾ teaspoon vanilla extract
½ teaspoon plus ⅛ teaspoon citric acid

1 Combine all of the ingredients in a bowl with an electric mixer on high speed for 1 minute or until the sugar has dissolved.

2 Pour the liquid into an ice cream maker and run until thick and creamy, 20 to 30 minutes.

3 You can eat the soft yogurt right away, or store it by transferring the frozen yogurt to a container and pressing a piece of plastic wrap gently down onto the frozen yogurt to keep the air out, then seal the container and freeze.

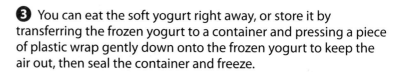

PINKBERRY POMEGRANATE FROZEN YOGURT

 First-Time Hack

 Active Prep: 5 min.
Inactive Prep: 1 hr.

 E Difficulty: Easy

 Yield: 5½ cups

Hacking Pinkberry's second most popular flavor is a matter of slightly altering my original flavor clone recipe (see page 206), then adding to it a pomegranate juice concentrate. The chain uses Pom Wonderful concentrate in the mix, which we can make easily by reducing 2 cups of juice down to one-quarter of its original volume. After the pomegranate juice cools, add it to the other ingredients and churn the mixture in a home ice cream maker until thick. Easy, cheaper, delicious.

2 cups Pom Wonderful pomegranate juice
2 cups fat-free plain yogurt
1 cup fat-free half-and-half

1 cup fat-free milk
⅔ cup granulated sugar
¾ teaspoon vanilla extract
¼ teaspoon plus ⅛ teaspoon citric acid

❶ Bring the pomegranate juice to a boil in a small saucepan over medium/high heat, then reduce to a simmer and cook until the liquid reduces to a quarter of its original volume, or ½ cup, and is thick and syrupy. This should take about 20 minutes. Cool for 20 minutes in your refrigerator.

❷ Combine all of the ingredients in a bowl with an electric mixer on high speed for 1 minute or until the sugar has dissolved.

❸ Pour the liquid into an ice cream maker and run until thick and creamy, 20 to 30 minutes.

❹ You can eat the soft yogurt right away, or store it by transferring the frozen yogurt to a container and pressing a piece of plastic wrap gently down onto the frozen yogurt to keep the air out, then seal the container and freeze.

First-Time Hack

Active Prep: 5 min.
Inactive Prep: 20 min.

E Difficulty: Easy

Yield: ½ cup

RAISING CANE'S CANE'S SAUCE

This chicken finger chain makes a big deal out its "secret" dipping sauce recipe, even requiring employees to sign a confidentiality agreement to protect any details about the recipe. As far as I can tell, it's a very simple recipe made with just a handful of pretty obvious ingredients. All you do is mix everything together and let it sit for a bit in the fridge. Soon you'll have a sauce that can be used on store-bought chicken fingers, or with a fresh clone of the chain's own delicious chicken fingers using my recipe hack on page 209. This may not be the exact recipe the chain uses, but it tastes the same, and that's all that matters.

½ **cup** mayonnaise
3 **tablespoons** ketchup
2 **tablespoons** Worcestershire sauce
¼ **teaspoon** ground black pepper
¼ **teaspoon** paprika
¼ **teaspoon** garlic powder
⅛ **teaspoon** onion powder

❶ Whisk together all of the ingredients in a small bowl.

❷ Cover and chill the sauce for at least 20 minutes. Stir again before serving.

RAISING CANE'S CHICKEN FINGERS

 First-Time Hack

 Active Prep: 20 min.
Inactive Prep: 24 hrs.

M Difficulty: Medium

Yield: 8 pieces

This chicken finger chain was born in Baton Rouge, Louisiana, in 1996 near the campus of LSU serving only fried chicken pieces, along with a top secret dipping sauce and a few sides. Perhaps it is the surprisingly simply menu that has helped this chain grow to more than 150 stores in fifteen states.

To get moist and tender chicken fingers like those you find at Raising Cane's, use chicken tenders and marinate the chicken in a brine for 24 hours, or at least overnight. Also, if your tenders are thicker than 1 inch wide, be sure to slice them in half lengthwise so that they better absorb the brine and are cooked all the way through when the outside reaches a nice golden brown color.

BRINE
2 cups water
1 teaspoon salt
1 teaspoon MSG (such as Accent seasoning)
⅛ teaspoon garlic powder
⅛ teaspoon onion powder

8 skinless chicken tenders
4 to 12 cups canola oil
1 large egg, beaten
1 cup milk

CHICKEN BREADING
1 cup all-purpose flour
1 teaspoon salt
1 teaspoon MSG (such as Accent seasoning)
1 teaspoon baking powder
¾ teaspoon ground black pepper
⅛ teaspoon garlic powder
⅛ teaspoon onion powder

1 Make the brine by combining all of the ingredients in a medium bowl. Add the chicken tenders (slice any tenders that are very thick in half lengthwise), cover the bowl, and marinate them for 24 hours.

2 When the chicken has marinated for 24 hours, remove it from the brine and rinse off each piece. Blot dry with paper towels.

3 Preheat the oil in a deep fryer or a large saucepan (the oil should be at least 3 to 4 inches deep) to 325 degrees F.

4 Combine the beaten egg with the milk in a medium bowl. Combine all of the breading ingredients in a shallow bowl or pie pan.

5 Bread each chicken tender by first tossing the chicken in the dry breading. Submerge the chicken in the egg/milk mixture, let some of the liquid drip off, then place it back in the dry blend. Roll the chicken around in the breading while pressing down so that a thick coating of breading forms on the chicken. Let the chicken sit for 5 minutes or so in the dry ingredients so that the breading sticks.

6 Gently drop each tender (if your fryer or saucepan is big enough you can cook 4 at a time) into the hot oil and fry for 5 to 6 minutes or until the chicken is golden brown. Drain the fillets on a rack or a plate lined with paper towels for 1 minute, then serve hot with a dipping sauce of your choice—I suggest the sauce from the recipe on page 208.

RED LOBSTER CHEDDAR BAY BISCUITS

👍 Improved Hack

🕐 Active Prep: 10 min.
Inactive Prep: 15 min.

E 🌡 Difficulty: Easy

👥 Yield: 9 biscuits

On the Red Lobster website the chain claims its recipe for these awesome biscuits served with each meal is a corporate secret. The site says, "That hasn't stopped home cooks and cookbook authors from trying to re-create them."

The company never reveals the real recipe but does offer two tips for making your own version of the famous biscuits. According to Red Lobster, baking soda is definitely one of the ingredients, and overkneading the dough is a no-no. My previous version of this recipe requires Bisquick baking mix—as do many of the recipes posted out there—which makes the recipe super easy, but does it really make for the best clone? I thought it was about time I worked on the ultimate hack of the world's most well-known cheesy biscuits, with all scratch ingredients, the way Red Lobster would most likely make them. And just because this new recipe is made from scratch with no baking mix doesn't mean it's hard. In fact, it's still a very easy clone and the finished product is lighter and flakier (thanks to the addition of cake flour) and more like the real thing than any other hack you'll try.

6½ ounces (1½ cups) **cake flour**
2½ ounces (½ cup) **all-purpose flour**
1 teaspoon **salt**
½ teaspoon **baking powder**
½ teaspoon **baking soda**
⅓ cup **cold shortening**
¾ cup **shredded** sharp cheddar cheese
¾ cup **cold water**
¼ **cup** buttermilk

GARLIC BUTTER SPREAD
¼ cup (½ stick) **unsalted butter**
1 teaspoon **garlic powder**
¼ teaspoon **salt**
¼ teaspoon **onion powder**
¼ teaspoon **dried parsley flakes**
⅛ teaspoon **granulated sugar**

1 Preheat the oven to 425 degrees F.

2 Combine the flours, salt, baking powder, and baking soda in a large bowl.

3 Add the cold shortening to the flour and mix well until no chunks of shortening are visible. You can also use a pastry cutter to cut the shortening into the flour until it is crumbly.

211

4 Mix in the cheese.

5 Add the water and buttermilk and mix gently with a large spoon JUST until the ingredients are blended. Do not mix too much or your biscuits may not be flaky.

6 Measure ¼-cup portions onto a parchment paper– or a baking mat–lined baking sheet. Bake for 14 to 16 minutes or until the biscuits are golden brown. Spin the pan around once halfway through the cooking time.

7 While the biscuits are baking, make the garlic butter spread by melting the butter in a small dish in your microwave for 30 seconds. Stir in the remaining ingredients.

8 When the biscuits come out of the oven, use a brush to spread the garlic butter over the top of each biscuit. Serve warm.

RED LOBSTER
PUMPKIN PIE
IN A JAR

First-Time Hack

Active Prep: 25 min.
Inactive Prep: 3 hrs.

Difficulty: Medium

Yield: 6 desserts

After the success of the chain's Strawberry Cheesecake in a Jar, Red Lobster introduced the Pumpkin Pie in a Jar for the 2013 fall holidays. The dessert, which the menu describes as "layered pumpkin and cream cheese mousse with a graham-cracker crust, topped with sugared pecans," quickly became a hit with customers and the online cooking blog community. I found a few interesting recipes posted online but none got it all right, so I thought it was time to break down my own Pumpkin Pie in a Jar to find out exactly what's going on in there. After getting the dessert back to the lab and separating all of the components, I hacked each layer, one at a time, so that I could now present you with this, the ultimate clone. You'll have to make several parts for this recipe, but they are each pretty easy and you can make them several hours or even a day ahead of when you plan to serve this. Once you've got all the parts whipped up, it's just a matter of layering everything into six 6-ounce canning jars (or drinking glasses if you don't have jars) for an impressive dinner party dessert or holiday meal finisher.

PUMPKIN LAYER
1 15-ounce can pumpkin puree
¾ cup half-and-half
½ cup (packed) light brown sugar
2 tablespoons granulated sugar
2 large eggs
½ teaspoon ground cinnamon
½ teaspoon salt
¼ teaspoon ground allspice

⅛ teaspoon ground ginger
⅛ teaspoon ground cloves

CREAM CHEESE MOUSSE LAYER
1½ cups heavy cream
8 ounces cream cheese, softened
1 cup marshmallow crème
¼ cup granulated sugar
½ teaspoon vanilla extract

WHIPPED CREAM TOPPING
1½ cups heavy cream
3 tablespoons granulated sugar
½ teaspoon vanilla extract

GRAHAM CRACKER CRUST
1 cup graham cracker crumbs
2 tablespoons granulated sugar
¼ teaspoon ground ginger
⅓ cup unsalted butter, melted

213

SUGARED PECANS
1 tablespoon water
2 tablespoons granulated sugar
½ cup chopped pecans

YOU WILL ALSO NEED
6 6-ounce canning jars (or 6 6-ounce glasses)

1 Make the pumpkin layer by combining all of the ingredients in a microwave-safe bowl and blending everything together with a mixer on high speed for 30 seconds. Heat the mixture in your microwave for 5 minutes on high or until very hot. Stir halfway through the cooking time. Cover and chill for at least 3 hours.

2 Make the cream cheese mousse layer by whipping the cream with an electric mixer on high speed until it forms stiff peaks (about 2 minutes). In a separate bowl, whip together the cream cheese, marshmallow crème, sugar, and vanilla until smooth. Combine the cream cheese mixture with the whipped cream and beat until smooth and fluffy. Cover and chill for at least 3 hours.

3 Make the whipped cream topping by combining all of the ingredients in a medium bowl and whipping with an electric mixer on high speed until the cream forms stiff peaks. Cover and chill this too.

4 Now for the crust: first, preheat your oven to 350 degrees F. Combine the graham cracker crumbs with the sugar and ginger in a medium bowl. Stir in the melted butter until all of the crumbs are moistened by the butter. Pour the graham cracker mixture into an 8 x 8-inch baking pan and press it down flat in an even layer that coats the entire bottom of the pan. Bake the crust for 8 minutes, or just until it starts to brown around the edges, then remove it to cool. When the crust is entirely cool, it will be crispy. Break the crust into tiny pieces.

5 Make the sugared pecans by combining the water and sugar in a small saucepan (a pan that is NOT nonstick, such as stainless steel, works best). Set the pan over medium heat and,

as soon as the water begins to bubble, add the pecans. Stir constantly until all of the water has evaporated and the sugar has become a glaze. Once you begin to see a little sugar crystallize on the nuts—it should take 2 to 3 minutes—remove the pan from the heat and stir rapidly. The sugar will then crystallize onto the nuts as they cool.

6 Now you can build your desserts: Spoon about 3 tablespoons of graham cracker crumbs into the bottom of a 6-ounce jar (or 6-ounce glass). Spoon about 3 tablespoons of cream cheese mousse into the jar, followed by 3 tablespoons of pumpkin. Add another layer of crumbs, pumpkin, and cream cheese mousse and then top off the dessert with a dollop of fresh whipped cream and some sugared pecans sprinkled on top.

ROY'S BRAISED SHORT RIBS OF BEEF

First-Time Hack

Active Prep: 30 min.
Inactive Prep:
4 hrs. 30 min.

Difficulty: Medium

Yield: 4 servings

There are recipes from various sources that claim to duplicate this delicious dish at the Hawaiian-themed restaurant chain, but not one of those formulas makes anything close to the braised short ribs of beef that is a signature item at Roy's. The closest recipe I found appears to be from Chef Roy Yamaguchi himself and it gave me valuable information about the braising liquid, but was otherwise different from the recipe used in the restaurant. Adapting parts of that recipe along with information gathered from restaurant employee interviews, I have created a new recipe that produces a finished entrée guaranteed to satisfy any fan of the original dish. Get the largest short ribs you can find without much fat on them and plan to make this recipe in advance since the short ribs will need to braise for 4 hours to reach the perfect tender texture of the original version.

2 tablespoons vegetable oil
4 12-ounce large beef short ribs (or 8 smaller 6-ounce short ribs)
1 teaspoon salt, plus more to season the ribs
½ teaspoon ground black pepper, plus more to season the ribs
1 small onion or ½ large onion, chopped (1½ cups)
1 large carrot, chopped (1 cup)
2 stalks celery, chopped (1 cup)
2 stalks lemongrass, bruised and chopped
5 garlic cloves, crushed and chopped
2 tablespoons peeled and diced ginger
3 cups beef stock
3 cups vegetable stock
2 teaspoons Kikkoman Teriyaki Marinade & Sauce

HONEY MUSTARD
2 tablespoons Dijon mustard
2 tablespoons whole grain mustard
2 tablespoons honey

GARNISH (OPTIONAL)
Mixture of diced tomato, onion, **and** chives

① Preheat the oven to 375 degrees F.

② Heat the oil in a roasting pan, large pot, or other large oven-safe pan (with a lid) over medium heat. Cut any excess fat off of the short ribs. Salt and pepper the short ribs and sear all sides of each short rib until browned in the pan, about 2 minutes per side. Remove the browned short ribs from the pan to a plate.

③ Add the onion, carrot, celery, lemongrass, garlic, ginger, salt, and pepper to the pan and cook for 3 to 4 minutes or until it's starting to brown. Turn off the heat and return the short ribs to the pan, then add the stocks. Add just enough water, if necessary, to bring the liquid to the top of the short ribs. Cover the pan and place it in the preheated oven for 1 hour, then reduce the heat to 300 degrees F and cook for 3 more hours. After 1 hour (2 hours total braising time), remove the short ribs from the stock and slice the bone away from the meat. Return the meat and the bones to the stock and cook for another 2 hours or until the meat is tender and flaky. Total braising time will be 4 hours.

④ Remove the short ribs from the pan and place them in a pan covered with aluminum foil. Strain the liquid through a mesh strainer to remove all of the cooked vegetables and bones. Measure 4 cups of the braising liquid and set it aside. Pour some of the remaining liquid into the pan (around ½ inch deep) with the short ribs, cover, and place them in your oven set to 225 degrees F to stay warm.

⑤ Add the 4 cups of strained braising liquid to a large saucepan and bring it to a boil over medium heat until it has reduced to ¾ cup, or around a fifth of its volume, and is thick and velvety. This will take around 30 minutes. When the sauce is done reducing, turn off the heat and stir in the teriyaki marinade.

6 Combine all of the ingredients for the honey mustard in a small bowl.

7 When you are ready to prepare the short ribs for serving, preheat your barbecue grill to high heat. You can also cook the short ribs using an indoor grill pan on your stovetop over medium heat.

8 Brush all sides of the short ribs with a generous coating of honey mustard. Grill the short ribs for 2 to 3 minutes per side or until nice grill marks are showing. Serve the short ribs with some of the braising liquid spooned over the top of each portion, and top with a garnish of minced tomato, onion, and chives, if desired.

ROY'S
MISOYAKI
"BUTTERFISH"

 First-Time Hack

 Active Prep: 30 min.
Inactive Prep: 9 hrs.

 Difficulty: Medium

Yield: 4 servings

I have seen a couple of recipes for this dish that come from either a chef at the restaurant or Roy's founder Roy Yamaguchi (who attributes the inspiration for the marinade recipe to Nobu Matsuhisa of the Nobu restaurant chain), and there is another version in Roy's seafood cookbook, but they are all different. After trying each one, I took elements that work from several of the recipes to create one master recipe that comes closer to the original dish than any single recipe has thus far. The quotes around the word "butterfish" are used in the menu because the fish isn't a true butterfish. It is actually Alaskan black cod, but when properly cooked it has a tender, flaky texture that is as soft as butter. If you can't find black cod, sea bass makes a great substitute. The recipe here makes much more tamari vinaigrette than you will need for the recipe, so you'll have plenty left over to garnish other dishes. It's easiest to make the vinaigrette if you have a food processor. Begin this recipe early in the day for a dinner meal, since the fish needs 8 to 12 hours to marinate.

MISOYAKI MARINADE
1 cup white miso
1 cup granulated sugar
½ cup sake
½ cup mirin

4 5- to 6-ounce Alaskan black cod fillets (or other oily fish such as sea bass)

TAMARI VINAIGRETTE
4 ounces (1 cup) diced white onion
4 ounces (¾ cup) diced daikon radish
2 ounces red bell pepper (½ cup, about ½ pepper), finely minced
2 ounces yellow bell pepper (½ cup, about ½ pepper), finely minced
4 cloves garlic, halved
1 teaspoon minced ginger
½ cup vegetable oil
¼ cup green onions (about 6 onions, green part only), finely minced
2 tablespoons finely minced cilantro
¾ cup plus 2 tablespoons (packed) dark brown sugar
⅔ cup tamari sauce
6 tablespoons rice wine vinegar
1 tablespoon lemon juice

❶ Combine all of the misoyaki marinade ingredients in a medium saucepan over medium heat. Heat until bubbling, then reduce the heat and simmer for 40 to 50 minutes or until the mixture is thick and a dark caramel color. Turn off the heat and cool, then pour the marinade over the fish fillets and chill for 8 to 12 hours.

② When the fish is just about done marinating, make the tamari vinaigrette by combining the onion, daikon radish, bell peppers, garlic, and ginger in a food processor. Pulse on high speed until the vegetables have been cut into bits about the size of rice. If you don't have a food processor, you can also finely mince the vegetables by hand. Pour the minced vegetables into a medium bowl. Heat the oil in a small saucepan over medium heat until the oil begins to smoke. Pour the hot oil into the mixing bowl with the vegetables and stir, then add the green onions and cilantro. Add the brown sugar, tamari,

vinegar, and lemon juice and stir well, then cover and set aside until needed.

③ To make the fish, preheat a heavy sauté pan over medium heat for a couple of minutes. Place the fish in the pan and cook for 2 to 4 minutes per side or until the fish is done and the surface is slightly blackened but not burned. If the pan is heavily smoking, your heat is too high.

④ Serve the fish with a little tamari vinaigrette spooned over the top, with rice and steamed baby bok choy on the side (as in the restaurant) or whatever sides you prefer.

ROY'S MELTING HOT CHOCOLATE SOUFFLÉ

👍 Improved Hack

🕐 Active Prep: 15 min.
Inactive Prep:
2 hrs. 20 min.

E 🌡 Difficulty: Easy

👥 Yield: 4 servings

I was able to find out exactly how Roy's chefs prepare their signature dessert when I ordered some food to go and told my server that I wanted the dessert to be as fresh as possible. With my food order he brought me an uncooked soufflé in a parchment paper–lined ring mold and gave me

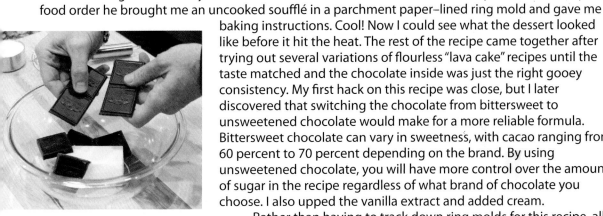

baking instructions. Cool! Now I could see what the dessert looked like before it hit the heat. The rest of the recipe came together after trying out several variations of flourless "lava cake" recipes until the taste matched and the chocolate inside was just the right gooey consistency. My first hack on this recipe was close, but I later discovered that switching the chocolate from bittersweet to unsweetened chocolate would make for a more reliable formula. Bittersweet chocolate can vary in sweetness, with cacao ranging from 60 percent to 70 percent depending on the brand. By using unsweetened chocolate, you will have more control over the amount of sugar in the recipe regardless of what brand of chocolate you choose. I also upped the vanilla extract and added cream.

Rather than having to track down ring molds for this recipe, all you have to do is start saving cans. You'll need four that have about a 2½-inch diameter. I found that 4-ounce cans of diced peppers work great.

4 ounces **unsweetened chocolate (100 percent cacao)**
½ cup (1 stick) unsalted butter
¾ cup plus 3 tablespoons granulated sugar
¼ cup heavy cream
2 large eggs
½ teaspoon vanilla extract
Pinch of salt

GARNISH
Raspberry sauce
Powdered sugar

ON THE SIDE
4 scoops of vanilla ice cream

❶ Melt the chocolate and butter together in a medium glass or ceramic microwave-safe bowl in your microwave on high for 1 minute. Stir. If the chocolate has not completely melted, zap it again for another 30 seconds and stir until smooth.

❷ Add the sugar and mix with an electric mixer on high speed for 1 minute. Add the cream, eggs, vanilla, and a pinch of salt and mix for another minute.

3 Open the top and bottom of four 4-ounce cans (such as the kind that hold diced peppers), remove the labels, and clean out the cans. Line the inside of each can with parchment paper. Make sure the paper is pushed all the way down to the bottom of the can so that the soufflé will slip out easily when cooked. Position each lined can on an additional piece of parchment paper on a baking sheet.

4 Fill each can with an equal amount of cake batter, cover all of them with plastic wrap, and chill for at least 2 hours.

5 When you are ready to bake the desserts, preheat your oven to 400 degrees F.

6 Bake for 20 minutes or until the dessert is starting to crack on top, then cool for 2 minutes.

7 Place each molded soufflé on the center of a serving plate. Carefully remove the can and peel away the parchment paper. Drizzle raspberry sauce onto the plate and dust the soufflé with a little powdered sugar. Add a scoop of vanilla ice cream to each plate and serve.

222

RUBIO'S
MILD SALSA

 First-Time Hack

 Active Prep: 10 min.
Inactive Prep: 2 hrs.

E Difficulty: Easy

Yield: 1⅔ cups

It was the delicious fish tacos he ate on a spring break trip with his buddies in San Felipe, Mexico, that became Ralph Rubio's inspiration for the first taco store he opened in San Diego in 1983. That one restaurant has now grown to nearly 200 throughout the West and Southwest serving a variety of seafood, chicken, and steak burritos, tacos, and salad bowls. The mild salsa is one of many choices in the restaurant's salsa bar, but it is also used in the kitchen on several tacos, including the Original Fish Taco (page 229). This recipe is mild but can be easily kicked up several notches by adding another jalapeño or a habanero pepper into the mix. You'll need a food processor or good blender to puree the ingredients to the same consistency as in the restaurant, then give it time to chill in the refrigerator for great flavor.

1 14½-ounce can diced tomatoes
¼ cup seeded and diced jalapeño
(1 medium pepper)

¼ cup diced white onion
1 tablespoon lime juice
½ teaspoon salt
2 tablespoons minced cilantro

1 Combine everything except the cilantro in a food processor or blender and pulse until the jalapeño and onion are chopped into fine bits.

2 Pour the salsa into a bowl and mix in the cilantro. Cover and chill for at least a couple of hours before using.

RUBIO'S
RED TOMATILLO
SALSA

 First-Time Hack

Active Prep: 15 min.
Inactive Prep:
2 hrs. 30 min.

M Difficulty: Medium

Yield: 1¼ cups

One of my favorite salsas from Rubio's is the Red Tomatillo Salsa, but you won't find it at the salsa bar because it only comes on select tacos such as the Grilled Gourmet Taco with Shrimp (cloned on page 226). The salsa is made with hard-to-find red tomatillos, which taste very similar to green tomatillos, so that's what we'll use in this recipe. You'll need a food processor or a good blender here to get the right consistency. There is a little habanero in the recipe for heat since the flavorful guajillo chilies are not very hot. You will need to use only one-quarter of a habanero to get the level of spiciness similar to the restaurant version, but if you're a chilihead like I am, you may want to add in more. Give the salsa a couple of hours to chill, and it'll be ready to pour over anything that needs a boost of spicy flavor.

1 pound **tomatillos**
1 ounce (3 to 4) **dried guajillo chilies,
    stems removed**
⅓ **cup diced white onion**
2 cloves **garlic**
¼ of a fresh **habanero pepper, seeded**
2 teaspoons **lime juice**
½ teaspoon **salt**
½ teaspoon **granulated sugar**
½ cup **water**
2 tablespoons **finely minced cilantro**

1 Preheat the broiler to high.

2 Remove the papery skins from the tomatillos and rinse them off, then place them on an aluminum foil–lined baking sheet and put them under the broiler on a rack that is about 4 inches from the heat. Broil for 5 to 7 minutes or until blackened on top, then flip them over and cook for another 5 to 7 minutes or until

nicely blackened. Remove the tomatillos from the oven and use tongs to put them in a bowl until you need them.

❸ Toast the chilies in a skillet over medium heat for 2 to 3 minutes per side or until some charring is visible. Place the peppers in a bowl, cover the peppers with hot water, and let them sit for 30 minutes so that they can rehydrate. Place another bowl on top of them to keep the peppers submerged.

❹ After 30 minutes, remove the peppers from the water and let the water drip off them. Give the peppers a coarse chop, then add them to a food processor along with the tomatillos, onion, garlic, habanero, lime juice, salt, sugar, and water. Process on high speed for 1 minute or until there are just small bits of chili visible.

❺ Pour the salsa into a bowl and stir in the cilantro. Cover and chill for at least a couple of hours before using.

RUBIO'S GRILLED GOURMET TACO WITH SHRIMP

First-Time Hack

Active Prep: 45 min.
Inactive Prep: 1 hr.

Difficulty: Medium

Yield: 8 tacos

There may be a slight wait for your food at Rubio's since everything is made fresh right there when you order it, including the shrimp for this taco that is grilled on a plancha, a Spanish flattop grill. That's great for me since it allowed me to peek into the kitchen to see exactly how they make these Grilled Gourmet Tacos. The secret is in toasting a cheese blend onto the tortilla before filling it. That's done by placing a pile of cheese on the griddle with the tortilla on top of it. When the cheese has browned, in about a minute, a spatula is inserted under the cheese and the tortilla is lifted and flipped, then it's loaded with the fillings. You don't need a plancha for the shrimp—any flattop griddle or preheated skillet will work just fine. This new hack will also show you how to duplicate Rubio's great chipotle cream sauce and shrimp marinade. Use my recipe for the Red Tomatillo Salsa on page 224 to finish off this copy of the best shrimp tacos at any chain restaurant.

SHRIMP

2 teaspoons ground black pepper
2 teaspoons garlic powder
2 teaspoons ground ancho chili pepper
1 teaspoon paprika
½ teaspoon salt
1 tablespoon lime juice
½ cup vegetable oil
¼ cup minced cilantro
½ cup water
32 small (51/60) raw shrimp, shelled and deveined

CHIPOTLE CREAM SAUCE

¼ cup mayonnaise
¼ cup sour cream
2 teaspoons pureed canned chipotle with adobo sauce **(see Tidbits)**

ONION/CILANTRO BLEND

¾ cup diced onion
3 tablespoons minced cilantro

CHEESE BLEND
4 ounces (1⅓ cups) shredded white cheddar cheese
1 ounce (⅓ cup) shredded Monterey Jack cheese
1 ounce (⅓ cup) shredded Mozzarella cheese

8 corn tortillas
½ cup Rubio's Red Tomatillo Salsa **(page 224)**
½ cup crumbled cooked bacon **(from 4 to 6 pieces of bacon)**
16 to 24 avocado slices **(from 1 large or 2 small avocados, respectively)**

❶ Make the shrimp marinade by combining the black pepper, garlic powder, ancho chili powder, paprika, and salt in a medium bowl. Stir in the lime juice and oil, making a paste. Stir in the cilantro and water, then add the shrimp. Marinate for 1 hour.

❷ While the shrimp is marinating, make the chipotle cream sauce by combining all of the ingredients in a small bowl. Make the onion/cilantro blend by combining all of the ingredients in a small bowl. And make the cheese blend by combining all of the shredded cheeses in a medium bowl.

❸ When the shrimp is done marinating and you are ready to make your tacos, preheat a heavy skillet (a cast-iron skillet works great if you've got one) over medium heat. Remove the shrimp from the marinade, add it to the pan, and cook for 2 minutes per side or until done.

❹ While the shrimp is cooking, prepare each tortilla in a nonstick skillet that has been preheating over medium heat. Sprinkle about ¼ cup of the cheese blend into the hot pan in a circle that is slightly smaller than the diameter of the tortilla. Place a tortilla on top of the cheese. After a minute or so, when the cheese has browned slightly, use a spatula under the cheese to remove the tortilla. Build each

taco by arranging 4 shrimp on the toasted cheese, followed by about 2 teaspoons of chipotle cream sauce and 2 teaspoons of the red tomatillo salsa. Sprinkle a heaping tablespoon of the onion/cilantro blend on next, followed by a tablespoon of crumbled bacon. Top off each taco with 2 to 3 avocado slices and serve immediately.

TIDBITS Puree the can of chipotle chilies and adobo sauce by dumping the entire contents of the can into a blender with ⅓ cup water and blend until the chilies are pureed. The sauce should be smooth with no pepper chunks remaining.

RUBIO'S ORIGINAL FISH TACO

🏅 First-Time Hack

⏱ Prep Time: 30 min.

M🌡 Difficulty: Medium

👥 Yield: 8 tacos

The hand-battered fish tacos are what started this Mexican food chain on its road to success back in the early '80s, so this dish has been high on my food-hacking to-do list. For this taco, wild Alaskan pollock is coated in a seasoned beer batter and fried until golden brown and perfectly crispy, then loaded into a corn tortilla with Rubio's white sauce, mild salsa, and cabbage. You can often find frozen pollock fillets at your supermarket, but you can also substitute with cod here. You won't need much—eight 2-ounce portions will do. The fish most likely will be available in 4-ounce fillets that you can slice in half. Use the Mild Salsa recipe on page 223 to top off your tacos.

6 to 8 cups vegetable oil

WHITE SAUCE
¼ **cup mayonnaise**
¼ **cup sour cream**

BEER BATTER
1 **cup all-purpose flour**
1¾ **teaspoons salt**
½ **teaspoon baking soda**
½ **teaspoon ground black pepper**
½ **teaspoon dried oregano**

¼ **teaspoon dried thyme**
¼ **teaspoon garlic powder**
1 **large egg, beaten**
10 **ounces (1¼ cups) Mexican lager beer**
   (such as Dos Equis or Tecate)

2½ **ounces (½ cup) all-purpose flour**
4 **4-ounce pollock fillets (or cod fillets),**
   sliced in half
8 **corn tortillas**
Vegetable oil
½ **cup Rubio's Mild Salsa (page 223)**
4 **cups finely shredded cabbage**

❶ Preheat the oil in a large saucepan with a thermometer attached to 350 degrees F.

❷ Combine all of the ingredients for the white sauce in a small bowl. Set aside until needed.

❸ Make the beer batter by combining the flour with the salt, baking soda, pepper, oregano, thyme, and garlic powder in a large bowl. Mix the egg and beer into the dry ingredients. Stir rapidly

with a whisk to break up any lumps. Pour the additional ½ cup of flour onto a plate or into a shallow bowl.

4 When the oil is hot, lightly coat each piece of fish with the flour, then dip it into the beer batter and immediately drop it into the oil. Turn the fish as it fries so that both sides are crispy and golden brown, about 4 minutes. Let the excess oil drain off the fish on a rack or paper towel–lined plate.

5 Assemble each taco by rubbing a corn tortilla with a little oil and warming it up in a skillet that is preheated over medium/low heat. Place the fried fish fillet in the center, then spoon over about 2 teaspoons of white sauce followed by 2 teaspoons of mild salsa. Top with about ½ cup shredded cabbage and serve.

TIDBITS If you prefer, you can replace the lager beer with a nonalcoholic beer and the recipe still works.

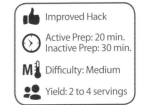

RUTH'S CHRIS STEAK HOUSE BARBECUED SHRIMP

Improved Hack

Active Prep: 20 min.
Inactive Prep: 30 min.

Difficulty: Medium

Yield: 2 to 4 servings

It's quite possible that I had come upon some information when writing the first version of this recipe that led me to believe the Barbecued Shrimp appetizer at this upscale 135-unit steakhouse chain was made under a broiler, and so that's the technique that I published. However, when I recently viewed an online demonstration video from the restaurant's kitchen, it became clear that today this dish is made entirely in a sauté pan. The cooking technique is explained thoroughly in the video, including the addition of the chain's top secret "barbecue butter," but exact measurements of the ingredients in this important component (which I did not include in my first recipe) are kept entirely under wraps. So, I did my thing and obtained an unused sample of the barbecue butter from the restaurant, which I then took home to analyze and hack. Now, I'm happy to share with you this much improved version of Ruth's Chris's popular appetizer that makes a serving twice the size as what you get in the restaurant.

BARBECUE BUTTER
¼ cup (½ stick) unsalted butter
1 teaspoon minced garlic
⅛ teaspoon crushed rosemary
½ teaspoon lemon juice
¼ teaspoon paprika
¼ teaspoon Tabasco pepper sauce
¼ teaspoon salt
¼ teaspoon ground black pepper
⅛ teaspoon Worcestershire sauce

Baguette or French bread
1 tablespoon canola oil
10 extra jumbo (16/20) peeled raw shrimp, **with tails left on**
2 tablespoons bias-sliced green onion (green part only)
¼ cup dry white wine
¼ cup heavy cream

GARNISH
Bias-sliced green onion (green part only)
Finely minced fresh parsley

❶ Make the barbecue butter by melting the butter over medium heat. Add the garlic and rosemary and cook for 1 minute, then turn off the heat and add the remaining ingredients. Pour the butter mixture into a small bowl and place it in your refrigerator for 30 minutes, or until the butter firms up. Mix the barbecue butter with an electric mixer on high speed until it's creamy, then continue to let it chill in the refrigerator until it's called up to service later.

2 Prepare the toast points by slicing baguette. Slice the bread flat on one end and at an angle at the other end. Butter both ends and toast the bread in a pan, angled side-down, in a 400 degree F oven for 6 to 8 minutes or until it's brown.

3 Heat up the oil in a medium sauté pan over medium heat. Add the shrimp and cook on one side for 1 to 2 minutes or until the shrimp begins to slightly brown on the surface.

4 Turn over each shrimp, then add the green onion and cook for another minute. Add the wine and cook for another 1 to 2 minutes or until the liquid reduces by half.

5 Add the cream and cook for another 1 to 2 minutes or until the cream reduces by half. Remove the pan from the heat.

6 Spoon the cold barbecue butter into the pan of sauce. Stir gently until it is melted into the sauce.

7 Prepare the dish by placing the browned toast points on their flat ends at one end of a warm serving dish or plate. Arrange the shrimp in the dish, then spoon the remaining sauce in the pan over the shrimp. Garnish by sprinkling the shrimp with a little sliced green onion and a couple of pinches of minced fresh parsley.

RUTH'S CHRIS STEAK HOUSE RUTH'S CHOP SALAD

 First-Time Hack

 Prep Time: 30 min.

M Difficulty: Medium

Yield: 4 salads

A dozen ingredients tossed in a refreshing lemon-basil dressing is what makes Ruth's Chris's signature salad taste so great, but the presentation of this dish is what brings out the "Wows." Now you can make a tower of salad just like the one at this fancy steakhouse chain after you track down some 3-inch PVC pipe at your local home improvement store. Saw a 4-inch length off the pipe and use sandpaper to smooth the edges, then find a glass or bottle with a flat bottom to use as a press. Once you prepare the dressing and crispy onions, and chop and toss the other ingredients, you can use this inexpensive mold to create your hacked salad masterpiece.

LEMON-BASIL DRESSING
½ cup **mayonnaise**
2½ tablespoons **lemon juice**
1 tablespoon **buttermilk**
1 tablespoon chopped **fresh basil**
1 teaspoon minced **garlic**
1 teaspoon **Dijon mustard**
⅛ teaspoon **salt**
Pinch of ground black pepper

CRISPY ONIONS
4 cups **canola oil**
1 **white onion, thinly sliced**
⅓ cup **all-purpose flour**

4 ounces (4 cups) chopped **iceberg lettuce**
1 ounce (1 cup) chopped **radicchio**
½ ounce (¼ cup) julienned **spinach**
2 ounces (1 cup) sliced **red onion**
1½ ounces (1 cup) sliced **white mushrooms**
1 ounce (¾ cup) small **croutons (classic cut)**
2 ounces (½ cup) sliced **hearts of palm**
2 ounces (½ cup) chopped **hard-cooked egg**
2 ounces (½ cup) **bleu cheese crumbles**
1½ ounces (⅓ cup) diced **cooked bacon
(from 4 to 5 slices)**
1 ounce (¼ cup) chopped **canned green olives
with pimientos**

GARNISH
6 **grape tomatoes**

❶ Make the mold for your salads by cutting a 4-inch-long section off of 3-inch-diameter PVC pipe. Sand the ends of the pipe to smooth it and then give it a good wash.

❷ Make the dressing by combining all of the ingredients in a small bowl. Cover and chill until needed. The dressing is best when it rests for several hours, or even overnight.

❸ Heat the oil in a saucepan over medium heat to 350 degrees F. Make the crispy onions by tossing the sliced onion with the flour

233

in a medium bowl. When the oil is hot, cook a handful of breaded onion slices at a time in the oil and fry until golden brown, 2 to 3 minutes on one side, then flip them and fry for 1 to 2 more minutes. Set the crispy onions aside when done, but do not cover them.

4 About 30 minutes before you plan to serve the salad, place the serving plates in your freezer.

5 When you are ready to assemble the salad, toss all of the salad ingredients (but not the crispy onions) in a large bowl, then pour on the dressing and toss gently with tongs.

6 Prepare each serving by dropping one-quarter of the salad into the PVC pipe mold on a cold serving plate. Press down semi-firmly on the salad with the bottom of a round glass or bottle that fits into the pipe mold. Do not press too hard or you will squeeze the dressing out of the salad, and that's not cool.

7 Place one-quarter of the crispy onions on the salad and use the glass again to press down onto the salad gently as you lift up the pipe mold.

8 Slice the grape tomatoes in half lengthwise and arrange three in a row on each plate before serving.

RUTH'S CHRIS STEAK HOUSE SWEET POTATO CASSEROLE

First-Time Hack

Active Prep: 20 min.
Inactive Prep: 2 hrs.

E Difficulty: Easy

Yield: 2 to 4 servings

A waitress at the restaurant told me that some customers will order this for dessert, along with a side of ice cream. You'll know why the moment you taste the sweet, caramel-like flavor topped with the perfect nutty crumble. Best of all, the prep is easy. Whether you whip this one up for the holidays or for just any 'ol day, I think you'll find that this is the best sweet potato casserole in the biz.

1 pound sweet potatoes (2 small or 1 large)
6 tablespoons granulated sugar
1 large egg
1 egg white
⅓ cup unsalted butter, **melted**
1¼ teaspoons vanilla extract
¼ teaspoon plus ⅛ teaspoon salt
⅓ cup heavy cream

TOPPING
⅓ cup (packed) light brown sugar
¼ cup all-purpose flour
⅓ cup finely chopped pecans
Pinch of salt
2½ tablespoons unsalted butter, **melted**

❶ Steam the sweet potatoes in a steamer basket over hot water in a covered saucepan for 1 hour or until the potatoes are tender. Slice the large potato in half if necessary to fit it into the pan.

❷ Preheat the oven to 350 degrees F.

❸ When the potatoes are cool enough to handle, remove the skin and mash them in a medium bowl.

❹ Combine the mashed sweet potatoes with the sugar, egg, egg white, butter, vanilla, and salt in a blender, then puree until smooth. When the mixture is smooth, add the cream and blend just until the cream is mixed in. Don't blend long once the cream is added or it may separate from the other ingredients.

5 Pour the sweet potato mixture into a medium casserole dish and bake for 50 minutes to 1 hour or until the top of the casserole begins to brown.

6 While the casserole cooks, prepare the topping by combining the brown sugar with the flour in a medium bowl. Add the pecans and salt and mix well with a spoon.

7 Drizzle the melted butter into the bowl

and mix it in with a spoon until the mixture forms crumbs.

8 When the casserole comes out of the oven, raise the heat to 425 degrees F.

9 Spread the pecan crumble over the top of the sweet potato casserole. Return the casserole to the oven and bake it for 8 minutes or just until the top begins to brown.

RUTH'S CHRIS STEAK HOUSE FILET

👍 Improved Hack

🕐 Active Prep: 15 min.
Inactive Prep: 15 min.

E 🌡 Difficulty: Easy

👥 Yield: 1 serving

Ruth's Chris Steak House has many great dishes, but as with any good steakhouse, the main attraction is the fabulous steaks. The chain claims the secret to producing juicy, flavorful steaks is the custom 1,800 degree F broiler designed by founder Ruth Fertel. According to restaurant chefs, the extremely high heat sears the outside of the steaks while locking in the flavorful juices. But, as I discovered back in 1997 when I created the first version of this recipe, you can get pretty much the same results with a home oven set to high broil. However, after recently unearthing some new information, I have now made some important changes to my original recipe to give you an even better restaurant clone of the chain's signature beef tenderloin filet.

First, you must trim the filet of fat so that your meat doesn't spatter under the high heat and smoke up your oven. Also, you should season the steak with sea salt for the best flavor. I found that Morton's sea salt is the perfect flake size for this. Pop a thick oven-safe ceramic plate into the oven on the bottom rack just before cooking your steak and you will have a 500 degree F serving plate that sizzles as in the restaurant. Try this easy technique the next time you're cooking up filets (you can cook as many steaks as you like at one time) and bring the upscale steakhouse experience into your own home dining room.

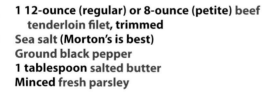

> 1 12-ounce (regular) or 8-ounce (petite) beef
>   tenderloin filet, trimmed
> Sea salt (Morton's is best)
> Ground black pepper
> 1 tablespoon salted butter
> Minced fresh parsley

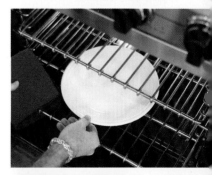

1 Preheat the oven to high broil for 15 minutes. This should put your oven temperature at somewhere between 550 and 600 degrees F. Set one rack at the bottom of your oven (for the plate), and another rack one notch above the first rack (for the filet). You want the filet to be 7 to 8 inches away from the intense heat of the broiler.

2 Trim the fat from the sides of the filet, then sprinkle sea salt over the top, bottom, and sides of the filet. Do the same with the pepper.

3 Place an oven-safe ceramic serving plate on the bottom rack of the oven to get it hot.

4 Place the steak on a rack over a foil-lined pan and place it under the broiler on the top rack. Cook the steak to your desired doneness according to this chart (flip the steak once):

Rare—4 to 6 minutes per side
Medium Rare—5 to 7 minutes per side
Medium—6 to 8 minutes per side
Medium Well—7 to 9 minutes per side
Well—8 to 10 minutes per side

5 When the meat is done, use a potholder to carefully remove the hot plate from the oven. Place the filet in the center of the hot plate.

6 Add 1 tablespoon of butter to the plate around the filet.

7 Sprinkle parsley over the top of the filet and around the plate on the sizzling butter. Serve immediately and be careful with that hot plate!

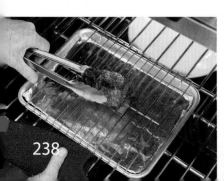

SABRA CLASSIC HUMMUS

👍 Improved Hack

🕐 Prep Time: 15 min.

E 🌡 Difficulty: Easy

👥 Yield: 1¾ cups

When I first hacked Sabra Hummus I thoroughly pureed the ingredients in a food processor for ten minutes to get a smooth consistency that closely matched the creaminess of the real thing. Recently, though, I've been using a technique for even smoother hummus in less time, and it's an easy tweak: just soften the garbanzo beans with heat before processing. When the beans are softer to begin with, your finished hummus will be as smooth as silk. Incorporating this technique into the recipe and making a few other adjustments to the ingredients, including the addition of a little sugar and cayenne pepper, will now give you an even better knockoff of the best hummus around.

1 16-ounce can **garbanzo beans (chickpeas)**, strained
½ **cup liquid from garbanzo beans**
½ **cup water**
¼ **cup sesame tahini (sesame seed paste)**

3 tablespoons **canola oil**
2¼ teaspoons **lemon juice**
1 teaspoon minced **garlic**
¾ teaspoon **granulated sugar**
½ teaspoon **salt**
¼ teaspoon plus ⅛ teaspoon **citric acid (sour salt)**
¼ teaspoon **white pepper**
Pinch of **ground cayenne pepper**

1 Pour the canned garbanzo beans into a strainer over a bowl to catch the liquid.

2 Combine the strained garbanzo beans, ½ cup of the liquid (toss out the rest), and the water in a small saucepan over medium/high heat and bring to a boil. Reduce the heat and simmer for 5 minutes. Remove the beans from the heat, cover the pan, and let them sit for 10 minutes.

3 Pour the hot garbanzo beans and all the liquid in the pan into a food processor and add the remaining ingredients. Process for 3 minutes on high speed until smooth. Store the hummus in a covered container in your refrigerator until chilled.

ST. ELMO
STEAK HOUSE
WORLD FAMOUS
SHRIMP COCKTAIL

 First-Time Hack

 Active Prep: 20 min.
Inactive Prep: 2 hrs.

 Difficulty: Easy

 Yield: 2 servings

When I was recently in Indianapolis for some live cooking demos I discovered the best shrimp cocktail I've ever tasted across the street from my hotel at St. Elmo Steak House, a 113-year-old institution in the heart of the city. The jumbo shrimp were tender and succulent, and the cocktail sauce was mind-blowing. Man, it was some powerful stuff! I knew right then I had a new hacking assignment on my hands, so I ordered some sauce to go and starting asking questions. I was told the secret is freshly grated horseradish in the sauce, which makes for a tastier and more nasal cavity–clearing sauce than typical cocktail sauces made with bottled horseradish.

When shopping for horseradish I discovered that the most flavorful horseradish roots are firm to the touch and not at all spongy, so give them the squeeze test before you buy. Once you peel, grate, and mince the horseradish, mix it with vinegar and a little salt to keep it from turning brown and to give it the right flavor. The dish isn't a complete success unless the shrimp are perfectly poached so that they are tender and not rubbery. I've got that technique for you here as well. Follow this recipe as described and you will have a great home kitchen copy of the famous restaurant appetizer that is sure to leave your diners breathing clearly and begging for more.

6 cups water
1 tablespoon salt
10 jumbo raw shrimp (21/25 per pound, with or without shells)

SAUCE
1 small, firm horseradish root
2 tablespoons white vinegar
Pinch of salt
½ cup ketchup
¼ cup water

GARNISH
2 lemon wedges

❶ Bring 6 cups of water to a boil in a 2- or 3-quart saucepan over high heat. Stir in the salt, turn off the heat, and set a timer to 3 minutes.

❷ After 3 minutes the water should be in the 160 to 180 degrees F range, which is the perfect heat for poaching the shrimp. Drop in the shrimp and set the timer for 2 minutes.

3 After 2 minutes remove the shrimp from the water and immediately plunge them into ice water for 1 minute to halt the cooking process. Remove any shells from the shrimp, dry the shrimp, and place them in a covered container in your refrigerator to chill for about 2 hours.

4 For the sauce, peel the brown skin from a firm horseradish root using a vegetable peeler. Grate the horseradish on a grater with holes that are about ¼-inch diameter, then mince it. Combine ½ cup of the horseradish with the vinegar and salt and let it sit covered in your refrigerator for at least 1 hour. Add the remaining sauce ingredients, stir well, then

cover and chill the sauce until your shrimp are cold and you are ready to prepare the dish.

5 To make each serving, place 5 shrimp in a dish or martini glass. Spoon a generous portion of sauce over the top of each serving and serve the shrimp cocktail with a wedge of lemon on the side.

TIDBITS You can keep any leftover horseradish for several weeks by mixing it with vinegar as described in the recipe: Mix every ½ cup of grated horseradish with 2 tablespoons of distilled white vinegar and a pinch of salt and you will have horseradish that's better than anything you'll buy in a bottle.

241

STARBUCKS BIRTHDAY CAKE POPS

🎖 First-Time Hack

⏱ Active Prep: 1 hr.
Inactive Prep: 2 hrs. 30 min.

H🌡 Difficulty: Hard

👥 Yield: 36 cake pops

No forks needed to eat this clone of Starbucks's portable pastry creation on a stick. The trend of cake pops on blogs and at specialty bake shops caught the attention of the world's largest coffee house chain. Starbucks research and development chefs figured out how to produce three different flavors: Rocky Road, Tiramisu, and Birthday Cake (to celebrate Starbucks's fortieth anniversary). The pops are each made by hand for the chain, just as you are now able to do with this recipe to create your own home copy of the most popular flavor. Find lollipop sticks, Styrofoam blocks, candy melts, and nonpareils at a craft store (such as Michaels) that carries cake decorating supplies.

1 18¼-ounce box **white cake mix (such as Betty Crocker
     or Duncan Hines)**
1¼ cups **water**
⅓ cup **vegetable oil**
3 large **eggs**
1 cup plus 2 tablespoons **vanilla frosting (from a
     16-ounce tub)**
2 14-ounce packages **pink Wilton Candy Melts**
White nonpareils (small balls)

YOU WILL ALSO NEED
36 4-inch paper lollipop sticks
3 12 x 4-inch Styrofoam blocks

1 Make the cake in a 9 x 13-inch baking pan following the directions on the box using the water, oil, and eggs. Cool completely.

2 When the cake is cool, gently crumble it into a large bowl using your hands. Make sure there are no large chunks of cake. Spoon dollops of the frosting into the cake and mix it up using a large spoon just until the frosting is mixed in.

3 Roll the cake into 1½-inch balls between the palms of your hands and arrange them on a baking sheet lined with wax paper. Freeze for at least 2 hours.

4 While your cake pops are chilling, use a lollipop stick to make 12 holes, about 2 inches apart, halfway down into each of the Styrofoam blocks. This is to hold your pops until they set.

5 When the dough balls have chilled, pour the candy melts into a microwaveable glass or ceramic bowl. Zap them for

1 minute and then stir until smooth. If the candy melts are not completely melted, pop them back in the microwave for another 15 to 30 seconds, then gently stir.

6 Now it's time to coat your cake pops. Take a few cake balls out of the freezer at a time on a plate. Press a lollipop stick about halfway into one ball, then swirl the ball into the candy up to the stick. Carefully bring it out of the candy and gently tap your hand on the side of the bowl so that the excess drips off. While the candy is still tacky, move the cake pop over another bowl and sprinkle the top with some white nonpareils. The sprinkles that do not stick will fall into the empty bowl and you can use them again. Place the finished pops into the holes in the Styrofoam and keep them in the refrigerator for a couple of hours until ready to eat. After they are chilled, you can also store the pops in bags in your freezer for a couple of months.

STARBUCKS HOLIDAY GINGERBREAD

First-Time Hack

Active Prep: 35 min.
Inactive Prep: 1 hr. 30 min.

Difficulty: Medium

Yield: 8 slices

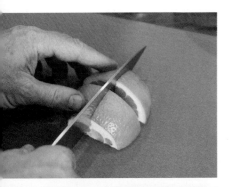

As you have probably figured out by the name, this moist spiced loaf of gingerbread is only available at Starbucks during the holiday season, but you don't have to wait until then to enjoy this popular favorite since you now have a clone recipe to re-create a spot-on version anytime you want. The secret ingredient is applesauce in the batter, which helps make the loaf moist and flavorful. Ground ginger and bits of candied ginger add the perfect ginger flavor to the loaf, and orange flavors come in from the zest, orange extract, and candied orange peel on top. With such an overwhelming aroma coming out of your oven as this bakes, the toughest step is waiting for the loaf to cool before frosting it so that you can dig into a slice.

CANDIED ORANGE PEEL
1 medium orange
½ cup water
¾ cup granulated sugar

GINGERBREAD
¾ cup (1½ sticks) unsalted butter, softened
1⅔ cups granulated sugar
3 large eggs
1¼ cups unsweetened applesauce
¼ teaspoon orange extract
2 tablespoons minced candied ginger
1½ teaspoons minced orange zest
11 ounces (2¼ cups) all-purpose flour
2 teaspoons ground ginger
¾ teaspoon salt
½ teaspoon baking soda
½ teaspoon baking powder
½ teaspoon ground cloves
¼ teaspoon ground cinnamon

CREAM CHEESE FROSTING
4 ounces cream cheese, softened
7 ounces (1¾ cups) powdered sugar
½ teaspoon vanilla extract
⅛ teaspoon orange extract

① Make the candied orange peel by slicing the top and bottom off of an orange. Sit the orange up on one of the sliced ends, then slice it in half. Use one half to make (with a zester) the 1½ teaspoons of orange zest to be added later to the batter. Chop the zest into small bits after zesting the entire orange half. Slice the other half of orange into quarters then slice the peel away from the orange segments. Try to remove most of the white pith, which is very bitter. Slice the 4 peel segments into ¼-inch-wide strips.

② Fill a small saucepan with 2 cups of cold water and drop in the orange peel strips. When the water begins to boil, set a timer for 5 minutes. When the peels have boiled for 5 minutes, strain them out of the water and repeat the process with another 2 cups of cold water. After the second blanching, pour the ½ cup of water into the saucepan along with the ¾ cup of sugar. Bring the sugar solution to a boil (the sugar will have dissolved), then reduce the heat to a simmer. Add the orange peels and cook for 20 minutes or until the white part of the peels is beginning to turn transparent. Do not stir or

the sugar may crystallize. Reduce the heat if necessary while cooking so that the solution is only gently bubbling. Remove all of the peels to a rack to dry. When the candied peels have dried, chop them into a very small dice. The peels will be sticky at first but will eventually harden on the outside.

③ Prepare the gingerbread by first preheating your oven to 350 degrees F.

④ Combine the butter, sugar, and eggs in a large bowl with an electric mixer on high speed for 1 minute. Add the applesauce, orange extract, candied ginger, and orange zest. Mix well.

⑤ Combine the flour with the ground ginger, salt, baking soda, baking powder, ground cloves, and cinnamon in a medium bowl. Pour the dry mixture into the wet mixture and mix well with the electric mixer on high speed. Transfer the batter to a 9 x 5-inch loaf pan that has been well coated with butter. Bake for 60 to 70 minutes or until the edges are dark brown and the center is firm to the touch. Cool completely before frosting.

6 Make the frosting by combining the cream cheese, powdered sugar, vanilla, and orange extract in a medium bowl with an electric mixer on high speed until smooth. Beat for 1 minute.

7 When the gingerbread has cooled completely, remove it from the pan. Frost the top of the loaf and sprinkle the top with the candied orange peel. Slice into 8 portions to serve.

STEAK 'N SHAKE CLASSIC MILK SHAKES

 First-Time Hack

 Active Prep: 5 min.
Inactive Prep: 1 hr.

E Difficulty: Easy

Yield: 1 16-ounce shake

The information that helped me the most in hacking this recipe was the calorie count. I first attempted to clone this milk shake using regular ice cream and whole milk. The resulting milk shake was an indulgent creamy delight, but seemed much richer than the version from the restaurant. I noticed ice crystals in the real thing that were not present in my version—a clue that led me to believe that there were lighter ingredients at use. Next, I calculated the total calories of my version and compared the numbers to the nutritional information located on the restaurant's website. My version with regular ice cream and whole milk resulted in a 16-ounce milk shake that tipped the scale at a diet-busting 1,345 calories. Steak 'n Shake's shakes came in at less than half that many calories. So, back to the supermarket I went to find "light" ice cream, which is made with mostly milk rather than cream. With that substitution, and replacing the whole milk with skim milk, my new shake dropped down to around 600 calories—exactly the same as the Steak 'n Shake original, and the flavor and consistency were perfect!

For this recipe to work the best, find a light ice cream, such as Breyer's Light. You can make the milk shake thick like the original by freezing the serving glass before pouring in the milk shake and then allowing the milk shake to firm up in the freezer for about an hour (if you can wait!) before diving in.

VANILLA
8 ounces (2 cups) light vanilla ice cream
½ cup skim milk
2 tablespoons Torani vanilla syrup

CHOCOLATE
8 ounces (2 cups) light vanilla ice cream
½ cup skim milk
3 tablespoons Hershey's chocolate syrup

STRAWBERRY
8 ounces (2 cups) light vanilla ice cream
½ cup skim milk
3 tablespoons Hershey's strawberry syrup

OPTIONAL
Whipped cream
Maraschino cherry

1 Place a 16-ounce glass in the freezer at least 1 hour before making the milk shake.

2 Combine the ingredients for the milk shake flavor of your choice in a blender and blend until smooth. If the ice cream is not blending in, turn off the blender and stir the mixture a bit, then blend again until smooth.

3 Pour the milk shake into the frozen glass and place it back in the freezer for about an hour to thicken. Add whipped cream and a maraschino cherry on top, if you like.

STEAK 'N SHAKE GENUINE CHILI

 First-Time Hack

 Active Prep: 30 min.
Inactive Prep: 2 hrs.

 E Difficulty: Easy

 Yield: 8 cups

Examining the list of ingredients on a can of this 500-unit midwestern chain's chili reveals a traditional chili con carne formula with beans as the only vegetable ingredient. There is no tomato sauce in the recipe, as stated by Internet copycats. Nor is there any chocolate or cola in the mix, as some recipes claim. Rinsing a portion of the chili through a wire mesh strainer reveals both small bits and large chunks of tender meat in the chili. But, what kind of meat is it? Well, considering the significant amount of fat floating on top of the chili and the tenderness of the chunks, I concluded that it's most likely an inexpensive, heavily marbled cut that braises well. Most likely chuck. Get 8 ounces ground up, and another 8 ounces that you slice into bite-size chunks. The flour and the cornstarch are added to the recipe to simulate modified food starch, and the dry beef bouillon punches up the flavor along with all the spices. After a two-hour simmer, serve this chili in a bowl on its own, or with shredded cheese and onion on top, or on top of spaghetti noodles in traditional midwestern style.

8 ounces **chopped chuck**
8 ounces **ground chuck**
1¾ ounces (⅓ cup) **all-purpose flour**
1¼ ounces (¼ cup) **cornstarch**
8 cups **water**
2½ tablespoons **chili powder**
5 teaspoons **dry beef bouillon (I used Maggi brand)**
2 teaspoons **ground cumin**
1¼ teaspoons **salt**
1¼ teaspoons **garlic powder**

1 teaspoon **ground oregano**
1 teaspoon **paprika**
¼ teaspoon **ground coriander**
¼ teaspoon **ground black pepper**
⅛ teaspoon **ground cloves**
⅛ teaspoon **ground cayenne pepper**
3 16-ounce cans **light red kidney beans, drained**

OPTIONAL
Shredded cheddar/Jack cheese
Diced onion
Spaghetti noodles

1 Brown all the beef in a 3- or 4-quart saucepan over medium heat for 5 minutes or until no pink is visible. Add the flour and stir it into the beef. Cook for 1 minute, stirring often, or until the beef is beginning to brown.

2 Whisk the cornstarch into the water and add it to the pan, then add all of the herbs and spices. Don't add the beans yet—we'll toss

those in later. Cook the chili over medium heat until it's bubbling, then turn the heat down and simmer, uncovered, for 1½ hours, stirring occasionally.

3 After 90 minutes of simmering, add the beans and cook the chili for another 30 minutes or until the big chunks of meat are tender. Serve in a bowl or over spaghetti noodles with shredded cheese and diced onion on top, if desired.

STEAK 'N SHAKE THE ORIGINAL DOUBLE 'N CHEESE STEAKBURGER

 First-Time Hack

 Prep Time: 20 min.

 Difficulty: Easy

Yield: 6 burgers

Rather than adding any seasoning, including salt and pepper, to their classic Steakburgers, Steak 'n Shake solely relies on the Maillard reaction for flavor. This is the browning that occurs when amino acids and sugars combine with high heat. I was able to peek into the grilling station at the restaurant to see cooks squashing ground beef "pucks" flat onto the hot grill to trigger the fast browning process. This was good information, but no amount of spying into the kitchen provided me with any information about which cuts of beef are used to make those burgers.

The term "Steakburger" doesn't tell us much since practically any cut of beef can be a steak until it's ground up, and there are conflicting reports about which cuts of beef are used. One article I found states that the burgers are made with chuck, rib eye, and brisket, while another claims it's a combination of ground round, sirloin, and T-bone steaks. A waiter at the restaurant told me it's all from porterhouse steak, which is both strip and tenderloin. Completely confused by my research, I decided to bust out the meat grinder and taste test all three combinations, plus several others. In the end I determined that the best clone of these burgers is made with the most flavorful, least costly cuts: top sirloin, New York strip, and chuck. So, grab a 9-ounce steak of each and have your butcher grind them up for you, or do it yourself if you have a meat grinder. Form the blend into a dozen 2¼-ounce pucks that are then smashed flat in a hot pan and cooked until caramelized to a dark brown. Build the burger just as shown here and you'll have a perfect match to the famous eighty-year-old Midwest original.

9 ounces ground top sirloin steak
9 ounces ground New York strip steak
9 ounces ground chuck steak
6 plain hamburger buns
6 slices of American cheese
6 leaves green leaf lettuce, **trimmed to fit**
6 tomato slices from 2 large tomatoes
6 thin slices of white onion
12 dill pickle sandwich slices, **trimmed to fit**

OPTIONAL
Ketchup
Mayonnaise
Mustard
Relish

① Gently combine the ground meats in a large bowl and use your hands to form twelve 2¼-ounce balls, then shape the balls into pucks that are 2½ inches across.

② When you are ready to make the burgers, preheat a large nonstick skillet or lightly oiled pan to medium heat. Brown the face of the buns in the hot pan. Remove the buns, then drop 2 beef pucks onto the hot pan. Cook for about 30 seconds, then flip the pucks over and press down on the meat, using a spatula, so that the patties squish down to about twice the diameter of the original puck—around 5 inches across. Cook the beef patties for another 3 to 4 minutes or until the meat has browned. Flip the patties over and cook for another couple of minutes or until browned. Place a slice of American cheese on top of one patty, then place the other patty on top of the cheese.

③ Build each burger by placing a leaf of lettuce on the bottom bun, followed by a slice of tomato. Stack the two beef patties on the tomato. Place a thin slice of onion on the beef, then lay 2 pickles on the onion. If you want ketchup and/or mayo on your burger, those go on the bottom bun before you build the burger. If you want mustard and/or relish on the burger, those go on the face of the top bun before you top off your sandwich.

252

TACO BELL CRUNCHWRAP SUPREME

 First-Time Hack

 Active Prep: 20 min.

 Difficulty: Medium

 Yield: 4 servings

I don't know the name of the food origami master at Taco Bell who created this perfectly portable hexagonally shaped flat wrap in 2005, but let me just give him or her a shout-out right now for inventing what would quickly become the chain's top-selling menu item—that is, until the Doritos Locos Tacos hit the scene in 2012. The Crunchwrap is pretty genius: a soft flour tortilla is folded around a crispy tostada shell separating the warm ingredients (beef and nacho cheese) from the cold ingredients (sour cream, lettuce, and tomatoes). The whole thing is pressed in a flat-iron grill until browned, keeping all its contents sealed up so well inside that it's a perfect on-the-go creation. Before a test group approved the name "Crunchwrap" for the once limited-time-only item, other proposed names included "Crunchilada," "Crunchwich," "Origami Tostada," and my personal favorite, the "Mexigon."

To make a perfect clone of the chain's seasoned ground beef, you'll need some oat flour or you can grind some yourself from rolled oats using a small food processor or coffee grinder. I get into more details about the chain's taco meat filling in the next recipe, the Taco Bell Mexican Pizza (page 256).

SEASONED GROUND BEEF (TACO MEAT FILLING)
1 ounce (¼ cup) oat flour (see Tidbits to make your own)
½ pound ground beef (20 percent fat)
2 teaspoons chili powder
1¼ teaspoons Knorr tomato bouillon
½ teaspoon onion powder
¼ teaspoon granulated sugar
¼ teaspoon unsweetened cocoa powder
⅛ teaspoon salt
⅛ teaspoon garlic powder
½ cup water

4 12-inch flour tortillas
½ cup Tostitos Smooth & Cheesy Dip
4 6-inch crispy yellow corn tortillas (tostadas)
¼ cup reduced-fat sour cream
½ cup thinly sliced lettuce
⅓ cup diced tomatoes

1 Combine all of the seasoned beef ingredients in a medium bowl. Use your hands to thoroughly incorporate everything into the ground beef until you have a pasty mixture.

2 Preheat a skillet over medium heat and add the ground beef mixture to the pan. Brown the beef mixture for 5 to 6 minutes or until cooked. Use a spatula or wooden spoon to break up the ground beef as it cooks to give a smooth texture without any big chunks.

3 To build each serving, place a flour tortilla on a plate or cooking surface and spread 2 tablespoons of cheese dip in the center.

4 Spread about ⅓ cup of seasoned ground beef on one side of the crispy corn tortilla. Turn the tortilla over, beef-side-down, onto the cheese dip.

5 Spread 1 tablespoon of sour cream onto the crispy tortilla.

6 Sprinkle about 2 tablespoons of lettuce over the sour cream, followed by a heaping tablespoon of diced tomato.

7 Fold one side of the flour tortilla all the way over onto the crispy tortilla. Work your way around, folding the flour tortilla 5 more times, until the wrap has six sides and the crispy tortilla is concealed. Turn it over onto the folded side to keep it from unfolding. Repeat with the remaining servings.

8 Preheat a nonstick skillet over medium heat. Working with one serving at a time, place a wrap into the hot skillet with the folded side of the tortilla down. Place a medium saucepan filled about halfway with water for weight (or a heavy cast-iron skillet) onto the wrap, pressing it down into the pan. Cook the wrap for 1 minute or until golden brown on the bottom. Flip the wrap over and press down again with the heavy pan and cook for another minute or until the second side is browned. Repeat with the remaining wraps and serve them hot.

TIDBITS You can easily make oat flour from rolled oats using a small food processor or a coffee grinder. Measure a heaping ¼ cup of rolled oats (such as Quaker Old Fashioned rolled oats—not instant) into the machine and grind for about 30 seconds to make a fine flour.

TACO BELL
MEXICAN PIZZA

👍 Improved Hack

🕐 Active Prep: 15 min.
Inactive Prep: 6 min.

M🌡 Difficulty: Medium

👥 Yield: 4 servings

It was in response to a lawsuit filed against Taco Bell in January 2011 regarding the exact ingredients in its seasoned ground beef that the company revealed that the taco meat filling was in fact 88 percent beef and 12 percent other ingredients to add texture and flavor.

Examining the ingredients list reveals that among the spices added to the meat is a significant amount of oats to help bind the meat together. This helps the taco meat filling stay inside of tacos where it belongs when customers take a bite. You can use oat flour you find in a store or make your own with rolled oats in a small food processor or coffee grinder (see Tidbits). If I had to name a "secret ingredient" for my clone, it would be Knorr tomato bouillon. This flavorful substance contains tomato powder, autolyzed yeast extract, cornstarch, and citric acid—many of the exact ingredients found in Taco Bell's taco meat filling—and it will help give your meat that distinct "Taco Bell flavor."

Once you've made the taco meat filling, it's just a matter of building your Mexican Pizzas on crispy flour tortillas, broiling them until the cheese melts, and sprinkling them with a little diced tomato. You can also add a garnish of green onion if you like. I list this here because it's how the chain used to make the Mexican Pizzas, although these days the green onion has been eliminated. Either way, you'll have a great, much-improved clone of one of the chain's top-selling items.

SEASONED GROUND BEEF (TACO MEAT FILLING)
- 1 ounce (¼ cup) oat flour (see Tidbits to make your own from rolled oats)
- ½ pound ground beef (20 percent fat)
- 2 teaspoons chili powder
- 1¼ teaspoons Knorr tomato bouillon
- ½ teaspoon onion powder
- ¼ teaspoon granulated sugar
- ¼ teaspoon cocoa powder
- ⅛ teaspoon salt
- ⅛ teaspoon garlic powder
- ½ cup water

- 1 cup vegetable oil
- 8 small (6½-inch) flour tortillas
- 1 16-ounce can traditional refried beans
- ½ cup mild chunky Pace picante salsa
- ½ cup shredded Monterey Jack cheese
- ½ cup shredded medium cheddar cheese
- ½ cup diced tomato

OPTIONAL
- ¼ cup chopped green onion (green and light green parts only)

❶ Combine all of the seasoned beef ingredients in a medium bowl. Use your hands to thoroughly incorporate everything into the ground beef until you have a pasty mixture.

❷ Preheat a skillet over medium heat and add the ground beef mixture to the pan. Brown the beef mixture for 5 to 6 minutes or until cooked. Use a spatula or wooden spoon to break up the ground beef as it cooks to give a smooth texture without any big chunks.

3 Heat 1 teaspoon of oil in a medium frying pan or skillet over medium heat. When the oil is hot, fry a tortilla in the oil for 30 to 45 seconds per side, or until crispy, and set it aside on paper towels. Repeat the process with each of the tortillas, adding 1 teaspoon of fresh oil to the pan before cooking each one. Use cooking tongs to pop any bubbles that form on the tortillas as they fry. Keep the tortillas flat.

4 Heat up the refried beans in a small saucepan over medium heat or in your microwave oven. Preheat the oven to high broil.

5 When the beef and tortillas are done, build each pizza by spreading about ⅓ cup of refried beans on one of the crispy tortillas. Spread ⅓ cup of beef on the beans, then place another crispy tortilla on top. Spread 2 tablespoons of salsa on the top tortilla,

then sprinkle 2 tablespoons of Monterey Jack cheese on top of the salsa, followed by 2 tablespoons of the cheddar cheese.

6 Place the pizzas on an aluminum foil–lined baking sheet and broil for 30 to 60 seconds or just until the cheese is melted.

7 Remove the pizzas from the oven and sprinkle each with 2 tablespoons of diced tomato. Slice each pizza through the middle twice to make four slices. Add a tablespoon of green onion on top—if you want to make it the old way.

TIDBITS You can easily make oat flour from rolled oats using a small food processor or coffee grinder. Measure a heaping ¼ cup of oats—such as Quaker Old Fashioned rolled oats (not instant)—and grind for about 30 seconds to make a fine flour.

257

T.G.I. FRIDAY'S LOADED POTATO SKINS

Improved Hack
Active Prep: 15 min.
Inactive Prep: 1 hr. 15 min.
Difficulty: Easy
Yield: 4 servings

When T.G.I. Friday's introduced loaded potato skins to the world back in 1974, the appetizer was such a big hit that other restaurants were soon cloning the dish for their own menus. I created my own clone recipe of the chain's creation in 1997 but have now modified the baking technique for the skins to give you a much better—and crispier—properly hacked signature appetizer. If you want to know what the original potato skins taste like, try this recipe.

5 medium **russet potatoes**
Vegetable oil
¼ **cup (½ stick) unsalted butter, melted**
Salt
1½ **cups shredded medium cheddar cheese**
5 slices **bacon, cooked and crumbled**
⅓ **cup sour cream**
1 **tablespoon chopped green onion (green part only)**

❶ Preheat the oven to 400 degrees F.

❷ Rub the potatoes with the oil and bake the potatoes for 1 hour on an aluminum foil–lined baking sheet. Cool the potatoes until you can handle them (around 10 to 20 minutes). Turn your oven up to 450 degrees F.

❸ Slice each potato lengthwise into thirds. The two outside slices will become the potato skins. Use the middle slice for another dish, such as mashed potatoes.

❹ Use a spoon to scoop potato out of each of the end slices, creating "boats" with about ¼ inch of potato left around the inside of the skin.

❺ Brush the entire surface of each potato skin, inside and out, with the melted butter. Sprinkle a little salt over the top and bottom of each potato skin. Bake the potatoes again on an aluminum foil–lined baking sheet for 15 to 18 minutes or until they are browned around the edges.

6 Put 2 to 3 tablespoons cheddar cheese into each skin.

7 Sprinkle about half of a slice of crumbled bacon over the cheese on each skin. Bake again for 1 to 2 minutes or until the cheese is melted.

8 Spoon the sour cream into a small bowl. Sprinkle the green onion over the top of the sour cream.

9 Serve the skins on a plate around the sour cream.

T.G.I. FRIDAY'S JACK DANIEL'S SAUCE

👍 Improved Hack

🕐 Active Prep: 30 min.
Inactive Prep: 10 min.

E🌡 Difficulty: Easy

👥 Yield: 1¼ cups

For almost twenty years, T.G.I. Friday's Jack Daniel's Sauce has been slathered over the chain's best-selling items, including the baby back ribs and the Jack Daniel's burger. Shortly after the sauce debuted at the chain, I was asked to hack it for an appearance on *The Oprah Winfrey Show,* and my original formula has been one of the most popular recipes on TopSecretRecipes.com. But I've always felt that there was room for improvement. For one thing, according to the most recent T.G.I. Friday's menu, the recipe includes Tabasco pepper sauce, which was absent from my first version. And the garlic, which was originally roasted in that earlier version, should be toasted. This method speeds up preparation of the recipe and makes it taste more like the real thing.

There are many other tweaks here, including less pineapple juice and the elimination of the water so that cooking the sauce will take less time. Spread this sauce over chicken, salmon, ribs, wings, pork chops, burgers, or just about any protein, but baste it on after cooking or serve it on the side for dipping since the sugar in the sauce will quickly burn if applied during the cooking step—especially over an open flame like on your grill.

4 teaspoons (3 to 4 cloves) minced garlic
1 tablespoon vegetable oil
¾ cup (1 6-ounce can) pineapple juice
1⅓ cups (packed) dark brown sugar
¼ cup teriyaki sauce (such as Kikkoman)
¼ cup lemon juice
¼ cup diced white onion
2 tablespoons canned crushed pineapple
1 tablespoon soy sauce
1 tablespoon Jack Daniel's Whiskey
1½ teaspoons Tabasco pepper sauce
⅛ teaspoon ground cayenne pepper

❶ Toast the garlic by combining the garlic and the oil in a medium saucepan over medium/low heat. Cook for 5 minutes or until the garlic becomes a golden brown color. Watch it closely so that the garlic does not burn. As soon as the garlic is golden brown, add the pineapple juice to prevent it from cooking any more.

❷ Turn the heat up to medium and add the other ingredients. Bring the mixture to a boil, then reduce the heat and simmer the sauce for 25 minutes or until thick. Watch the sauce closely to be sure that it doesn't bubble over. Remove from the heat, cover, and cool. Store in a sealed container in the refrigerator for several days.

T.G.I. FRIDAY'S DRAGONFIRE SALMON

 First-Time Hack

 Active Prep: 20 min.
Inactive Prep: 25 min.

 Difficulty: Medium

  Yield: 4 servings

One of my favorite dishes at T.G.I. Friday's is the Dragonfire Salmon. The spicy kung pao sauce is flavorific and the sweet pineapple pico de gallo is a perfect bright garnish. Best yet, each of these components is super easy to make from scratch. You can even prepare them a day in advance if you like, then when you're ready to make the dish, crank up your grill and cook up the salmon. It helps if you can find freshly sliced pineapple in your produce or deli section for the pico de gallo so that you don't have to buy a whole pineapple. The chain uses Norwegian salmon but any salmon will do here, and you may want to serve the fish over a bed of rice with a side of steamed broccoli just as they do at the restaurant chain, so add that stuff to your shopping list.

PINEAPPLE PICO DE GALLO
1 cup finely diced fresh pineapple
1 cup finely diced Roma tomato (2 tomatoes)
¼ cup finely diced red onion
2 tablespoons minced jalapeño
2 tablespoons minced cilantro
1 tablespoon lime juice
⅛ teaspoon salt

KUNG PAO SAUCE
1 tablespoon vegetable oil
4 teaspoons minced ginger
1 tablespoon minced garlic
¼ cup water
⅓ cup (packed) dark brown sugar
3 tablespoons rice vinegar
4 teaspoons soy sauce
2 teaspoons chili sauce (sambal)

4 6- to 8-ounce salmon fillets
Vegetable oil
Salt
Ground black pepper

GARNISH
1 11-ounce can mandarin orange segments
4 teaspoons minced fresh parsley

1 Preheat your grill to high.

2 Combine all of the ingredients for the pineapple pico de gallo in a medium bowl, then cover and chill until later.

3 Make the kung pao sauce by heating the oil, ginger, and garlic in a small saucepan over medium/low heat for 5 minutes or until the garlic just begins to brown. Add the water to stop the garlic from browning. Add the remaining ingredients, then turn the heat up to medium. When the mixture begins to bubble, reduce the heat and simmer for 10 to 15 minutes or until thick. Turn off the heat and cover.

4 Brush the salmon fillets with the oil, then lightly salt and pepper each fillet. Cook the salmon on a well-lubricated barbecue grill or grill pan on your stovetop over medium heat for 6 to 8 minutes per side or until the fish flakes easily.

5 Serve each salmon fillet on a bed of rice, if desired. Brush each fillet with some of the kung pao sauce, and spoon some pineapple pico de gallo over the top. Add some mandarin orange segments next, and sprinkle each serving with about a teaspoon of minced parsley.

TONY ROMA'S
BABY BACK RIBS

👍 Improved Hack

⟳ Active Prep: 16 min.
Inactive Prep: 4 hrs.

E🌡 Difficulty: Easy

👥 Yield: 2 full racks

A barely watched YouTube video uploaded by Tony Roma's in 2013 revealed the secret to the cooking process for the "world famous" baby back ribs at the chain. In the video, Executive Chef Bob Gallagher demonstrates the secret steaming technique used by Tony Roma's (and many other restaurants who don't use a smoker) to give the ribs a smoky flavor and fall-off-the-bone tenderness. In the video, liquid smoke is added to a little water in a pan with the ribs, then the pan is covered and baked in the oven for a couple of hours. The steam from the water makes the ribs tender while the liquid smoke fills the ribs with hickory flavor. After the ribs cool, they are grilled and brushed with sauce several times. It's a very easy process and a good way to make tender, smoky ribs if you don't happen to have a smoker.

Chef Gallagher recommends cooking the ribs for 2 hours, but I found that the ribs need more like 3 hours to achieve perfect tenderness and great smoky flavor. While your ribs are baking, you have time to make your choice of the two most popular sauces from the chain in the following recipes (Original and Carolina Honeys), or just use a cup of your favorite bottled barbecue sauce. Try to find baby backs that are on the small side so they better fit into a 11 x 15-inch roasting pan.

2 full racks trimmed pork baby back ribs
4 cups water
1 tablespoon hickory liquid smoke
1 cup barbecue sauce

❶ Preheat the oven to 350 degrees F.

❷ Trim the ribs of any excess fat and meat. The rib meat should be a consistent thickness across the ribs. Also, remove the silver skin from the bone side of the ribs. This is the very thin white opaque connective tissue. Use a sharp knife to nick through the silver skin so that you can grab it. Use a paper towel to hold an edge of the sliver skin and pull it away from the ribs.

❸ Add the water to an 11 x 15-inch bake and roast pan along with the liquid smoke. You may need to slice a bone off the end of the ribs so that your racks fit flat into the pan. You can slice the racks in half and overlap them to make them fit. If you are using a 9 x 13-inch pan, you will most definitely have to slice each of the racks in half so that they fit overlapped in the pan. Place the ribs in the pan with the bone sides down and cover the pan tightly with aluminum foil. Bake for

3 hours or until the meat is fall-off-the-bone tender. Uncover the ribs and remove them from the pan and let them cool for an hour so that they do not fall apart when grilling.

4 Preheat your barbecue grill to medium heat while the ribs are cooling.

5 Place the ribs on the grill with the bone sides facing down. Brush the sauce over the top of the ribs as they cook, completely covering the surface of the ribs with sauce. Cook for about 4 minutes, then flip the ribs over and apply sauce to the bone side. Cook the ribs for 2 to 3 minutes or until the sauce begins to char on the other side. Flip the ribs over and apply sauce again. Cook for 2 to 3 minutes, flip the ribs once more, apply sauce, and cook for another 2 to 3 minutes. Flip the ribs one last time and brush the top once again with sauce. Cook for another 2 to 3 minutes, then serve.

TONY ROMA'S ORIGINAL BARBECUE SAUCE

 Improved Hack

 Active Prep: 10 min.
Inactive Prep: 25 min.

E Difficulty: Easy

 Yield: 1 cup

My quest to re-hack this award-winning sauce took me to the busiest Tony Roma's in the world at The Freemont Hotel and Casino in downtown Las Vegas. Thirty minutes after opening its doors, the restaurant was completely packed and a line had formed out the door winding through the slot machines. I've never seen anything like it. I'm glad I went, though, because the first time I hacked this recipe I targeted the bottled sauce that Tony Roma's sells in stores, which happens to be totally different from the stuff you get at the restaurant. The bottled sauce is good, but the restaurant version of the sauce has a much better, more complex flavor with a distinct hint of cinnamon that's not found in the bottles. Make the recipe here and you'll have a clone of the award-winning sauce served at the restaurant with a flavor that totally trumps the bottled version. Use it on your favorite rib recipe or on the Tony Roma's Baby Back Ribs hacked in the recipe on page 264.

1 cup ketchup
¾ cup water
6 tablespoons white vinegar
3 tablespoons dark brown sugar
½ teaspoon vegetable oil
½ teaspoon dry mustard powder

¼ teaspoon plus ⅛ teaspoon salt
¼ teaspoon paprika
¼ teaspoon onion powder
¼ teaspoon garlic powder
¼ teaspoon hickory liquid smoke
⅛ teaspoon ground cinnamon

1 Combine all of the ingredients in a small saucepan over medium heat.

2 Bring to a boil, then reduce the heat to medium/low and simmer for 25 to 30 minutes or until thick. Remove from the heat, cover, and cool.

TONY ROMA'S CAROLINA HONEYS BARBECUE SAUCE

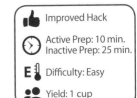
👍 Improved Hack

🕐 Active Prep: 10 min.
Inactive Prep: 25 min.

E 🌡 Difficulty: Easy

👥 Yield: 1 cup

I wonder why the version of this sauce at the restaurant is so different from the bottled sauce that you can find in stores. You can clearly see the difference in the color: the bottled version is so dark that it's almost black. And the bottled sauce has much more molasses flavor in it—way too much, in fact, if you ask me. That's why this time around I hacked the restaurant version of this great barbecue sauce. Dump everything here into a saucepan on your stovetop and you're less than 30 minutes away from a sauce that you can use on your favorite pork ribs, beef ribs, or chicken; or use it with the recipe for the Tony Roma's Baby Back Ribs hacked on page 264.

1 cup **ketchup**
¾ cup **water**
¼ cup **white vinegar**
3 tablespoons **dark brown sugar**
2 tablespoons **molasses**

1 tablespoon **honey**
¼ teaspoon plus ⅛ teaspoon **salt**
¼ teaspoon **paprika**
¼ teaspoon **hickory liquid smoke**

1 Combine all of the ingredients in a small saucepan over medium heat.

2 Bring to a boil, then reduce the heat to medium/low and simmer for 25 to 30 minutes or until thick. Remove from the heat, cover, and cool.

WAFFLE HOUSE WAFFLES

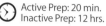

👍 Improved Hack

🕐 Active Prep: 20 min.
Inactive Prep: 12 hrs.

E 🌡 Difficulty: Easy

👥 Yield: 6 waffles

I was able to improve upon my previous hack of the best waffles in the biz when a very helpful server at a Waffle House in Indiana gave me an empty 3¼-pound bag of waffle mix. The preparation instructions printed on that bag of dry mix said to add 2 quarts of half-and-half to the mix along with 4 eggs, then refrigerate overnight. I had the overnight chilling part correct in my first recipe (you can use the batter right away if you really want to), but the amount of half-and-half in the formula is now more accurate. That tweak, plus a few other small adjustments based on the ingredients list on that waffle mix bag, makes what was already a good recipe even better.

1 **large** egg
½ **cup** granulated sugar
1 **teaspoon** salt
½ **teaspoon** vanilla extract
1 **cup** half-and-half
¼ **cup** buttermilk
2 **tablespoons** shortening, **melted**
3 **tablespoons** unsalted butter, **melted**
8 **ounces** (1⅔ **cups**) all-purpose flour
¼ **teaspoon** baking soda
Nonstick spray

ON THE SIDE
Butter
Maple Syrup

❶ Combine the egg, sugar, salt, and vanilla in large bowl with an electric mixer on high speed for 1 minute.

❷ Add the half-and-half, buttermilk, shortening, and butter and mix well.

❸ In a separate medium bowl, combine the flour with the baking soda. Add the flour to the wet mixture and mix well with the mixer. Cover and chill the batter overnight for the best results, or you can use it right away if you like.

4 When you are ready to make the waffles, preheat a waffle iron. Spray the waffle iron with a little nonstick cooking spray, then spoon ⅓ cup to ½ cup of batter (depending the on the size of your waffle iron) onto the center of the waffle iron.

5 Cook the waffles for 2 to 3 minutes or until golden brown. Serve with a pat of butter on top and maple syrup on the side.

WENDY'S CHILI

👍 Improved Hack

🕐 Active Prep: 15 min.
Inactive Prep: 2 hrs.

E🌡 Difficulty: Easy

👥 Yield: 12 servings

When I hacked this recipe in my first book, I must not have done a "sieve analysis." Recently, I took ½ cup of Wendy's Chili and rinsed it through a fine mesh strainer. The solid stuff that was left behind told me a lot about how I could improve this recipe. I found a lot more vegetables in the Wendy's version than in my earlier version—twice as much, to be exact. So doubling the onion, chilies, and celery was the first step to making this famous chili recipe a greatly improved clone. Through further examination, I found that there was too much tomato sauce in the mix, so I left out the sauce and replaced it with canned petite diced tomatoes. I also fine-tuned the seasoning and added some cornstarch to help thicken up the finished product. Now try the ultimate Wendy's Chili clone, which, I think, is the best-ever hack of the most famous chili in America.

2 tablespoons **vegetable oil**
2 cups diced **white onion** (1 large onion)
1 cup seeded and diced **Anaheim chili**
(2 medium peppers)
⅔ cup diced **celery** (2 stalks)
2 pounds **ground beef**
3 tablespoons **cornstarch**
2 cups **water**

3 15-ounce cans **petite diced tomatoes**
1 29-ounce can **dark red kidney beans** (with liquid)
1 29-ounce can **pinto beans** (with liquid)
3 tablespoons **chili powder**
1 tablespoon **granulated sugar**
2½ teaspoons **salt**
2 teaspoons **ground cumin**
1½ teaspoons **ground black pepper**
1½ teaspoons **garlic powder**

TOPPING (OPTIONAL)
Shredded, cheddar cheese
Chopped onion

❶ Heat the oil in a large pot over medium heat. Add the onion, chili, and celery and cook for 5 to 8 minutes or until the onions become translucent.

❷ Add the ground beef and cook for 5 minutes or until no pink is visible. Be sure to crumble the beef as it cooks so that there are no big chunks in the pot.

❸ Dissolve the cornstarch in the water and add it to the pot along with the remaining ingredients. Bring the chili to a boil, then reduce the heat and simmer, uncovered, for 2 to 3 hours or until thick. Stir every 15 to 20 minutes. Top with shredded cheddar cheese and chopped onion, if desired.

WENDY'S PRETZEL BACON CHEESEBURGER

First-Time Hack
Active Prep: 35 min.
Inactive Prep: 1 hr. 15 min.
Difficulty: Hard
Yield: 4 burgers

Wendy's profits were on a roll after the summer 2013 introduction of the "pub-style" bacon cheeseburger, which was served on the first pretzel bun in fast-food history. The dense, chewy pretzel bun is the main attraction, but the delicious combination of sliced cheddar cheese, honey mustard sauce, cheese sauce, thick-sliced bacon, and spring lettuce greens makes this a burger unlike any you'll find at other fast-food chains. The Pretzel Bacon Cheeseburger is Wendy's most successful product launch in the last eleven years, and now you can make a great copy in the comfort of your own HQ from scratch, including a perfect pretzel bun! This recipe will make four burgers, so you'll have a couple of buns left over for other sandwich creations since the recipe here makes a total of six fresh pretzel buns.

PRETZEL BUNS
3 tablespoons granulated sugar
1¼ cups warm water (105 to 110 degrees F)
1 pkg. (2¼ teaspoons) active dry yeast
1¼ teaspoons salt
16 ounces (3 cups) bread flour
3 tablespoons vegetable oil
3 tablespoons baking soda
4 cups water

HONEY MUSTARD SAUCE
¼ cup mayonnaise
4 teaspoons Grey Poupon Country Dijon mustard
2 teaspoons honey
1½ teaspoons granulated sugar
1 teaspoon yellow mustard
¼ teaspoon paprika
⅛ teaspoon liquid smoke

1 pound ground beef
Salt
Ground black pepper
4 deli-style cheddar cheese **slices**
2 tablespoons Cheez Whiz, **warmed**
6 slices cooked thick-sliced bacon (applewood-smoked is best)
2 cups spring mix lettuce greens
4 large tomato **slices (or 8 medium-size slices)**
2 red onion **slices, separated into rings**

1 Make the pretzel buns by dissolving the sugar into the warm water in a medium bowl. Add the yeast and stir to dissolve. Let the yeast sit for about 5 minutes or until a foam forms on top of the solution.

2 Stir the salt into the flour in a large mixing bowl, then pour in the yeast solution and oil. Use a kneading hook on a stand mixer or mix by hand until the dough forms into a ball. Knead for 10 minutes, either with the dough hook or by hand until the dough is smooth, without any lumps. Let the dough sit in a bowl, covered with a towel, in a warm spot for 1 hour or until doubled in size. When the dough has doubled, punch it down and form 6 4-ounce balls of dough. Press them down onto a nonstick or silicone mat–lined baking sheet until 4 inches in diameter and let them rise for another 15 minutes.

3 Preheat your conventional oven to 400 degrees F (or 375 degrees F for a convection oven).

4 Combine the baking soda with the 4 cups of water in a medium saucepan over medium heat.

5 When the baking soda solution begins to bubble, drop one bun at a time into the solution. Use a large spoon or spider to flip the bun over after 20 seconds and let it sit in the solution for another 20 seconds. Remove the bun from the solution with the spider, allowing the excess liquid to drip off, and place it on the baking sheet. Repeat the process with the remaining buns. Before placing the buns in the oven, use a very sharp knife with an oiled blade to score an "X" that is about ½ inch deep in the top of each bun. Wipe the blade of the knife clean after each slice. Bake the buns for 12 to 15 minutes or until dark brown. Cool.

6 Make the honey mustard sauce by combining all of the ingredients in a small bowl.

7 Form the ground beef into 4 square patties that measure approximately 4 inches across.

8 Preheat a large nonstick skillet over medium heat. Slice 4 of the pretzel buns in half and brown the faces of those buns in the hot skillet.

9 Cook the ground beef patties in the skillet for 2 to 3 minutes per side or until done. Lightly salt and pepper each of the beef patties as they cook.

10 Build each hamburger by placing a slice of cheddar cheese on the bottom bun, then stack a beef patty on top of the cheese. Spread about 1½ teaspoons of honey mustard sauce on the beef patty, followed by 1½ teaspoons of warmed Cheez Whiz.

11 Break the cooked bacon slices in half and arrange 3 halves side by side on the patty. Add a handful of lettuce greens on top of the bacon, followed by a tomato slice (or 2 slices if your tomatoes are smaller) and 2 rings of red onion. Top off the burger with the top bun and serve immediately.

TIDBITS You may want to warm up the pretzel buns by zapping the burgers in your microwave for 15 to 20 seconds before serving.

274

TRADEMARKS

Applebee's and Fiesta Lime Chicken are registered trademarks of Applebee's International, Inc.

Arby's is a registered trademark of Arby's, Inc.

Auntie Anne's is a registered trademark of Auntie Anne's, Inc.

Ben & Jerry's is a registered trademark of Ben & Jerry's Homemade, Inc.

Boston Market is a registered trademark of Boston Market Corporation.

Bubba Gump Shrimp Company is a registered trademark of Landry's, Inc.

Burger King and Stuffed Steakhouse Burger are registered trademarks of Burger King Corporation.

Cafe Rio is a registered trademark of Cafe Rio, Inc.

The Capital Grille is a registered trademark of Darden Concepts, Inc.

Carrabba's Italian Grill is a registered trademark of Bloomin' Brands, Inc.

The Cheesecake Factory is a registered trademark of TCF Co., LLC.

Chick-fil-A is a registered trademark of CFA Properties, Inc.

Chili's is a registered trademark of Brinker International.

Chipotle Mexican Grill is a registered trademark of Chipotle Mexican Grill, Inc.

Cinnabon is a registered trademark of Cinnabon, Inc.

Cracker Barrel is a registered trademark of CBOCS Properties, Inc.

Dippin' Dots is a registered trademark of Dippin' Dots, LLC.

Domino's is a registered trademark of Domino's IP Holder, LLC.

El Pollo Loco is a registered trademark of El Pollo Loco, Inc.

Frito-Lay and Cracker Jack are registered trademarks of Frito-Lay North America, Inc.

Fudgsicle is a registered trademark of Unilever.

Gatorade is a registered trademark of Gatorade, Inc.

Girl Scout Cookies, Samoas, Caramel deLites, and Trefoils are registered trademarks of Girl Scouts of the United States of America.

Hostess and Twinkie are registered trademarks of Hostess Brands, LLC.

Houston's is a registered trademark of Hillstone Restaurant Group.

IHOP is a registered trademark of IHOP IP, LLC.

IKEA is a registered trademark of Inter IKEA Systems B.V.

Jack in the Box is a registered trademark of Jack In The Box, Inc.

KFC and Original Recipe are registered trademarks of Yum! Brands, Inc.

Legal Sea Foods is a registered trademark of Legal Sea Foods, Inc.

Lofthouse Cookies is a registered trademark of ConAgra Food, Inc.

Long John Silver's is a registered trademark of Long John Silver's, LLC.

Marie Callender's is a registered trademark of Marie Callender Pie Shops, LLC.

Mauna Loa is a registered trademark of The Hershey Company.

McDonald's, McCafé, Big Mac, McRib, and McWrap are registered trademarks of McDonald's Corporation.

The Melting Pot is a registered trademark of The Melting Pot Restaurants, Inc.

Mrs. Fields is a registered trademark of Mrs. Fields, Inc.

Nordstrom is a registered trademark of Nordstrom, Inc.

Nuts 4 Nuts is a registered trademark of United Snack, Inc.

Olive Garden is a registered trademark of Darden Concepts, Inc.

Orange Julius is a registered trademark of American Dairy Queen Corp.

The Original Pancake House is a registered trademark of Original Pancake House Franchising, Inc.

Outback Steakhouse, Bloomin' Onion, and Kookaburra Wings are registered trademarks of Bloomin' Brands, Inc.

Panera Bread is a registered trademark of Panera Bread, Inc.

Pepperidge Farm and Milano are registered trademarks of Pepperidge Farm, Inc.

P.F. Chang's is a registered trademark of P.F. Chang's China Bistro, Inc.

Pinkberry is a registered trademark of Pinkberry, Inc.

Raising Cane's is a registered trademark of Raising Cane's U.S.A., LLC.

Red Lobster and Cheddar Bay Biscuits are registered trademarks of Red Lobster Hospitality, LLC.

Roy's is a registered trademark of Bloomin' Brands, Inc.

Rubio's and the Original Fish Taco are registered trademarks of Rubio's Restaurants, Inc.

Ruth's Chris Steak House is a registered trademark of Ruth's Hospitality Group.

Sabra is a registered trademark of Sabra Dipping Co., LLC.

St. Elmo Steak House is a registered trademark of St. Elmo Incorporated.

Starbucks is a registered trademark of Starbucks Corporation.

Steak 'n Shake and Steakburger are registered trademarks of Steak N Shake, LLC.

Taco Bell and Crunchwrap are registered trademarks of Taco Bell Corp.

T.G.I. Friday's is a registered trademark of Friday's Inc.

Tony Roma's, Tony Roma's Original, and Carolina Honeys are registered trademarks of Tony Roma's Inc.

Waffle House is a registered trademark of WH Capital, LLC.

Wendy's is a registered trademark of Oldemark, LLC.

INDEX

279

More *Top Secret Recipes*® from
Todd Wilbur

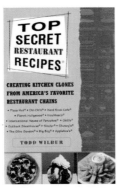

www.TopSecretRecipes.com

PLUME
An imprint of Penguin Random House LLC
www.penguin.com